Shop Different

Shop Different

HOW RETAIL REVEALED APPLE'S GENIUS

Ron Johnson

Creator of the Apple Store

with Zander Nethercutt

HarperCollins*Publishers*

This book is based on my personal experiences and my best recollections of conversations and events. Dialogue has been re-created from memory to reflect the essence of the conversations that took place. In some instances, I have consulted with others to verify details; however, this remains a subjective account and does not represent the official position of any past employers.

HarperCollins*Publishers*
1 London Bridge Street
London SE1 9GF

www.harpercollins.co.uk

HarperCollins*Publishers*
Macken House, 39/40 Mayor Street Upper
Dublin 1, D01 C9W8, Ireland

First published by HarperCollins*Publishers* 2026

1 3 5 7 9 10 8 6 4 2

A catalogue record of this book is available from the British Library

HB ISBN 978-0-00-876639-9
PB ISBN 978-0-00-876640-5

Printed and bound in the UK using 100% renewable electricity at CPI Group (UK) Ltd

To the employees of the Apple Store
and twenty-five years of enriching lives.

Choose kindness.

Contents

PROLOGUE Meeting Steve xi

CHAPTER 1 In the Beginning 1

CHAPTER 2 I Love Retail 21

CHAPTER 3 Good Design Doesn't Have to Be Expensive 34

CHAPTER 4 A Significant Opportunity 50

CHAPTER 5 Visions Emerge 68

CHAPTER 6 Genius Is Revealed 97

CHAPTER 7 The Difficult Early Years 118

CHAPTER 8 Love Works 139

CHAPTER 9 Wouldn't It Be *Great*? 165

CHAPTER 10 "This Is the Moment We Built the Stores For." 181

CHAPTER 11 The Most Important Person Is the One in Front of You 199

CHAPTER 12 People Want to Do Significant Things 219

CHAPTER 13 "How Much Success Do You Need?" 240

CHAPTER 14 When Vision Becomes Blinding 254

CHAPTER 15 What's Next, Now? 282

CHAPTER 16 Choose Kindness 290

Acknowledgments 301

PROLOGUE

Meeting Steve

On a cool fall day in November 1999, I sat in a black leather chair outside of a corner office on the fourth floor of Building 1 at 1 Infinite Loop in Cupertino. My interview to develop and lead a retail strategy for Apple was scheduled for 5:00 p.m.

I glanced at my watch.

It read 5:03 p.m.

With no cell phone to look at, my eyes found a copy of *Time* on the table in front of me. Steve's face was on its cover. I'd never met him. I knew precious little about him. At Target, where I'd been for the past decade, we didn't use computers for everyday work. In fact, few people I knew in Minnesota used a computer.

I picked the magazine up off the table.

"Steve's Jobs," the cover read. I leafed through it. Steve wasn't running just Apple but Pixar, too. And at Pixar, he was full-time CEO. At Apple, he was still interim CEO. I had known little about this prior to opening the magazine. As I closed it, I caught another photo of Steve on another magazine cover.

This guy gets a *lot* of attention, I thought.

"He saved Apple with his hot new iMac," the subheading read. "He struck gold at Pixar with digital movies like *Toy Story 2*. You'd think he'd learn to chill. Think different."

Think different, I thought. I like that.

My watch now read 5:09 p.m. I put down the issue and picked up another with Steve on the cover. This time, *Fortune*.

"And Now, for My Next Trick . . ." it read. Before I had time to discover what the trick was, I looked up to see a knee sticking out of a ripped pair of jeans.

This must be Steve, I thought.

We introduced ourselves, then entered a conference room attached to his office. The sun had been dipping below the mountains west of Cupertino as I'd entered the building, and what light remained danced on the walls through a window that faced south into the courtyard. I sat, and Steve drew the shades before sitting down adjacent to me. He fidgeted, his hands shifting in and out of a prayer position as he got settled and placed a foot on the table. His eyes bore into mine, his right eyebrow raising just slightly relative to his left. I met his gaze, thinking I had some idea of what would come of our conversation.

I did not.

□

Poet and philosopher David Whyte coined the term *the conversational nature of reality*. If reality is a conversation, attempts to control it will always shrink it. The best conversations happen when both parties relinquish control; when they accept that neither can—or should—be able to predict what happens next. This creates space for what Whyte calls "the frontier." Not a copy of the past or compromise on the future, but a dynamic, ever-evolving present.

The power of presence appears all over Whyte's writing. For him, it is directly tied to the idea of "genius." When we think of genius today, we think of individuals and the things they create or discover—say, Steve and the iPhone, or Einstein and relativity. But for Whyte, genius isn't a person or an object so much as a way of observing the world. It is the quality of your attention. It is the capacity to hear what is being asked of you, then answer in a way that continues the conversation.

Whyte would argue that the genius of the iPhone was downstream of how Steve related to his surroundings. It was a result of his presence: the *quality* of his attention. The insights that led to the iPhone revealed themselves in Steve's conversations with Jony Ive, who designed it; Scott Forstall, who created its software; Phil Schiller, who marketed it, and others. These conversations were intense because Steve set incredibly ambitious goals for himself and his team—and with the iPhone, it was none other than reinventing the phone. Still, while Steve had a knack for seeing the big picture ahead of everyone else, he knew that the most important work was in the small details. He understood that the insights revealed in conversations among a small group of people might not look like insights at first, and thus required a profound level of focus to notice. But he also understood that those insights, when caught and combined, could reveal something genius.

I understood this when I met Steve, too, even if I couldn't have articulated it. I was coming off a decade at Target, and the best ideas for how to serve our customers had always emerged through conversation. The best conversations tended to happen between people with diverse personal geographies, defined as everything we've experienced in our work and life: where we grew up, where we've lived, what we've learned. And while Steve's and my "geographies" couldn't have been more different—he was a technologist from Silicon Valley, and I was a retailer from Minnesota—we shared genius as Whyte describes it: an ability to be truly present with one another and thus hear what we needed from each other. Our first conversation revealed ideas that became a store many would describe as "genius," and one that would reveal Apple's genius. But that store, too, emerged from conversations I had with myself, which were shaped by the conversations I shared with Steve, my team, and everyone else.

To understand what I brought to those conversations, we have to go back to the beginning.

CHAPTER 1

In the Beginning

Unconditional love is the greatest gift a child can receive, and it was the first thing I knew.

My earliest memory is walking to Cornelia Elementary with my mom. I'm four years old. My interview with the principal and a few teachers will determine if I'm ready to start school a year ahead of plan. The principal asks a question.

"What color is George Washington's white horse?"

I pause. I look at my mom. I turn back to the principal.

"Black!" I exclaim.

The interview ends. My mom takes my hand, guides me outside, then stops me, bends down, and gently grasps my shoulder before looking me straight in the eyes.

"Ronnie," she says. "No matter what happens, I will always love you."

My mom's reminder that I was loved no matter what I did was the ultimate gift: freedom from fear. It also drew me to beginnings.

Those who know me well know that my three favorite words are "in the beginning." I've always been drawn to newness. I love new opportunities, new friends, new relationships. I love new stores, new merchandise. And I love finding new ways to serve people.

I credit my mom for this, too. When I think of her, I think of her serving others. I can still hear her gentle tiptoeing past my brother's and my bedroom in the morning, its barely audible pitter-patter a reminder that she was thinking of us while doing something for us. I can hear our station wagon's engine turning over in our driveway before sunrise, its low din a reminder that my mom was racing the postman to the mailbox of whoever had a birthday that day. I can even see what she used to bake for kids' birthday parties, too—train cakes, each car frosted with the name of one of the kids attending the party. My mom's desire to make others feel at home knew no end, and it gave me an innate sense of places where I felt like I belonged.

One of those places was stores.

To this day, my favorite thing to do is visit stores. I do it regularly, walking through malls, or the best shopping streets in the world. Even today, I can recall great presentations in store windows I visited on Bond Street forty years ago, or the Ralph Lauren polo shirt display from a visit to the Houston Galleria in 1982. The vision of starched folded shirts on a mahogany table—a white, blue, pink, yellow, then a blue stripe and a pink stripe—will never leave me. The stores I remember were always filled with colors.

A few years after my first interview at Cornelia Elementary offered little hope for the one that I'd share with Steve four decades later, I sat in the back seat of our car as my mom drove south from Edina down to Bloomington. I followed dutifully as she ushered me out of the car into a gigantic parking lot and toward a single-story store that was bigger than any I had ever seen. I recall entering to lights, music, and red concentric circles. The store was the fifth location of a new retail concept: a gamble by Douglas Dayton—whose family owned and operated the most significant retailer in Minnesota, the Dayton's department store—that there existed a middle ground between bare-bones discounters and upscale department stores. Perhaps portending the accuracy of the gamble, he named it Target. It was in 1962 in Duluth, he later said, that he first heard someone call it "Tarzhay."

Dayton had been willing to bet big on Target for several reasons. One of them was that, by the late 1950s, another bet was beginning to pay off. In 1952, Douglas's brother Donald—who was then president of Dayton's—had commissioned a study to quantify the commercial impact of Minnesota's bone-chilling winters. The study found that Minnesota had only 126 days of ideal shopping weather each year. Those born after 1956 might be wondering why weather had any bearing on people's tendency to visit indoor malls. The answer is that prior to 1956, indoor malls didn't exist. Working with an Austrian architect, Victor Gruen, Donald Dayton envisioned a climate-controlled shopping environment with shops turned inward. Together, the two men developed plans for Southdale Center. When it opened in 1956, Southdale was the first indoor shopping mall in the world. I was born two years later, two miles away.

Growing up, my brother, Dwight, and I biked to Southdale. In the winters, our parents brought us there with them. They were there for the merchandise, but Dwight and I didn't care about that—at least, not at first. What we cared about was the experience. And Southdale was an experience. The year after it opened, Southdale hosted the *Truth or Consequences* game show with host Bob Barker in their exotic "Garden Court." At the center of that court was a twenty-one-foot-tall brass cage filled with canaries and parakeets. Trees reached upward along widely set, wood-paneled escalators as planters flanked restaurants and hung from second-floor railings. Atrium cafés overflowed with customers gathered under colorful, tasseled umbrellas and awnings with entrances marked in movie poster fonts. Gruen's glass skylights shed Edina's ceaseless snow and bathed the atrium in a warm, gentle light. And people frolicked in that light. They conversed, they smiled, they laughed—and yes, they shopped. Southdale wasn't a mall. It was a neighborhood. It was the result of two men who looked at everything that had come before and decided to create something different.

The more time I spent at Southdale, the more I felt at home in stores. Our local toy store, Clancy's, encouraged kids to come in and walk the aisles, touch and open boxes, and play with the toys. Our local sporting goods store, Kokesh Athletic, was the place to get geared up for every season of youth sports—and come high school, I would work there. Even stores whose merchandise didn't particularly matter to me found ways to make themselves destinations. Korner Plaza, a multicategory specialty store that my mom loved, put a bowl of candy out at their jewelry counter—five round, colored chocolates wrapped in cellophane. Gabberts, meanwhile—a furniture store that remains in its same location fifty years later—had a kids' area in its basement complete with a koi pond, tables covered with coloring books and crayons, and TVs that played the cartoons we could never watch at home. In the winter, they put out hot chocolate and animal crackers. As a teen, I came back to Southdale with friends. As an adult, I came back with my kids. In a mall that felt like home, stores became playrooms. And what is more fun, I thought, than play?

Of course, there were no bigger playrooms than the department stores. Southdale was anchored at each end by one of them: Dayton's to the north and Donaldson's to the south. Those were the "big" stores. The "little" shops—sixty-four of them—then sat in between along an enclosed arcade. As the years went on, this model would be tested and tweaked; initially, Southdale had a grocery store, which was carved into smaller stores once it became clear that those who shopped for groceries didn't tend to linger in the mall. But soon, the mall caught its stride and began growing quickly. Sixty-four little shops became 107. This expansion was completed a decade and a half after Southdale first opened, and a third department store was introduced to anchor growth. Its name wasn't significant to me then, though it later would be: JCPenney.

I spent some time at JCPenney during those years. But I spent more time at Dayton's. The year after JCPenney opened at Southdale, my brother, Dwight, participated in a carolers group that sang every night for thirty days at Dayton's flagship department store in Minneapolis. Every night they performed, my mom would drive me, Dwight, and our sister, Diane, along a frozen highway 12 into downtown, where we would follow the singers through the store, up all the escalators, through the men's, women's, and home departments, before finally reaching the elaborate winter wonderland display on the tenth floor. No sooner had we arrived there than I realized it was the same place I'd first met Santa Claus years earlier. Every meaningful moment of my life, it seemed, was attached to a store. Prom tuxedo fittings, haircuts for school pictures, cleats for baseball. I wouldn't have known who I was without the stores I grew up in. Maybe that's why today, my favorite thing to do is walk through stores. Maybe that's what Steve sensed as the sun set on our first meeting and I was still talking about them.

□

When I caught up with Steve's recruiter Dan Walker in the process of writing this book, he explained that I "had Steve at hello." My knowledge of retail was important to him, but how I treated him made a stronger impression.

This shouldn't be surprising. Steve did not have the same monopoly on the word *nice* that Minnesota did. But he was unapologetically himself, and that courage gave others a chance to give him what I believe he struggled to give himself—kindness. I was not the only kind person in his life. Steve Wozniak, Tim Cook, Jony Ive, and Steve's wife, Laurene—all of them were kind. Not pushovers, mind you. But kind.

Being kind has always been in my nature, and it has benefitted me throughout my life. I first learned this in middle school. To that point, the world had been small. Cornelia Elementary was a few blocks from my house. The teachers all knew me. The students did, too. I walked to and from school every day with my brother, Dwight, and when school ended, he and I would play Wiffle ball in our backyard with our best friends, the Mootys. Around 7:00 p.m., my mom would ring the bell for dinner, the Mootys would head home, and Dwight, Diane, and I would gather around the dining room table with our parents. It was, in virtually every way, the true all-American childhood.

If I grew up in a cocoon, middle school was the first time I left it. More than that, middle school was the first time I even noticed it was there. I boarded a bus for the first time on a warm September day in 1969, not having realized how nervous I was until I took my first step past the driver. I stared down the aisle and saw a bunch of bigger, older students leering at each other—and, it seemed, at me. Pressed forward by the kids behind me, my eyes darted around for a seat. I found one and threw myself into it. My imagination, once filled with images, was empty. All I could see was what was in front of me: the cracked brown leather of the seats, the fabric of my backpack, and—once the bus started rolling—the unfamiliar neighborhoods passing by. I didn't know where I was, but I knew exactly where I wasn't. Home. For those earliest days in middle school, I thought of little else.

Out of that experience, I grew in what felt like a different way than I'd been growing. I wanted to feel connected to those around me: the popular kids, the athletes. For a time, that meant wanting to be like them. I wanted the confidence and security it seemed like they had. I wanted to do what it seemed like they did: throw clothes on, flip my hair across my face, and walk out of my house feeling handsome and confident. I wanted my arrival at school to coincide with girls smiling and waving or whispering to each other as I walked by. But with parents who exemplified the importance of earning what you had, I also didn't want any of it. I was in desperate need of connection, but I also felt like the connections I wanted would turn me into something I didn't recognize. The dissonance quickly became all-encompassing. In fact, all I remember from middle school is tiptoeing along the fence between who I was becoming and who I wanted to be.

Eventually, I picked a side. I chose the version of myself that I felt like I'd always been: the sweet, if shy, kid. The one who listened and observed. The one who noticed, as he attended middle school, that he wasn't the only one who felt like he didn't belong. I began to see in others what I felt in myself: the same lack of belonging, the same need for connection. My dad told me that everyone liked to talk about themselves, so instead of seeking the kindness I needed, I began offering it. And in offering it, I found it. So I continued to be kind. I asked the kids who were quiet like I was how their day was going. I learned about them. We sat together at lunch, studied together, and greeted each other in the halls. The connections weren't deep, but the need they served—for me and others—was.

I couldn't have identified this at the time, of course. It didn't occur to me that my kindness was affecting others' opinions of me. But then in eighth grade, the assistant pastor at our church—Mount Olivet Lutheran—announced that my confirmation class of 250 kids would be electing a confirmation president. He passed voting slips around. Upon returning to the chapel the following Wednesday, he announced the results.

"As confirmation president," he began, "the class selects Ron Johnson!"

I looked around for this "Ron Johnson," and 502 eyeballs stared back at me.

Wait, I thought. That's *my* name.

It's hard to overstate how surprised I was. It was unimaginable that when asked to nominate a confirmation president, anyone would even *remember* my name, let alone write it down. Except, they did both.

It turned out, too, that the confirmation president was responsible for giving a speech to a packed church of two thousand people at our confirmation graduation ceremony. Prior to having been elected, this would've been unimaginable. But having been elected by my classmates gave me confidence. The speech I delivered dwarfed anything I'd believed myself capable of before. It also taught me two things. The first was that kindness earned me the right to lead others. The second was that once I had others' support, there was no limit to what I could accomplish.

Both lessons followed me into high school, where I was eventually nominated as captain of my varsity soccer team. With the support of my teammates—and the belief that it was a captain's responsibility to lead—I found myself imagining where we could go. And there was one place that I really, *really* wanted to go: Minnesota's state tournament. There was just one problem. We had won only two games the year prior.

It didn't matter. I called a meeting for those interested in soccer, outlined my vision, and was as surprised as anyone when the room of nearly a hundred kids erupted in support of it. People, I learned, *wanted* to do big things. And in the end, we *did* a big thing. A team that had won two games the year before eventually entered the state tournament in Minnesota, not as an underdog but as the number one seed. And while I hesitate to speak in platitudes in a book, I'm hard-pressed to do any better; if there was anything our state tournament run showed me, it was that, well, *anything was possible.* There were no limits. We could do anything we put our minds to.

A lot of people noticed what we did that season. But it was my dad who recognized what *I* could do as a result. He saw the fire I'd lit in the heart of my team. And in that ability, he saw something he'd seen before. My dad had worked as a politician during the 1950s in Washington, DC, and was exposed to great leaders. He named my brother, Dwight, after one of them. But what he observed about them—about people like Eisenhower, John F. Kennedy, or our Minnesota senator, Hubert Humphrey—was that they didn't actually "do" so much. Instead, they were people around whom things got done; their success, as another author I loved would later put it, came in the energy they stirred in other people. And while an unlikely state tournament run for a high school soccer team out of a well-to-do Minneapolis suburb might not have seemed predictive of much, for my dad, I believe it planted an idea in his imagination—that maybe I had a flicker of the same ability he'd seen in the leaders he respected; maybe I had the spark in me that could eventually light others' souls on fire. And maybe it was his job, as my dad, to fan the flames.

Of course, I can't know any of this for sure. All I can know is what I remember, and what I remember is my dad speaking highly of men like Humphrey, Kennedy, and Eisenhower. I also remember him putting on our living room table a 1973 issue of *Time* that had Minnesota governor Wendell Anderson—who was elected by Minnesota's engaged, educated populace on the promise of *higher* taxation to support programs for people. But as of 1975, I did not see myself as I believe my dad saw me. I was honestly just having fun. I liked the idea of being on a mission with other people, and taking a two-win Edina West Cougars team to the state tournament in a sport that really didn't matter yet to Minnesota felt like a mission. I found that it was an easy way to make friends, too, and to feel connected. And I did feel connected to them, to the point that I didn't really want to *leave* them. That fall, I applied to Stanford, and I encouraged most of my friends to apply as well—especially those on the soccer team. People told me I was crazy, that this would "hurt my chances." But that hadn't occurred to me. I just wanted to go with my friends.

In the end, I did. Twenty-five kids from our class applied to Stanford. Nine—including my best friends from the soccer team, Tom Virden and Mike Anderson—got in. It was more admits to Stanford out of Edina West than there had ever been applicants. And it was more proof to me that the things I believed *sounded* great—like going to Stanford with close friends—would actually *be* great; it was more proof to me that I could lead, and more evidence for my dad that others would want to follow.

Naturally, when I arrived at Stanford, I came in assuming both things were true. I don't think it was arrogance, mind you, but maybe it was. I had assumed something that would catch up to me years later, too: that the geography of the place I'd arrived would resemble that of where I was from.

It didn't.

California was different from Minnesota. And the people were different, too—slightly less trusting, slightly more skeptical. In me, I wonder if they saw someone who was too nice, too good to be true—someone whose manipulative nature would reveal itself the moment they let their defenses down. But the defenses signaled by my openness weren't hiding. Instead, they simply weren't there. I'd never really had to develop them. All I'd developed was an ability to play offense—with kindness, imagination, creativity. But I needed other people to believe in me to make anything out of those abilities, and that required believing in myself. On the pitch with the Cougars at Edina West, I'd believed that if I worked hard, I could be great, that the team could be great. The latter might've been true at Stanford, but the former didn't seem to be.

I had gotten to Stanford a few weeks before school started because, like at Edina West, I'd be on the soccer team. But while I started in every game as a freshman, I realized very quickly that I was not special on this team. I was *good*, but everyone around me was *great*. Soccer had provided extraordinary meaning to me in high school, but it wouldn't do the same at Stanford.

I needed a new path.

To find it, I did what I'd always done: I practiced kindness and service. They were my default modes, having been raised in the love-your-neighbor-as-yourself culture of Minnesota. I grew up in a home where service was just what you did; my mom encouraged me and my siblings to shovel snow from our neighbor's driveway after her husband passed, and then, twice a week, brought us to either volunteer in a home for the mentally disabled or read for the blind. There was something innately grounding to me about serving others. So I sought opportunities to be of similar service at Stanford.

Twice a week, I made the hour-long walk from my dorm to the Ronald McDonald House to physically pump mucus from the lungs of patients with cystic fibrosis. Perhaps honoring my dad's belief that I had some future in politics, I ran for—and was elected to—the Stanford student government, where I worked to shape a better future for the student body. Then, during my senior year, I worked as a resident adviser and helped students adjust to life on campus. But while these activities filled my calendar at Stanford, they weren't filling my soul. Service felt good, and I knew it was the right way to spend my days. But I didn't yet see how it could be what I would do with my life.

By the time I left Stanford, I also knew that I'd just spent four years among many of the greatest athletes, artists, and scientists in the world. It felt like a missed opportunity. Greatness, I determined, would require focus. The problem was that I still had no idea what to focus on.

□

When we are uncertain about the future, we can do one of two things: look outward or inward. The former—listening to what others tell you to do, or mimicking what others are doing—is easy and natural. The latter—looking inward—is harder. But even when we look inward, the question tends to be: What do I want? What we tend to ask less is: What does the world want from me?

I wouldn't have asked this question of myself as a twenty-two-year-old if not for my dad. It was in my early twenties, after I left Stanford, that he first started using a word that would become familiar: *significance*. That, he seemed to suggest, was what I had the opportunity to achieve in my life. And I loved my dad. He was my hero. I wanted to honor that belief, to prove him not wrong but right. The problem was that achieving "significance" would require first understanding what it meant, and I had no idea. So I asked my dad. Again and again and again. And each time, he declined to give me a definition. So, finally, I went to the dictionary.

"Has meaning," read its definition.

Okay, I thought. Then I looked up *meaning*.

"Significance," the dictionary read.

Great, I thought. Perfect.

The point might've been lost on me then, but it became clearer to me as time went on. No one could define *significance* for me. The circularity of its definition—significant things had meaning, and meaning meant significance—was the point. Every person is their own source of meaning; each one of us has to define significance for ourselves. And we define it, my dad seemed to suggest, through what we choose to do.

For my dad, significance meant public service. In his twenties, he worked in Washington, DC, and when he returned to Minneapolis, he ran for the Minnesota state legislature. He later forfeited a life in public service for a job at General Mills, and while that was hard for him, it was what our family needed, and he obliged. In the meantime, his passion for politics grew. He loved our politicians and was proud to be one of their constituents. He respected Humphrey, Anderson, and Eisenhower. He admired their courage, their character. And part of him saw me in them, or them in me. Part of him hoped I'd find my own path to public service. And I would. It just wasn't my dad's.

I could say here that I always knew I wanted to be in business. I don't know if that's true. But I do know that as I left Stanford, it felt like everyone I knew was going off to a job consulting in Los Angeles, or doing finance in New York City, with the plan to eventually return to business school. That felt right—or at least, not wrong. The shadow of Watergate was still looming large; business felt like a more natural path to significance, now, than politics. I applied and was accepted to a job in the consulting arm of one of the big accounting firms in Minneapolis, Peat Marwick Mitchell. I would cut my teeth there. Then I, too, would apply to business school.

In the meantime, I'd catch glimpses of a truth I'd relearn repeatedly throughout my career: that often, new paths reveal themselves once you're already on a journey. Getting to Peat Marwick required my walking through the Minneapolis Skyway System—a physical path—designed by the Dayton family to reinvigorate Minneapolis's decaying downtown in the wake of post–World War II suburban flight. And once I entered that skyway system, getting to the elevator bank to reach Peat Marwick's offices on the fortieth floor of the IDS Center required walking through a store.

A department store.

Dayton's department store.

Chance, maybe. Or, perhaps, fate.

Over the next two years, I became familiar with Dayton's. Part of the reason why was their security guard—their loss-prevention officer—Jim Fuhrmann. Slight, balding, and well into his sixties, Jim was hardly the picture of intimidation, and he didn't try to be. Instead, he was warm. He was kind. He was, in many ways, like I was—always up on the balls of his feet, ready to greet people with a handshake and a smile.

"Good morning, Ron!" he'd exclaim as he saw me coming. "How are you?"

"Jim!" I'd say back. "If I were any better, I'd be you!"

Those interactions might have seemed insignificant. To me, they were anything but. I found that I cared about Dayton's because I cared about Jim, and I cared about Jim because Jim cared about me. My heart beat faster in Dayton's. I could see their fixtures in my mind's eye even when I wasn't in the store. I had to set my mind to consulting, but I couldn't keep my mind off retail. What I didn't realize yet was that this voice was my intuition—my inner voice trying to tell me what I would find significant—and that its insistence was an indicator that perhaps, I hadn't just found where the world wanted me to be. Perhaps I'd found where I wanted to go.

For a time, I did what most of us do when our intuition speaks: I failed to listen. I'd created a map of my future. Retail wasn't on it. In fact, it didn't even occur to me as I walked through Dayton's that retail *could* be on it. Getting into the best business school did not depend on my wonderings about how Dayton's could reposition their shoe fixture to maximize foot traffic. So, day after day, I pored over hospital feasibility studies at Peat Marwick, reminding myself that they were significant—that they "had meaning"—because they led to the construction of hospitals that served people. I was helping the world and earning a reputation that would follow me into it.

That, at least, is what I told myself.

Less than a year after starting at Peat Marwick, I was in the office at 4:00 a.m. alone. The long hours had recently paid off with a promotion—a reminder that I was on the path to the same greatness I'd had no chance of achieving playing soccer at Stanford. I got up, stretched, and walked to the window, gazing out at the smaller structures below.

I've *made* it, I thought.

Made *what*? the voice in my head asked.

It was a great question.

A reputation? I wondered. A path to business school? To financial success?

Yes.

But . . . did any of that matter? Did any of it feel significant to *me?*

No, I thought. The right answers suddenly felt wrong.

I stood there for a while. I gazed out at Minneapolis's skyline, the lights winking at me in the buildings below. The office was quiet, dark. I found comfort in knowing I was good at what I did, but none in the idea of doing it forever. I didn't want to spend ten weeks on a project. I wanted to spend ten years on a *mission.* I wanted to make something, build something. A career. A life. Myself.

What, I wondered, could I build? And from where could I build it?

More than that: What would light me on fire?

Somewhere, forty floors below, was the answer.

□

Steve, I would come to learn, had somewhat of a similar experience to the one I had at Dayton's in his early twenties. After dropping out of college at Reed, he dropped in on a calligraphy class, and around the same time I was figuring out my future, he was ensuring that the original Macintosh would ship with multiple typefaces and proportionally spaced fonts. There would've been no way for Steve to "connect the dots" looking forward, no way for him to know how what he was doing would influence what he would later do. There was only the ability to do things, to try things, then have faith that the knowledge he accrued would resurface later, when necessary.

I tried a few things after I graduated Stanford. I worked at Peat Marwick. I volunteered with Minneapolis's Citizens League. I was assistant coach of Edina's American Legion baseball team—my former squad. Meanwhile, I played on every recreational sports team I could: softball, basketball, and soccer. Then, in 1982, I applied—and was admitted to—Harvard Business School. Whatever I was going to do—consulting, finance, retail—I needed to be on an equal playing field with the best to do it. But from the moment I arrived at Harvard, something felt off. I wanted a training ground. Harvard felt like a victory lap. The sense I got from many around me was that we had all "made it" simply by virtue of having been admitted to Harvard. And in some ways, this was true. We were on the stepping stone to the best consulting and financial firms in the world—to Wall Street, to "success." But a year past the realization that I didn't want to be great at consulting, nothing about being stuck on the path to doing it for the rest of my life felt comfortable. I was trying to make a leap to a destination I couldn't see.

But I was catching glimpses.

Often, the CEOs who were subjects of the cases we were reviewing would visit our classes and present. Those I admired most had made it to the top of their respective industries by making permanent, lasting impacts. When they explained the nature of those impacts, every one of them shared the same message: They absolutely *loved* what they did. Whether that love was a result of their success or a predictor of it, what they said stuck with me. It was a lesson my dad emphasized, too. If I was going to be significant at something—whatever that meant—I needed to pick an industry I loved and commit to it for a lifetime.

So, what did I love? Toward the end of my first year at Harvard, I sat in my dorm room and tried to figure it out. I sifted through the four-hundred-some-odd cases next to my desk to find my favorites. After fifteen minutes, I had two piles. In the bigger one sat the cases I didn't love: finance, operations, organizational behavior. In the smaller pile sat the cases that lit me on fire: marketing, retail. I thought back to Southdale, to Dayton's. Coupled with the memory of Jim's greetings, it was all starting to feel something like an invitation.

□

I didn't say yes to retail immediately. In fact, part of me tried to bury the knowledge I'd unearthed in the letter I'd opened. I accepted an offer the summer after my first year at Harvard to intern at an investment bank, Salomon Brothers, in New York City. It was the expected thing, the "Harvard" thing. I thought, too, that appeasing the outer voices would do the same to my inner voice. The opposite happened. The quieter the outer voices got, the easier it was to hear my own. And the more I tried to ignore that voice, the louder it got.

That feeling sat inside me with all the comfort of a hot coal through my internship that summer. And at Salomon Brothers, the stakes were higher than they'd been at Peat Marwick. The work was more demanding, the hours longer, the job more intense. I was drawn in by the challenge and the rewards of meeting it: the suit, the status, the salary. But as I did the work, I couldn't justify the rewards I was getting with the value I was creating. I *did* think about it constantly, but only because I had to continue rationalizing it to myself. I missed retail, where the thoughts came to me unbidden. I missed Jim. Armani suits and Rolexes didn't fill the hole in my heart. The only thing I liked about being fifty floors up was my ability to look out.

On a trip home that summer, I spoke to my dad about retail. The rubber was meeting the road, so to speak: I was careening toward a decision that would shape my life. My dad listened, as he always did, and later set up a conversation with a family friend, Dick Schall, who was then the vice chairman of the Dayton Hudson Corporation. I shared my thinking with Dick, and he introduced me to an idea. There was a different place I could consider: a mid-tier department store chain on the West Coast, Mervyn's, which was then Dayton Hudson's fastest-growing subsidiary. If I were interested in retail, Dick told me, that was the place to go.

I was more than interested. The dots were beginning to connect; I found myself reliving moments with Dwight at Gabbert's, or with Diane at Dayton's. I was giddy thinking of creating the same environments in which I'd once felt so at home. I thought, too, about my years engaging in service, about how success in retail meant serving the customer well, and about how serving people well began with kindness. I also thought about how, years after abandoning soccer, retail was, in many ways, like sports. There was a manager, a team, and a scoreboard—the sales report—and at the end of the day, you got to see how you'd done. Then you got to improve on it—not the next week, like in soccer, or the next year, like in most businesses, but the next *day*. Every day was a new game, a new chance to play.

Sure, retail didn't carry the status of Salomon Brothers, but it carried an energy and potential that just seemed fun. No industry felt more dynamic, and no place felt more like home.

Of course, there was one other thing about retail that scared and thrilled me: *very few from Harvard were considering it.* In fact, I'm not even sure friends thought that *I* was truly considering it. But I was. I visited Mervyn's corporate headquarters and fell immediately in love with their culture of humility and kindness. But I was a kid in business school, and I was drawn to what so many of my classmates seemed drawn towards, too.

Goldman Sachs.

On a Saturday in September of 1983, I made it to a "bake-off" at Goldman—their term for a competition meant to see who could stand the heat. Ten hours later, I was still going. Whistles would blow, and we would switch offices. The exhilaration of the competition made me forget that this wasn't what I wanted to do. Then, hours after I left, I got a call offering me the chance to do it.

In the moment, I was excited. Friends were, too. I called Tom out in California, told him the news, and accepted his congratulations. Of course I was going to accept the Goldman offer, he seemed to say. Good old Ronnie, good-natured, good family, off to a great company. And I was off to a great company.

It just wasn't Goldman.

When I told Tom, he was incredulous. No one turned down Goldman. No one did it to go into retail. And no one would *ever* do it to go where I was going: the stockroom. But I'd gotten some good advice from Dick.

"The net present value of your life is greater than the net present value of your bank account," he said.

That was the last push I needed to pick Mervyn's. That, and the bouquet of flowers they sent me. Something to care for. I liked that.

Also, for as crazy as Tom thought my decision was, there was upside to it for him. I'd be in Hayward, California. He was working for a company based not far from there, a startup, and they'd gone public just before he'd arrived, netting their CEO, some guy with a funny last name, $250 million.

"Dude's a *genius*," Tom had said.

"What's the company?" I asked.

"Apple Computer."

I had never used a computer coming out of business school, and I didn't know the first thing about them. Tom told me I would—that maybe someday, we all would.

Maybe, I thought. Someday.

In the meantime, now, I had a different industry to learn.

CHAPTER 2

I Love Retail

The best foundations—the ones from which you can build the highest—go deep. And for the next several years, I went deep. I *buried* myself in retail.

First came Mervyn's Glendale Galleria store in Los Angeles's San Fernando Valley, where I met one of the best bosses I ever had, Brian Bee. I learned a lot from Brian, but most important was how I wanted to make other people feel. I followed him dutifully as he bounced through the store's aisles, connected with each employee individually, by name, and shared a quick moment with them. And I listened when Brian explained to me that if he did his job right, he could have a 20 percent impact on the store's sales that day.

I aspired to eventually do much more than that.

Over the next six months, I had more fun at work than I'd ever thought possible. I unloaded trucks, stocked shelves, and rang up customers. I scraped gum off the floor. I celebrated employees' birthdays and had my own celebrated. And I played softball with the team on Thursday nights, too. All of this was formative. It was also *fun*.

When I eventually returned to Mervyn's corporate headquarters in Hayward, I threw myself into work with a similar gusto. I started off as an assistant buyer in swimsuits and activewear before getting promoted to unit control manager of twenty-five people in the jewelry, cosmetics, and accessories division. I had so many thoughts on how things could be done better, and I flooded my team with ideas, thinking that everyone would be as excited as I was.

They weren't.

On Halloween in 1987, my boss pulled me into a conference room for my quarterly review. I was wearing some sort of costume, which, when I realized what was happening, felt more than a little ridiculous. Then, when she said what she said, I felt even more ridiculous than that.

"This isn't working," she said.

"What . . . the costume?" I asked. "It's Hallo—"

"No," she said. "Not the costume. You. Your team *likes* you, but they don't like working *for* you."

"*What?*" I said. "But I spend so much time with them!"

She took a deep breath.

"That might be part of the problem," she said. "They say that every time they bring you an idea, you say, 'That's good, but wouldn't it be great if we did *this*?'"

I do say that, I thought.

"I'm trying to lead them," I said.

"You're not leading them," my boss said. "You're suffocating them."

Suffocating.

The word stuck with me. It made me doubt my instincts, my intuition. Everything that had felt right suddenly felt wrong.

I didn't know what to do. All I'd been doing was what I'd learned to do in business school. Management, as I understood it from Harvard, was about setting goals and holding people accountable to them. And I had a high bar for what those goals could be. But instead of inspiring anyone, I was smothering them. This was making them fear me. I saw in their eyes a version of myself that I didn't want to recognize. I saw who I had never wanted to be.

I'd like to say that I turned things around right then and there. I didn't. Part of this was circumstantial. Not long after that conversation with my boss, I was promoted to the position of senior buyer in Mervyn's men's shirts and ties department. I had a small team but was mostly free to indulge myself. So, I did. And it was fun. I *loved* being a buyer. I would wake up at 4:00 a.m. every day, go directly to the office, and race the sales report to the printer so I could be the first call to New York to reorder what had sold best. Then, on Saturday mornings, I would visit JCPenney, Macy's, and Nordstrom in nearby Hillsdale Shopping Center to see what might sell even better. I loved seeing those stores' leaders on buyer's trips, asking them how a new line was doing, and seeing their eyes widen. They might have wondered how I knew, but it wasn't a secret. I just loved retail.

My first chance to do something significant came in Mervyn's men's shirts and ties department. At the time, Mervyn's was trying to position itself as an upscale but still value-focused department store. We offered better value and were more approachable than the typical department store, but we had better quality merchandise and fashion than the typical discounter. Still, most of our fashion was private label merchandise, and at the time, department store assortments were roughly 80 percent branded. If we were trying to go upscale, being 100 percent private label felt wrong. The problem was that brands believed, correctly, that our reliance on discounts for sales would lead us to devalue them. So, instead of going after brands that would laugh at the idea of being in Mervyn's, I went to a department store we were competing with—JCPenney—and took note of two brands that were popular with the middle-class shopper at the time: Arrow and Van Heusen. My divisional merchandise manager and I brought the idea of partnering with Mervyn's to Arrow, and they said no. But Van Heusen said yes. I made them 40 percent of the department, and sales rose 40 percent.

My confidence grew by more than that.

Around the time I turned thirty, I moved back to Minneapolis and joined Target. It was the next logical step in the progression I'd been making; Target had supplanted Mervyn's as Dayton Hudson's hottest and fastest-growing subsidiary (and would later become the company's namesake), and continuing my ascent through retail would start with landing there. But there remained the problem I'd been ignoring: I hadn't made any meaningful progress toward finding a way not to suffocate people as a leader. Given the nature of my role, I hadn't needed one, and at Target, the same would be true. I interviewed for the position of senior buyer, got it, and was given the choice of department.

I picked toys.

When I made this decision, a lot of people told me I was crazy.

"Toys is the *hardest* department to buy for!" they said.

I wasn't sure I agreed; in toys, vendors—like Hasbro and Mattel—would tell us what they were planning to market, so a lot of the work was just battling for allocation. But if anything, that gave me confidence. I was thirty and single, loved building relationships with vendors—playing golf, taking them out to dinner—and had time to do it. But I also knew the stakes: Toys was extraordinarily seasonal, so if you were going to make a big bet, you had to be sure. If you got it wrong, you weren't making it up in the spring or fall. The holidays were it.

I remember thinking this pressure was appealing. Target was locked in a battle with Walmart, whose cheaper real estate and more spartan stores had given them a lower cost structure than we had. We couldn't win long-term on price, but toys—if we bet on the right products—could help us win on convenience. If people shopped Target for toys during the holidays, they weren't going to Walmart for wrapping paper, or ribbons, or cards, or sweaters. They were coming to us for *everything.* As the old saying goes: So go toys, so goes the company at holiday. The old retailers had it right.

How would I change Target's toys department? How would I make it *better*? These were the questions that ran through my head as I walked the aisles it was my job to fill. And I noticed that along with carrying a brand that I knew both parents and their kids loved—LEGO—we were also carrying all their so-called competition. I say "so-called" because to my mind, nothing could beat LEGO. So why were we carrying anything else?

Well, in retail, what I was seeing was considered *safe.* Cover all the price points, make sure nothing is left out. But as I checked the shelves, the only thing "left out"—that is, *on* the shelves, *by* customers—was *all of LEGO's competition.* And sure, it might be picked up by last-minute holiday shoppers. But that didn't seem like a reason to keep stocking it. I didn't think customers were picking it so much as they were getting stuck with it. I believed that everyone wanted LEGO, and I knew we could give it to them.

In the fall of 1989, I made a big bet: I filled every inch of every shelf in one of our aisles with LEGO, devoting 48 linear feet of space to a single brand. This allowed us to carry more LEGO than any other retailer, and when Christmas rolled around and customers had learned to associate us with LEGO, we became the brand's top priority; they kept us in stock all the way through the season. By committing, we earned commitment—from customers first and *then* from our vendor—and the echoes of the initiative's success were felt throughout Target. I was learning that doing big things wasn't just meaningful. It was effective. It was, in a very real sense, a business strategy.

Still, a business strategy was all that my work in toys was. And it was all that branded dress shirts had been at Mervyn's, too. And that was nagging at me. I'd joined a church when I returned to Minneapolis and begun exploring my calling in Bible study, and as much as pure business success was nice, it didn't feel like a calling. What did feel like a calling was the way in which Jesus described love: not as a romantic feeling but as a decision to secure the good of those who came into your path. This made sense to me; I had always felt called to treat people this way. The question was how to do it through my work.

The answer was not immediately clear. At no point in my two years at Harvard Business School had a professor talked about "love," or loving people. And I could see why. Loving people, as I understood it from my life, meant trying to constantly get clear on what they needed from me. Managing people, as I understood it from Harvard, was about constantly trying to *make* clear what I needed from them.

Nothing had ever felt more foreign.

This had something to do with the comfort I found in my buying positions at Mervyn's and in toys at Target. I was working with small teams—not "managing" so much as collaborating. And this would be fine so long as I stayed a buyer, but my success in toys was catching the eyes of those responsible for helping me move up. I was promoted to be the divisional merchandise manager for Target's kids department in 1990, and with fifty people reporting to me, most of whom were years—or decades—my senior, I quickly realized I needed a new way to look at leadership.

The answer came in a book. *A Return to Love* by Marianne Williamson. I picked up a copy in an airport bookstore before a trip to

Singapore—my first with my team in kids. In that store, I read a few pages. Then, on the plane, I read the whole book.

Marianne described the world as a garden of which we are all given a piece to transform—a piece that is our relationships and our circumstances, yes, but also our work. She also explained that it wasn't necessarily our circumstances that needed to change. Rather, it was *us.* Our fundamental nature is love, and it is that nature to which we must return.

"Love is what we are born with," she wrote. "Fear is what we learn here. The spiritual journey is the relinquishment—or unlearning—of fear and the acceptance of love back into our hearts. Love is the essential fact. It is our ultimate reality and our purpose on earth. To be consciously aware of it, to experience love in ourselves and others, is the meaning of life."

I read her words repeatedly. Nothing had ever so elegantly captured what I believed. I thought of my first memory, my mom's reminder that I was loved unconditionally. That was how I wanted those I led to feel.

These thoughts accompanied me that night as I got to Singapore, checked in at the Shangri-La Hotel, and stopped by the hotel bar. I wanted to go for a run the following morning, and I asked the bartender where he thought I should go. He told me there was a bus every morning that took guests over to the Singapore Botanic Gardens. It was a twenty-minute ride, he said, but one that was more than worth taking if I'd be up at 6:00 a.m. the following day. I told him that I probably would, as it would be early evening back in Minnesota, where I'd come from. I also liked the idea of running through a garden.

The following morning, I woke up early, took the twenty-minute bus ride, exited, then began my run. No sooner had I broken a sweat than I was surrounded by the most beautiful plants I had ever seen.

Every day for the remainder of that trip, I returned to the garden, and every night, I reread Marianne. I realized that everyone on my team needed a light to grow toward and support as they did, but every person's unique geography meant that they—like every plant—needed something different, too. Some needed space; others needed praise. Some needed encouragement; others needed a firm hand. It was my responsibility to tend my teams like one might tend plants in this garden—to figure out what they needed and do my best to give it to them. Clear vision, high standards, and excellent support. That, I realized, was how I could secure my team's good, will their success, and create a climate in which everyone could thrive.

When I got back from Singapore with my team, I found that conversations in this new leadership style were fun. People responded well to being treated like people: inherently good, trying their best, and uniquely capable of great things. Those conversations also began giving shape to a vision for our kids' department that was better for Target and better for our customers. And in my efforts to realize that vision, I would find myself—for perhaps the first time since that 1975 soccer season—on a mission.

□

By the time I got to Target's kids' department, our Walmart problem had only gotten worse.

Target and Walmart shared the same founding year: 1962. Ever since, the two brands had been locked in a battle over the loyalty of the discount customer. Walmart served them in rural locations with spartan stores, while Target went with urban real estate and nicer store environments. And while the two brands had existed for thirty years in a fragile peace, as of my arrival at Target, Walmart was beginning to threaten it.

The threat came in the form of Walmart's encroaching on Target's urban territory, and the risk for Target was clear immediately. Walmart had a lower cost structure than Target, which meant they would eventually win on basic products like toothpaste, which every retailer sold for the same market price. So, in the late 1980s, Target's CEO, Bob Ulrich, had announced a new strategy for Target: differentiation. Every department needed to find a way to make itself different—and not just from Walmart but from all of Target's competitors: Macy's, JCPenney. This included the department I had just joined: kids.

By the time I got to kids, I had been walking through the same departments in our competing stores for years. All were differentiated in some unique way.

We were not.

This *should* have mattered to Target. The reason it didn't *seem* to have mattered was because the department's performance appeared, from the numbers, to be good. I remember seeing 15 percent year-over-year growth and being impressed. But walking through the department, I was underwhelmed. The presentation was confusing. The merchandising was poor. I knew what Gap, Macy's, and JCPenney were doing. I knew how a world-class kids' department felt, and Target's did not feel like one. But the message I got when I asked questions about our performance was clear.

"Don't upset the apple cart."

Still, I couldn't not upset the apple cart. My intuition told me that the department simply couldn't be growing as much as everyone said it was. But then I'd check and recheck the reports, and the numbers would be right there in front of me. There had to be some other explanation for our growth.

Surviving the battle with Walmart, it turned out, wasn't just about differentiating from them. It was also about growing alongside them.

And for Target, this expansion corresponded with approximately 10 percent year-over-year growth in new stores. Kids' growth, in other words, was mostly just *Target's* growth.

This might not have been such an issue if not for two other things I was noticing. The vast majority of Target's new-store growth, I knew, was in the suburbs, and most of our marketing was geared toward young moms (versus Walmart's older customer). The suburbs, too, were *filled* with young families—and I knew from my time in toys just how hard Target was trying to reach them. We had wanted to establish relationships with young moms who would eventually shop Target for all their kids' needs and had been positioning ourselves—for years—to do exactly this. So, to my mind, our kids' department—far from just barely beating the pace of Target's growth—should've been blowing its doors off. Kids, in other words, had the opportunity to be the fastest-growing department in Target.

As I thought about how to turn the kids' department into what I imagined it could be—and how to do something with that department that would permanently improve Target—the first thing I noticed was our size. We couldn't add more variety into our limited footprint unless we changed how we organized within that footprint, and at the time, we were organizing like all our competitors—with a kids' section and an infants' and toddlers' section. Kids was then divided into girls and boys, which were then divided into subsections corresponding with size ranges. For girls, the smaller range was 4–6x, while the larger one was 7–14; for boys, the smaller range was 4–7, while the larger one was 8–20. There was a gap between each range, and kids who fell into it were left without anything that truly fit. When I asked why we were doing it this way, the answer was the same one I'd come to expect.

"Because *everyone* does it this way."

I couldn't help wondering if there were opportunities in being different.

I also noticed that our styles often made no sense for the kids who wore them. The smaller size ranges offered juvenile styles, while the larger ones catered to adolescents. Put another way: an older, smaller boy—who I could imagine already having a tough time at school—might be limited to shirts that, because they were covered in farm animals, or cartoon characters, would be certain not to make a tough time any easier. When I asked why we hadn't addressed this, the answers were, again, the same.

"Everyone does it this way."

Except, weren't we trying to be different?

"The numbers are *good.*"

But . . . were they? No, they weren't. And neither were *kids' experiences in our clothes.*

These were not the only problems. As I spoke to my buyers, many of whom *had* kids, I learned that one of the biggest problems they faced was actually keeping their kids in clothes. To do it, most parents bought one or two sizes ahead. This solved the problem of having to shop more often, but it also meant that their kids were walking around in shirts that looked like smocks. There had to be a way to help parents shop less while also giving their kids clothes that fit *and* looked good.

Several years earlier, Gap had launched Gap Kids. Their presentation stood out every time I walked into one of their stores. Instead of launching sections for infants, toddlers, and little kids, Gap Kids had one size range—2–20—that covered all of them. They also offered each shirt in a size range—say, a 6–7—versus individual sizes. This could've been a gimmick, but it wasn't. The clothes fit better, lasted longer, and their uncluttered presentation made shopping easier. If copying sounds obvious, you can imagine how excited I was when I realized we could be the first of our true competitors to do it.

Of course, copying Gap would have been easy if we hadn't already been doing something else. Historically, Target would have one rack for boys' polo shirts in sizes 4–7, then another for sizes 8–20. But if we collapsed the sections and dedicated only one rack to sizes 4–20, that would free up another to offer something fun and seasonal like a soccer jersey in the fall. It was a formative moment for me: Being new to the department, a lot of people said it would be easiest to "start small." My experience was precisely the opposite. In retail—an industry in which every decision has ripple effects—I was learning that it was often easier to think big than small. The people working for me also wanted to do big things. They wanted to make parents' lives easier, kids' days better. Securing customers' good also secured employees' good.

Still, everything I wanted to do hinged on one massive bet: To overhaul kids, we would have to change our sizing patterns.

This was my craziest idea yet, and a lot of people pushed back on it. The decision would require remeasuring thousands of kids, developing all new patterns, and convincing vendors to use them for every item they sold to Target. But if we did it, parents could buy any size in any brand for their kids and know it would fit the same way. Also, Target's buyers in the kids' department would be set up for success in the years that followed; even if they didn't pick the right merchandise, they'd have the wind at their back with sizing.

We launched the "standardized sizing" initiative in 1992. For the first six months, our department's numbers plummeted.

Then they stabilized.

Then they *hockey-sticked.*

To that point, I hadn't really had Target's attention. I'd come into toys, which I saw as a relatively easy department, and done a fun thing. Great, cool, fine. But overhauling the kids' department . . . that was a different beast, and my team was a different team. Everyone, Target's head of HR later told me, wanted to work for me, to grow in my garden.

"You're the pied piper," he said.

"Maybe," I replied. Being from Minnesota—and from the family I was from—I knew the importance of being humble . . . or at the very least, the importance of *appearing* humble. But I'll be honest: I didn't feel particularly humble. I knew what I was capable of, what the teams I *led* would be capable of. I knew, too, that I had Target's attention, and that I now had the opportunity to do something even bigger than I'd done.

What I couldn't know was the attention I'd attract—and the man I'd attract it from—as a result.

CHAPTER 3

Good Design Doesn't Have to Be Expensive

All throughout the 1990s, Target's push to differentiate drove us toward fashion. As early as the late 1980s, Target had started filling a Sunday circular that had once bragged of great low prices with models in high-waisted acid-wash jeans, crop-top T-shirts, and chunky platform sneakers. Department store customers who had once whispered about Target at their country clubs were suddenly bragging about their latest find at "Tarzhay."

The problem with using fashion to differentiate was that while it commanded a higher initial markup, markdowns eventually led us to earn the same profit as we did on basic products like toothpaste. And even on basics, our focus on differentiation was hurting the customer. I'd see us buy toothpaste tubes that were four ounces to Walmart's three, then double their price. This was "different"; it was also *worse*. In 1997, I was given the opportunity to lead Target's home department, and when I got there, I sensed an opportunity.

We could make Target not just different, I believed, but also better—and that meant preferred.

Establishing preference for Target was, in many ways, the final act in a play that had begun with listening to CEOs at Harvard Business School in 1984. I had wanted to have a permanent, positive impact—to do something significant—and making Target preferred would certainly qualify. Home was also the hottest retail category in the world in 1997, with Pottery Barn and Crate & Barrel supplanting Gap and The Limited as Americans' favorite places to shop. The question was how to capitalize—how to make something significant out of what felt like a significant moment. How, I wondered, could I use the opportunity as leader of Target's home department to do something that would elevate the brand forever?

How, how, *how*.

Well, as it turned out, there had been a wind blowing, and as the years had gone by in retail, I'd learned to sail. The job, I understood, was as much about understanding what was happening in the world as it was about understanding what was happening in stores. And 1997 was an interesting year. It was the year Steve returned to Apple. It was also the year that he began work on what would become the iMac—an elegant, egg-shaped computer that would bring design to consumer technology. That iMac wouldn't come out until the following year, but as of 1997, Steve must've been seeing the same thing I was seeing: an explosion in design around the world.

As early as the 1980s, the culture around design had been shifting. Then, in the 1990s, a fault opened. In 1993, designer Philippe Starck collaborated with Alan Heller, founder of upscale furniture brand Heller Inc., to release the now iconic Excalibur toilet brush. Per its namesake, the handle of the brush protruded from behind a plastic shield so that when you used it, toilet water wouldn't get on your hand. The Excalibur was sold in London's upscale, design-focused home store The Conran Shop, and it eventually landed in every hip restaurant and home in the city. Later in the nineties, Alan Heller took over the Milan furniture fair with the Bellini Chair. In the corporate world, too, business guru and coauthor of *In Search of Excellence* Tom Peters had recently declared design to be "it," thus giving businesses permission to think aesthetically. Then, in 1997, Volkswagen launched its iconic New Beetle. And all the while, Steve was in Cupertino working on a computer whose smooth edges and svelte figure looked, like the Beetle, *different*.

Design's emergence was being helped along by an unprecedented boom in Americans' economic fortunes. I was one of those Americans. I was attending dinner parties, going to friends' houses, seeing function evolve toward form. Products not only *could* be more than functional—to truly matter, they *had* to be. But I also knew that the homes I was spending time in were not the homes of those who spent meaningful time shopping in Target. And so, it didn't really click for me that we might be able to offer some version of the products I was seeing until I visited a place where everyone had access to them.

Europe.

I was there in February 1997. The occasion was my first buyer's trip to London with my team in home. On a cool morning, I gambled on a foreboding sky and took a walk from Chelsea to South Kensington—an upscale, hip neighborhood filled with influential stores. When the sky opened up, I walked into a small home-goods boutique. Surrounding me were dozens of beautifully designed, essential home items. Each was presented like a work of art, with a placard next to it describing its designer—often, an architect—and what inspired them.

Everyone deserves products like this, I thought.

And then . . .

Target could deliver them.

The idea was obvious. In fact, it was more than obvious. Everyone deserved products that made them smile. And, *and* . . . I thought, design commanded the markup Target had been pursuing with fashion, but *unlike* fashion, good design was timeless—and thus *never had to be marked down.* Doing design would make Target what I believed it could be. Different *and* better. Preferred. Forever.

The vision, as per usual, was not one that anyone else at Target shared. In fact, even my team balked at first.

"Design is *expensive*!" they said.

And sure, it was. But it didn't have to be. I knew designers. They wanted their products to reach as many people as possible. If their products were expensive, it wasn't because of them, but because of the manufacturers or retailers for whom they designed products. And Target was the retailer who could help them sell their products at a price *everyone* could afford.

Still, this was part of the problem. Few thought that a designer would want to work with a mass-market retailer, or that Target's customer, long seen as discount-focused, would embrace sophisticated products that sold for a premium. Fewer still thought that we could adopt a concept associated with a customer we didn't serve and execute it such that it not only attracted them but also appealed to our existing customer. At the highest level, virtually no one thought it would be possible for Target to reach everyone, all at once.

The attitude of other executives reflected this understanding.

"Why don't you test it?" they asked. "Throw a few items on a back endcap and see if customers bite?"

It was a defensible suggestion, but this wasn't a defensive initiative. Target had been trying to serve young moms for years, and I had, too—in our toys and kids' departments. But with design, we could go slightly upstream and earn the loyalty of men and women in their late twenties living in cool, upscale neighborhoods, then continue serving them as they got married and had families. I had just gotten married, too—to my wife, Karen—and we'd started a family when our daughter Lizzey was born. *We* were the customers I believed existed.

I told my buyers that we'd be making a big cut to make room for design: 10 percent of our existing assortment. We would find a partner to launch the initiative and add well-designed products to every category we could. I was certain that this would help us achieve preference.

My buyers thought it was insane.

A 10 percent cut in favor of an unproven initiative wouldn't happen in a vacuum. Vendors might not understand or have the ability to design products to our specifications, and they might shift to designing products for Walmart. And vendors' concerns would be tied to the belief that Target's customer shopped us for basic, functional products, and thus wouldn't adopt design. But that was exactly why we couldn't test it—exactly *why* we had to go big. We would only earn commitment from designers if we committed to design. And yet, this line of thinking did little to comfort my buyers, who were still struggling to imagine who Target's customer could become. So, I found myself searching for more ammo. And I found it in, of all places, Walmart.

I had known for years that Walmart was encroaching on our territory. What I wondered now was whether they were also tightening their assortments. If they were, and if they now had fewer home products in each category than we did, I could position a 10 percent cut as a step towards expanding our home assortment and reaching a new customer without sacrificing our competitiveness with Walmart.

It was a hypothesis.

Now, I needed evidence.

A week later, Karen and I traveled down to Naples, Florida, to visit her parents with Lizzey. Every day, Karen exercised, so I took Lizzey for a few hours. On our first day in Naples, I looked down at her, all of twenty months old, those big blue eyes staring back up at me.

"We're going to *Walmart* today," I said, scrunching my face into a frown. Her ever-present smile turned into a scowl.

That's my Lizzey, I thought.

I took her out to the car we'd rented, got her into her car seat, and we drove across town. Then, after parking at Walmart, I plopped her into her stroller. No sooner had we walked into the store than she'd fallen asleep.

Walmart's home department was huge. Thirty aisles, each just wide enough for two shopping carts to fit next to each other. (Any narrower, and you're hurting the shopping experience; any wider, and you're sacrificing selling space.) Each aisle then had two "runs," or sides of an aisle, and each was thirty-two feet long, six feet tall, and two to three feet deep. The first run I found was filled with toasters. I counted. Walmart had twenty-six. Target, I knew, had thirty-one. But that was just toasters. I got through a few more product categories before Lizzey started to stir, and we left. But luckily, Karen exercised every day, and Lizzey needed to nap every morning. So, for the next three days, I returned to Walmart and completed my count. And in every category, Walmart had *fewer* products than we did.

What excited me most about this realization was understanding how big the opportunity with design was, and how little risk there was to doing it. Walmart had just proven to me that we could cut 10 percent of our existing assortment without losing our existing customer. And design didn't even have to be all that productive off the bat—the point was that it would attract a customer we hadn't yet had, who, even if they didn't buy design, would purchase other things they needed at Target. That new customer's shopping Target would also give buyers in every department the opportunity to go slightly more upscale with their products. Vendors would start imagining what they could design, or how they could improve their packaging. Customers would start thinking of Target for basics *and* design. We could then convince better brands like Bodum and Calphalon to sell their products on our shelves. Over time, the ripples of design would be felt throughout Target.

All my excitement about how great design would be for Target's customer and Target itself allowed me to temporarily ignore the biggest question I faced in getting the products onto our shelves.

Who was going to *design* them?

As it turned out, Target had spent the past few months planning for the launch of our first store in Washington, DC, and had been searching for a way to generate press. To do it, they had accepted an offer to sponsor the construction of scaffolding for a much-needed restoration of the Washington Monument. This would require an architect. Target's CMO, Bob Thacker, hired Michael Graves. A brilliant creative mind whose star had fallen just slightly since its peak in the 1980s, Michael was a perfect fit for the project.

He also turned out to be a perfect fit for me.

Not long after Michael had agreed to do the scaffolding project for Target, Bob visited him at his office in Princeton, where Michael was a professor. A delayed train gave the two men time for a tour, and Michael took Bob up to a conference space. Countless tracings lay on the table. Some, as Bob had expected, were of scaffolding.

Many more were of home goods.

Bob knew I was running Target's home department, but he had

no idea that I'd just determined Target could bring great design to everyone. Even so, he called me and said there was someone I might want to meet, then asked if I could come to Dayton's the following week. I asked who it was that I'd be meeting.

"Michael Graves," Bob said.

"Michael Graves . . ." I repeated. The name sounded familiar. "Wait, like *designer* Michael Graves?"

"Yeah," Bob said. "Can you make it?"

Can I *make* it, I thought.

It was clear from the moment Michael and I met that we saw the world similarly. Within minutes of shaking hands, he was explaining to me that he'd wanted to do a large, low-cost collection of products for years. No one he cared about could afford any of what he'd created. Alessi, who commissioned many of Michael's designs and controlled their pricing, made his bird-whistle teakettle—which Michael had wanted to be competitive with the $50 Revere kettle—*$125.* A tea set Michael designed was later priced at *$10,000.* None of this made him happier. The point of great design wasn't to make money. It was to improve lives, to make people smile. At those prices, Michael's products weren't doing either one.

At Target, they could do both.

The scale of the impact we could have together revealed itself when I brought Michael to our Minneapolis Target store a few weeks later, handed him a stack of Post-its, and asked him to put one on every product he thought he could improve. Michael eyed the stack, looked around, then turned back toward me.

"You're not going to have enough Post-its," he said.

The two of us shared a passion for a world in which everyone could afford great design, and that passion eventually filtered into the team we created. Our ability to collaborate was borne of

Michael's and my playful, boyish friendship. I loved every team I worked with at Target, but I *especially* loved that team. We were, in every way, like a family.

But we didn't start off that way.

□

It's worth pausing here to acknowledge that buyers are accustomed to being treated like royalty. They get to go on lavish overseas trips, stay in posh hotels, spend time talking to vendors, fondling products, being wined and dined. Meanwhile, the first meeting to which I brought my buyers was in Princeton.

Princeton, *New Jersey.*

Princeton, New Jersey, in *February.*

Now, had Michael's team been interested in meeting us, we might've gotten off to a better start. But they weren't, and we didn't. It turned out that they had been begging Michael—as my buyers had been begging me—*not* to pursue this partnership. It would hurt their reputation with their client base, they told him. Alessi, too, implored Michael not to work with us, arguing that it would erode everything they had worked for. But, of course, "everything they had worked for" had, to Michael, felt more like everything *Alessi* had worked for.

Michael wanted something different.

But his desire to bring great design to everyone did not spread easily to his team. It didn't spread easily from me to my buyers, either. For them to buy that good design didn't have to be expensive, they would have to know two things. The first was that the physical products Michael and his team had designed for us would be priced somewhere in the range of what Target's customer could conceivably be expected to pay. The second was how those products would look and feel, which meant foam models. Ideally, Michael's team would've also put those models in an open, uncluttered space.

They did . . . none of the above.

I'll admit fault here. I could've done a better job of communicating what my team would be expecting to Michael so he could communicate it to his team. But I didn't, so he couldn't. As a result, the room we ended up in—far from resembling any of the gorgeous showrooms my buyers had come to expect—was about the size of a broom cupboard. Second, the products—which were crammed into every inch of shelving on the wall—were not those we would be selling at Target. Rather, they were the same products that had made my buyers so hesitant to believe in this partnership in the first place: $150 teakettles and $10,000 tea sets. And *third*, the products that Michael and his team had created to show us were not modeled in foam but scribbled on paper. It didn't matter that this was how designers worked. My team took it as a signal that they weren't taking us seriously, and thus couldn't be taken seriously.

It was not a promising start.

Still, I tried to keep us moving forward. That was always the most important thing: keep people's eyes on the vision, keep things moving. I encouraged my buyers to peruse the drawings and find those they liked, understanding that I would have to speak with Michael about how to get our teams on the same page. My buyers obliged, but only out of obligation. One of my best buyers and closest friends, Bruce Tominello, grabbed the drawings and began sorting them, in front of the entire room, into two piles: a "no" pile and a "maybe" pile. When Michael, who had not attended the meeting, later ran into Steve Sikora—one of the external partners I had worked with on the campaign—in the bathroom, he asked how things were going.

"Bumpy," Steve said.

That was an understatement.

And yet, a lot of good came out of that meeting. The conflict was necessary. It revealed that we spoke different languages, and I knew that those who partnered up—in any domain—often did. I told Michael that my buyers expected models they could touch, and when we came back a few weeks later to his team having created those models, my buyers got excited. It had taken time for people's vision to adjust, but it always takes time. This was a lesson I learned, even if it was one that I would eventually forget.

□

As early as that first meeting between my buyers and Michael's team, it was clear that presentation of the products was going to matter. Target had no salespeople, so the burden of selling a premium-priced product was on the packaging itself. Meanwhile, a typical mass-market package in the nineties was as visually loud as possible, begging for attention with pictures and feature callouts.

Ours needed to look different.

Working with Michael, his team, Design Guys (Steve Sikora's firm), and my team at Target, we modeled our package on the industry icon: the Tiffany box. We picked an elegant color for the boxes, too—a light shade of blue that we ended up calling "Graves blue." Then, instead of feature callouts, we had each box display a faithful photo of the product inside and its name—say, "teakettle." We also settled on a smooth matte finish for the boxes, which had the added benefit of obscuring the dust thrown up by Target's nightly floor polishing. And the boxes themselves were designed with the understanding that most customers would still expect to be misled by packaging and would thus try to open it to see the product inside. Most brands responded by making their packages harder to open. We made ours easy. Latches allowed customers to open the box and see that the product inside looked and felt as luxurious as its packaging suggested. Leading with design would require not being misleading.

Still, as we neared the launch of design, we ran into one final hiccup: the original box we'd been designing proved too expensive, and we nixed it. The problem was that we had been designing two separate gondolas (free-standing, double-sided shelving units)—one for kitchen products, and one for home décor—with that original box's dimensions in mind. The new, smaller box, though it maintained the latch and materials of its predecessor, would make the presentation look cluttered. But this, too, proved to be an opportunity. The extra space gave us the chance to do what I'd seen done in that London boutique and explain the products. We could also introduce Michael so everyone knew who he was. This made our "exhibit" approachable. Every decision we made represented a brushstroke, and the gondola was our canvas.

□

When we finally completed work on design, we'd created a work of art. And it wasn't a somber, heady thing.

It was lighthearted.

It was *fun*.

And perhaps as a result, we planned our launch event at a venue we thought would be fun: the Whitney Museum on Madison Avenue in New York City. Steve Sikora and his wife, Lynn, took the lead on organizing the event, and the sense they got was that New Yorkers had "seen everything," so we needed to keep it short.

No one, we were told, would linger.

Except, well, everyone did.

The truth we learned on the night of the launch was that while

New Yorkers might've *seen* everything, they hadn't *heard* everything. Not this story. Not *our* story.

The one we told them had been two years in the making, but that night, it began curbside at the Whitney. A Graves blue carpet emerged from the front entrance of the museum and snaked across a concrete bridge that passed over a tented outdoor sculpture garden. Rows of silver garden luminaries lined—and lit—the pathway. Michael had designed a set of glass vases as part of the collection, and Lynn had lined up dozens of them at reception, filled them with water and live goldfish, then backlit them. The light cast glimmers off each goldfish's scales that danced on the walls.

And that was just what people saw *before* they entered the museum.

At check-in, guests received a lanyard that included their name and a red coach's whistle, which was meant to resemble the spout on Michael's teakettle. The connection would not be hard to make. Mounted to a Graves-blue wall built in front of the Whitney's bookstore were seventy prototype teakettles, each with its own signature whistle. The kettles were then perched on clear acrylic shelves in front of hidden speakers, creating a sound sculpture. To the left of the teakettle wall stood an enormous silver bull's-eye composed of Graves clocks, and while Target had yet to adopt the bull's-eye without Target's name underneath it as its logo, this sculpture offered an early glimpse of its power. Meanwhile, the adjacent atrium housed three massive chandeliers composed of inverted cake layers of Michael's stainless-steel cooking tools. For the chandelier draping, we selected highly reflective material, then used theater projection lighting to cast it with the Graves color palette. I remember looking around at Lynn, Steve, Michael, Bruce—everyone who had been involved in getting this initiative off the ground.

Above us was a disco ball.

Around us was a *party.*

Finally, an hour or so into the festivities, I took the stage. I introduced Target to the audience over some brief comments, then handed the microphone over to Michael. This was *his* moment, and—in contrast to the forced seriousness of his discipline—he was quite funny. By the end of his comments, those in the audience were blowing the red plastic whistles dangling from their press credentials in approval. No one had known what to expect, and those who had predicted a muted reaction were wrong. Even as Michael's speech took place an hour into the event, the atrium was full and the audience was engaged. When the food was taken away, the crowds lingered. Around 10:00 p.m., the lights came up, and *still* they remained. Even after the bars closed, I watched—with Michael—as people wandered around trying to take it all in. And while it had felt for the entire year that we'd been working on design like we'd been paddling into a swell, that was the first night we realized we were in the middle of a wave. I looked up at the thousands of cooking tools, the hundreds of clocks. Lynn had stacked them to create a sense of abundance. Design was no longer for the few. A new era—design for *all*—had begun.

Of course, it was one thing to believe this standing in the Whitney Museum. It would remain to be seen if a similar excitement would emerge in the hundreds of Target stores around the country. Each store, I knew, was slightly different; each team would put their own unique spin on their presentation. But this didn't make me nervous. It made me excited. I was extremely curious to see how those presentations looked and how customers would react to them. So, on the first day the products were in the store, I drove around to all fifteen Target stores in Minneapolis to see them. I began on the southwest side of Minneapolis at Southdale, then drove north. Ridgedale, Bloomington, St. Louis Park, Eden Prairie. Eventually, I made it to every store in Minneapolis and even a few in St. Paul. And while the presentation everywhere looked great, it was what I saw at Ridgedale that told me it would work.

At Ridgedale, I watched as a man and a woman in their late twenties stood there taking it in, separate from each other, then began talking—and flirting—in front of the products. Minutes later, they exchanged numbers. In that moment, I knew design would have the impact I'd imagined. I just knew. I knew that the Whitney event would demonstrate if we had appeal to the sophisticated New York crowd but that the stores would show if we also appealed to the younger, up-and-coming generation. And those two proved it. They showed me that we had revealed a market that we could continue to serve in the years that followed—a market that we could communicate with, grow with, evolve with. What they needed would become what we needed. They gave me confidence to sign a second designer, Philippe Starck, to a much larger range of products for Target. I had seen the future, and I got all the benefits: praise, interviews, awards.

And then I got something else.

A call.

From a recruiter.

At *Apple.*

Steve used to say that people don't know what they want until you show it to them. Many have since taken this to demonstrate arrogance: that Steve thought he knew what other people wanted before they did. But all I've since taken it to mean is that our desires are inherited. We can't ever really know what we want until it's shown to us. And we often don't understand the nature of where we've been until we find ourselves somewhere else.

My first meeting with Steve would reveal what I had been coming to realize about where I was: that for all the potential I saw in Target's future, setting us up for it had been a struggle. I was willing to keep fighting, but I was open to frontiers on which I might not have to. Thus, by the time I was in that conference room with Steve in 1999, I was primed for an opportunity to lead with an inner voice whose pitch and cadence had been finely tuned by years of speaking up for everyone: customer *and* company. I was open to a place where I *could* make big bets, where it was *easier* to think big than small, where I would be *encouraged* to ignore the outer voices in favor of my inner voice—my intuition.

I was ready, in every sense of the word, for something different.

CHAPTER 4

A Significant Opportunity

There are certain conversations you never want to end. In my experience, they're usually the ones in which it feels like you're cocreating a reality with someone else. With Steve, that's what was immediately clear to me. I wouldn't be working for him.

I'd be creating *with* him.

I think Steve felt at home talking to me, and I felt at home talking to him. I could see my passion reflected in him. I also realized how much I could learn from him. My perception was that people used computers for work. Steve explained that people would use them to create.

"If Apple is going to win, we're going to win on innovation," he said. "But you can't win on innovation without a way to communicate with customers."

It was a simple expression of the same idea I'd acted on to launch design at Target.

Steve explained that he had returned to Apple in 1997 after having been ousted in 1985, cut expenses, and launched the iMac. He had envisioned it as a computer for everyone, but after a strong uptake by Apple's installed base, sales had slowed. Around that same time, Apple had hired McKinsey to assess the feasibility of stores. Their conclusion was that Apple lacked point of sale advocacy, and employees in traditional retail stores couldn't speak to the advantages of Apple's higher-priced products relative to Windows computers. Still, some of Apple's board pushed back on Steve investing in his own stores. Retail was expensive and hard, and it was better to lean on someone who had already taken the risk of doing it than go at it alone. This led Steve to create a mini store inside one of the biggest sellers of PCs in the US at the time: CompUSA.

When I asked Steve about the performance of the mini store, he explained that it was better, but it still wasn't great. Apple was selling most of its computers to the customer it already had: creative pros. Steve had been working on consumer versions of the same "apps" that those pros were using on the Mac—iMovie, for instance, was the consumer version of Final Cut Pro. He believed that opening his own store could broaden Apple's appeal from creative pros to consumers with creative interests, and that this could double Apple's market share and help the company reach twenty-five million more customers. But some on Apple's board weren't convinced. They believed that Steve should improve the reseller experience and invest in an internet strategy like Dell.

I told Steve there was merit to the board's opinion. There was little reason for him to invest in an Apple Store to reach a narrow customer segment with a goal of doubling Apple's small market share. But the board also hadn't told Steve what I knew from my experience at Target: that the true power of a store was in its ability to help a brand reach the customer they didn't yet have by showing them what they hadn't known they needed. Apple had 5 percent of the PC market in 1999, and only 50 percent of Americans were using computers. The opportunity that revealed itself to me in that moment was interesting, obvious, and *huge*.

"You don't need stores to go after the creative pro," I said to Steve. "But you would need stores if you wanted to go after everyone—*especially* the fifty percent who don't yet understand why they need a computer."

This was *exactly* what Steve wanted to hear.

From there, our conversation took off. We spoke about how a store that introduced the Mac to all Americans would work. I shared what design at Target had taught me: that the power of a store was in revealing customers' unmet needs and that it seemed like we could break the customers Apple didn't yet have into two groups: those who had never owned a computer and those who owned a Windows machine. An Apple Store would show the former why they needed computers, and it would show the latter why they needed to switch away from PCs. We could use presentation the same way I'd used it at Target to educate and inform—to demonstrate to those who hadn't yet used computers that they didn't have to be intimidated by them, and to show the Windows user that we could offer them a better experience. Steve's attention never wavered. He asked clear, direct questions, then listened.

"Where would you put the store?" he asked. It was the next obvious question, and I thought about it. If we were going after everyone, we needed to locate where people lived their lives. My mind, of course, went directly to places like Southdale, which had once attracted customers by making itself a destination.

"You need to be in malls," I said.

Steve's face darkened.

"I *hate* malls," he said. "They're ugly and full of crappy stores."

"'Everyone' disagrees," I said. "In most cities, malls are people's preferred places to shop."

We stared at each other for a while, neither of us backing down. Still, I sensed a level of respect from Steve regarding what I knew about retail and what I thought Apple could accomplish with it, and believed that at some point, this would bring him around. He did eventually indicate as much, telling me that he knew nothing about retail and that few at Apple did, either. Unlike at Target, I'd get to build everything—the team, the culture, and, ultimately, the store—from scratch.

My heart leapt.

Steve later asked me, too, about store size. This, it turned out, was less retail wisdom than marketing wisdom; the size of a store, I told Steve, signaled the size of a brand. If we were going to go after everyone, that meant we would be competing with Windows. And if we were competing with Windows, we needed a big store. Steve asked how big. I thought about the best brand in the mall, Gap, and one whose CEO—Mickey Drexler—Steve had said was on Apple's board.

"Is Apple as big of a brand as Gap?" I asked.

"Bigger," Steve said.

I smiled.

"Then you need a big store," I said. "At *least* as big as Gap. Otherwise, you won't be relevant."

Most CEOs would not have loved this idea, but Steve did. He explained how his mentor, Mike Markkula, had believed that a great brand should "impute" its values through everything it did. If an easy-to-use product needed simple marketing and elegant packaging, a brand like Apple needed a store whose size demonstrated its importance. A store the size of Gap—six thousand square feet—would do exactly this.

But there was one thing that stuck out to me about the idea of a six-thousand-square-foot store. It wasn't occurring to Steve, of course, because he wasn't a retailer. He didn't know what he didn't know. But I knew that conventional wisdom in retail said that stores should maximize their products per square foot. At Target, this wasn't hard; we had 100,000 SKUs.

Apple had *four.*

And yet, as I sat there across from Steve thinking about Bruce Tominello's cramming into a broom cupboard years earlier only to encounter shelves *filled* with products, I realized that a small product line was an opportunity. The Apple Store wouldn't have to be cluttered. Its geography could be open and inviting. Showing people what they could do with technology wouldn't require filling shelves with it. The best teachers always kept things simple.

When Steve's and my conversation did finally wind down, the light from the setting sun had long since ceased casting streaks along the white walls. The only light in the room came from the computers on the credenza. I must've glanced at my watch.

It was 8:00 p.m.

Steve and I had talked for *three hours.*

I told him that I had a flight to catch, a place to get back to.

"When can you come back *here*?" he asked.

I felt my heart skip a beat.

Uhh . . . *Tomorrow*? I thought. Whenever?

But I settled for playing it cool.

"What works for you?" I asked.

"How about the Monday after Thanksgiving?" he asked. "Two weeks from today."

Two whole weeks . . .

"Sure," I said. The word came out with a casualness I did not feel.

"And when you get back to Minneapolis, can you send me an email on how you'd go about building the store?"

An email, I thought. Have I ever sent an email?

"I'm going to need one of those," I said, gesturing toward the iMac.

"You don't have a *computer*?" Steve asked.

I shook my head.

"I'll get you one," he said. "I'll have it sent to your house. My guy Simon will call you and help you set it up. I can even have him fly out if necessary."

"If that's necessary, we have a bigger problem," I said.

Steve laughed.

"Fair enough," he said.

There was a moment of silence.

"Thanks for coming out," Steve said.

"Thank *you*."

The feeling of being with Steve followed me out of that conference room, into the elevator, out the door of 1 Infinite Loop, and into the car I'd rented. It stuck with me as I drove north on 280, my headlights cutting swaths through the fog rolling in over cypress trees and golden hills. At Target, I'd been pushing water uphill for a decade. And while I thought I'd been dreaming big at Target, Steve showed me that I hadn't been dreaming nearly big enough. With design at Target, I'd been trying to create a better store. With Steve, I could create a better *world*.

I still didn't have a definition for significance, but this felt pretty darn close.

□

In the two weeks that followed, I worked nonstop to capitalize on the opportunity in front of me. The first call I made was to my dad. I told him about Steve, about his vision for the world, about his need for a store and his ask for a write-up. And my dad listened, as he always did, then asked questions. Several of them were about the write-up. But I was way ahead of him. I had already been in CompUSA.

I had gotten home around four the morning after Steve's and my meeting. Normally, I slept on planes. But nothing about the conversation I'd had before that flight was normal, so neither was my experience of the flight. For approximately five hours, I imagined a store for everyone. I caught two hours of sleep, maybe, once I got home. Then, at 6:00 a.m., I all but erupted out of bed. Two hours after *that*, I was in CompUSA's parking lot.

I was also the *only* one in CompUSA's parking lot.

Now, an empty parking lot in front of CompUSA wasn't necessarily a sign that they, in Steve's words, "sucked." First, it was 8:00 a.m. Second, people bought computers once every few *years*. It would be kind of weird if CompUSA's parking lot *was* full. I was trying—hard—to give them the benefit of the doubt. But when I walked into the store, I found that I no longer could.

The weather was typical for late November in Minnesota: bad, cold—not like it had been in Cupertino. But the store itself did not make me feel warmer. No one greeted me when I walked in. No one seemed to even notice I was there. Apple's "store within a store" was in the back. I liked the concept itself—it was cool. But few who weren't looking for it would ever find it. And they were who I—and now, Steve—wanted to reach.

The picture wasn't much better at Apple's independent, locally owned reseller, FirstTech. The bell on the door tinkled as I walked in, but not one of the three bearded men behind the store's counter even looked up as I entered. They all kept their eyes downcast as they tinkered with parts of the machines that sat in pieces on the wall. The displays reminded me of those in Michael's office: cramped, cluttered. Printers and third-party monitors filled every inch of shelves that sagged under their weight, and keyboards, cords, and mice had been shoved haphazardly in what few nooks and crannies remained. The wall itself was a mass of sepia and beige, and even if the employees were passionate, they weren't creating the connection with me that would enable me to share in it. I'd heard Apple was a cult, but cults made people feel like they belonged. This store didn't. I left without saying another word.

On my way across town, I dropped by Circuit City. They had carried the Mac for a few years before deciding that its volume wasn't making up for their low margins. Across the street from Circuit City was Best Buy, which was succeeding by selling all the products Apple didn't—camcorders, digital cameras, MP3 players. These were the two best technology stores in the country, and given Apple's brand, they were exactly where I would've expected the Mac to be. Instead, it was in *Sears*. Next to the vacuums. And while I admired Sears' merchandising of products that literally "sucked," I felt nothing looking at them. A great store had a heartbeat. Sears needed a defibrillator.

Over the next two weeks, I condensed my observations into a write-up using the iMac Steve had sent me. I outlined the research I'd done on the computer industry, went into Apple's strategic position, and described the issues I saw with the company's go-to-market strategy. I also did a quick competitive analysis by reviewing publicly available data from Gateway—a rival computer maker that was pursuing a strategy like the one I had recommended Steve pursue with Apple. Finally, I concluded by outlining how a retail concept for Apple would work. We would champion design excellence, of course. And—perhaps inspired by my experience from a decade at Target—I told Steve that customers valued relationships and that we would design environments in which customers could build relationships with our products.

I attached my write-up to an email—the first time I'd ever done this—then hit Send.

Steve replied quickly.

"Thank you, I got it," he wrote.

For the next week, a five-word email was all I had to go on.

□

When I got back to Cupertino—after interviewing with several members of Steve's leadership team—I was anxious to hear his thoughts.

There was a long pause as I waited for him to mention the memo.

I waited.

And waited.

And *waited.*

"So . . ." I finally said. "What did you think of the write-up?"

"Oh, it was okay," Steve said.

It was *okay*? I thought.

"Actually, to tell you the truth, it wasn't what I was looking for," Steve said. "But I'm going to offer you the job anyway."

"Wow!" I said, thanking him for the vote of confidence. I don't think Steve really cared what I'd written about the stores. All he wanted to do was get back to creating them together.

"We *should* be in malls," he said.

That's a one-eighty, I thought.

"Yeah," he continued. "We can't get customers to drive ten *miles.* But we can get them to walk ten feet!"

I nodded. He was excited, and I was excited. Now, it was just a matter of getting those in my life excited, too.

This would not be easy. Karen was happy raising our kids—Lizzey, yes, and our second, Will—in Minneapolis, and had made great friends. She was naturally concerned by the stories about

Steve "firing people in the elevator," and I could only imagine how she'd feel when she learned he was doing this as *interim* CEO (or the abbreviated "iCEO"). I explained to Steve that it would be hard to uproot my family and leave a great career at a thriving company to join Apple, which had recently been on the verge of bankruptcy. Steve told me he understood.

"Why don't you come back out for Macworld in January?" Steve asked. "You and Karen can look at housing and schools. And attend Macworld."

"Sure!" I said. I'd never attended a Macworld, and it sounded fun.

I had no idea what was coming.

In the weeks leading up to Macworld, I had the necessary conversations with those in my life about Steve's offer to join Apple. I spoke to Karen; to my siblings; to my sister's husband, Mark—a good friend from business school. I also spoke to my boss at Target, Gregg Steinhafel. And then, eventually, I spoke to my dad. We shared a long breakfast and talked through the offer. He asked questions, as he always did. Then, after, he sent me a letter outlining what he'd heard from me, what he'd learned from others, and what he now understood.

"Most people who talk to you come away convinced you have made your decision, to your own satisfaction," he wrote, "and are merely *appearing* to be still weighing alternatives."

True, I thought.

The letter continued.

"All your life you have made very quick decisions, sometimes without counting ten," he wrote. "Once you reach your decision you tend not to want to hear—though you are very polite—unfavorable thoughts or information."

Hence you *writing* me a letter, I thought. My dad always saw me. More than that, he always helped me see myself.

In this case—and in most cases—he was right. I hadn't wanted to hear dissenting opinions about overhauling kids, and I *really* hadn't wanted to hear them about design. Skepticism had always gotten in the way of my creativity. I wanted people who would tell me how things could work—not just why they wouldn't. Steve was like that, too.

This thinking had shaped the team Steve had put together when he returned to Apple. Jon Rubinstein ("Ruby"), who Steve had recruited from HP, was leading hardware engineering. Tim Cook, who Steve had lured away from Compaq in 1998 to oversee Apple's operations, had fixed the company's issues with inventory and improved its supply chain. Avie Tevanian, who Steve had brought with him from NeXT, was handling software, and Sina Tamaddon, who had risen quickly through Apple's ranks during Steve's time away, was building the Mac's apps. Together, their work led to everything Steve would present at Macworld 2000.

I couldn't have known it at the time, but the January 2000 Macworld would prove to be one of the most important presentations Steve ever gave. That, combined with his Macworld presentation twelve months *later* in 2001, laid out the company's strategy for the next decade. Steve had seated Karen and me between Vice President Al Gore and Gap CEO Mickey Drexler, and as Steve walked out and the room exploded, Mickey turned to me.

"Advantage: Steve," he said. "Wait till you see what he does."

When Steve took the stage, the audience treated him like Bono, or the Beatles. I had never seen anything like it. Steve opened the presentation by pulling up a four-quadrant matrix. In it sat the four computers I'd seen in our first meeting. The first was Apple's consumer desktop, the iMac. The second was its pro desktop, the Power Mac G4. The third was its pro portable, the PowerBook. And the final computer was its consumer portable, the iBook.

The numbers Steve shared on the iBook and iMac were telling. He explained that a significant portion of those buying them were new to Apple, and over 90 percent of people had gotten on the internet since purchasing them. This was relevant because Steve was then thinking about the value of the iBook and iMac in terms of helping people get online and take advantage of the internet, and that day, he unveiled a free suite of internet services—iTools—that would help them do it easily and safely. KidSafe protected children from chatrooms and other dangerous things on the internet. Mail—with the domain name @mac.com—made email simple and easy. HomePage helped people create personal websites. iDisk offered people internet storage. Steve demoed the tools, then outlined a twelve-month launch schedule. It was by January 2001, Steve said, that OS X would be fully rolled out—and if I joined Apple, we'd be aiming to open the stores a few months before.

But, of course, it wasn't just the internet—and iTools—that made Apple's computers appealing. It was also the apps that Steve had been working on. iMovie, in particular. Steve spoke about the FireWire port that he'd built into the new iMac, which allowed people to connect digital camcorders from Sony or Canon, upload videos to their computers, and edit them, effectively turning anyone with a Mac into a moviemaker. Steve showed three different advertisements he had been working on with his ad agency partner, Chiat\Day, and asked us in the audience to make ourselves an "applause-o-meter" to demonstrate which one we liked best. The most popular was an ad showing Sina's kids, both about Will's and Lizzey's ages, smiling, waving, and hugging each other. The video was set to "Good Riddance (Time of Your Life)" by Green Day. As a parent, I found it utterly magical. I wasn't the only one. Many in the audience wept. Steve wasn't selling a computer so much as an amplifier of human creativity. He was reminding us—and me—of what truly mattered.

For the latter half of the presentation, Steve went into painstaking detail on every design decision made for OS X. He talked about how things "moved" and "behaved." He unveiled a new feature, the "Dock," which organized everything people could do with OS X. Then he clicked an icon in the dock, and the audience gasped as it expanded onto the screen like a genie from a lamp.

"Isn't that *cool*?" Steve asked. "I could just play with it all day long, actually."

By the end of the presentation, I was all in—save for one thing. There remained that one pesky problem, that little issue of Steve's temperament combined with his status as interim CEO. It would make Karen and me more comfortable if Steve could somehow demonstrate that he was committed to this company for the long haul. And then, just as it seemed that Steve was about to end the presentation, he announced that there was, in fact, one more thing.

"I got back to Apple, along with several other people, two and a half years ago," Steve said. "What we found was a great company that needed a little bit of help, a lot of *incredibly* talented people. As a matter of fact, while I'm on that, I would like all the folks from Apple that have been working on OS X, and have been working on our internet stuff, to stand up, and I'd like to give them a hand."

Applause echoed throughout the auditorium, and I turned to see the team standing and taking it in.

"We also have some incredible partners we work with," Steve continued. "CKS on the graphics side, Chiat\Day on the advertising side. Can you guys just quickly stand up for a minute?"

More applause.

"Everybody at Apple has been working really hard these two and a half years," Steve said. "And during this time, I've been the interim CEO. I have another job at Pixar as the CEO, which I love. And so

I was the interim CEO of Apple. Well, I hope, after two and a half years, that we've been able to prove to our shareholders at Pixar and our shareholders at Apple that maybe we can pull this dual CEO thing off. And so I'm not going to be changing any of my duties at either Pixar or Apple, but I'm pleased to announce today that I'm going to drop the interim title."

The room erupted. Everyone leapt out of their chairs. Mickey, me, Al, Karen. One thought ran through my head repeatedly.

We're in.

Meanwhile, Steve waited in vain for the applause to subside. After what felt like minutes, he attempted to speak, but the audience wouldn't allow it. People stamped their feet. Chants echoed through the auditorium.

"Steve, Steve, Steve, Steve."

He opened his mouth, then closed it again, then smiled, almost sheepishly, seemingly taken aback by the reaction.

"I, uh—thank you," he said.

"We love you, Steve!" came a shout from the back of the auditorium. Steve paused and smiled again. Then he continued.

"You guys are making me feel funny now," he said. "I get to come to work every day and work with the most talented people on the planet at Apple and at Pixar. But these jobs are team sports."

Not since Edina West had I been so excited to play on a team.

That night, Karen and I went to dinner with Steve. We met his wife, Laurene, for the first time. Fred Anderson was there, too, with his wife, Marilyn. The six of us ate at Steve's favorite restaurant: Late for the Train in Palo Alto. We talked family, schools, housing. We spoke about our kids, about Pixar, about movies and values and responsibility. It felt real, familial, joyful. More than that, it just felt *right.* I needed to be here in Cupertino with Steve. I had never been more certain of anything in my life.

Still, for as clear as Steve had made his commitment to Apple's future onstage that day, he hadn't mentioned anything about retail. There wasn't one word about the go-to-market strategy. Some on the board, I knew, hadn't wanted stores and had only begrudgingly agreed to test them. I was certain that Steve was no longer testing the waters at Apple, but I couldn't uproot my family—or even hire a great team—if he was going to "test" stores.

The question in my mind—and Karen's, most likely—was simple: Was he all in on retail?

The following morning, I would get my answer.

□

Steve and I had planned to have breakfast before Karen's and my flight back to Minneapolis. But minutes before 8:00 a.m., I got a call from his assistant Andrea asking if I'd be willing to skip breakfast and go to Stanford Shopping Center instead.

"Yes, of course," I said. I loved malls!

Steve pulled up to my hotel a few minutes after 8:00 a.m. in a silver, two-door Mercedes without a license plate. I clambered in next to him. Bob Dylan played through the speakers.

"Thought you *hated* malls!" I said.

"If we're putting stores in them, we may as well go visit one," Steve said.

For the time being, his words pushed any concerns about a test to the side.

Steve continued, explaining how it really wasn't that he hated malls. It was just that he couldn't visit them like an average person. Once Apple had gone public in 1980, he'd become a celebrity. Large public spaces were hard. Large public spaces full of "crappy" stores were harder. But when we arrived at Stanford Shopping Center, he didn't seem judgmental. He seemed curious. The stores were sources of endless fascination.

"Where's the best spot in the mall?" Steve asked.

"It depends," I said. And it did. Most often, the best spot was at "center court," or the fifty-yard line. But at Stanford, this wasn't as true. You could tell from the stores' sizes, I explained. Those in the middle were tiny relative to the behemoths—the department stores—at each end. Neiman Marcus was one of them. Macy's was another, and had two stores—their main one, which was dedicated to women, and another for men. Stanford exemplified what was then true of flagship malls across the country: the best spots were occupied by department stores.

Long before Stanford Shopping Center existed, I told Steve, every city had their own department store. Marshall Field's in Chicago. Bloomingdale's in New York City. Dayton's in Minneapolis. During World War II, people flooded cities to support the war effort, creating a bit of a secondary—albeit, temporary—golden age for department stores. When World War II's end gave way to postwar suburban flight, the same department stores that had once benefitted from the war began languishing. Suddenly, suburban mall operators had the leverage to convince department stores to anchor new suburban developments. Most department stores, recognizing the precarity of their position, capitulated. But some negotiated a deal. They would anchor those developments, but only if they didn't have to pay rent. Perhaps surprisingly, I told Steve, most suburban mall operators agreed.

For a time, the deal seemed to work for everyone. Suburban malls attracted more people. Those people got access to the department store. And department stores flourished as malls' "anchors." But it was clear from the get-go that department stores had accepted a bit of a Faustian bargain. The influx of customers into malls spurred innovation, which opened every tenant up to competition. This should've been a golden opportunity for the department stores, because they were well positioned to stay ahead of it. But, maybe because of the quality of their economics—remember, they weren't paying rent—many got tired, lazy. They didn't innovate. Instead they let retail innovators siphon customers away from their stores by picking one of their departments and specializing in it. This, I explained to Steve, was the birth of the "specialty store." Gap was one. Pottery Barn was another. And many stores like that now surrounded the department stores at Stanford, relishing the opportunity to better serve the department store's customers than the department stores themselves could.

I'm not sure Steve had ever thought about retail this way, and suddenly it was a lot more interesting.

As we approached 10:00 a.m., I thought about Steve's mention of large public spaces being hard and asked him if he wanted to leave.

"No," he said. "We can stay."

I nodded. Steve walked into Eddie Bauer. I followed him. He said he liked the dual entrances. I didn't. I explained what was true about them.

"They make the store's layout harder to understand," I said. "And they offer us less space for a stockroom."

Steve nodded. We agreed that our store—at least to start—would have one entrance. For everything I'd heard *about* Steve, I found myself surprised by how easy it was to work *with* him. If something made sense, we'd make it work.

We kept walking, talking, designing the store. It felt like we were already working together, and I still hadn't accepted the job.

Steve asked me why, and the thoughts I'd been having that morning came rushing back. The only difference was that now, I also had the benefit of our having discussed virtually every meaningful element of our store.

Why on earth would we *test* it? I thought. Why wouldn't we just *do* it?

I explained all of this. The concerns in the context of the opportunity. Then, I summed it up.

"I can't come here for a test," I said. "I can't uproot my family for a test. And I won't be able to hire anyone good for a test!"

Steve nodded.

"I know you're all in on Apple," I said. "I need you to be all in on retail."

A long pause.

"Ron," Steve finally said. "I have four billion in the bank. If I could spend *one* billion right now and have a hundred stores, I would do it."

I nodded.

Steve was all in, and now, so was I.

CHAPTER 5

Visions Emerge

When I arrived for my first day at Apple, I introduced myself to the security guard only to find that I had been given a code name: John Bruce. It wasn't exactly the warm welcome I was expecting, but it was an early introduction to Steve's emphasis on secrecy.

When I got to the executive team (ET) meeting that morning and sat down next to the guys I'd interviewed with a few weeks earlier—Phil, Tim, Sina, Avie, Ruby, and a few others—Steve told me he wanted to keep the store, code-named "Project Nexus" internally, confidential. Most of Apple's revenue was still coming through resellers like CompUSA, and if we demonstrated a commitment to creating a new channel, CompUSA might cut us off from theirs. Still, as much as I understood the desire for secrecy, I wasn't sure we could maintain it. Every store we built would involve countless people—landlords, contractors. Also, we were putting them in malls. Not places one went, I thought, if they were trying to hide.

The emphasis on secrecy followed me everywhere. I wasn't exactly sure who I could speak to, what I could say. But then, a few weeks later, I was invited to attend Steve's annual "Top 100" meeting—a collection of the people Steve said he would take with him on a lifeboat to his next company—and I happened to sit next to Apple's senior director of retail sales, Jim Mallekoote, on the bus. He was one of a few people who knew we were opening stores, and it felt good to have someone to talk to about them. I was hopeful, too, that as a retailer, he'd grasp the vision that had been starting to emerge in my imagination. But instead, he did what smart people do: He asked questions. And those questions made *me* ask questions—like if this very expensive dream I had for the Apple Store would work as well in reality as it seemed to in my head.

"Where are you putting the stores?" Jim asked.

"Malls."

"That's costly real estate."

"We need it to reach the Windows customer."

"For a product they buy once every few years?"

"No," I said. "To create a place where they can come back for help and training."

"How are you actually going to get them to buy a Mac?"

"By creating a comfortable place where people want to come and hang out," I said. "And by offering world-class service."

"What about commissions?"

"No commissions," I said. "I want our employees looking in customers' hearts, not their wallets."

"So, let me get this straight," Jim said. "You're pouring money into real estate, removing employees' incentives to recoup it, and having them focus primarily on service?"

"Exactly."

There was a long pause.

"I'll be honest with you, Ron," Jim said. "I'm not sure that's going to work."

Jim wasn't the only one with doubts. Not long after Steve hired me and told the board that he was proceeding with three hundred stores, one of Apple's strongest board members, Ed Woolard, resigned. Genentech CEO Art Levinson called the stores "crazy." And when I got to the Top 100, I realized it wasn't just the board. I hadn't expected Steve to say anything about the stores given the emphasis on secrecy, but then he told the room that one of the priorities for the year was to develop his own retail strategy and asked me to introduce myself. I looked around at the faces in the audience as I spoke and saw mostly blank stares. A few things became clear to me in that moment. First, products were Apple's main event, and retail was, at best, a sideshow. Second, most at Apple seemed to believe that if enough effort went into perfecting the products' user experience, those products would sell themselves.

I didn't think this was true, of course. Coming from Minnesota, I found computers intimidating. I didn't know what everyone around me knew about them—and I didn't think most Americans would, either. Still, if any team could've made a computer that would sell itself, it was this one. I thought I'd been around smart people in my life—in Minnesota, then at Stanford, Harvard, Mervyn's, and Target. But as I listened to the people in the room present, the conversations I'd once had at Target began to seem downright juvenile. Retailers tended to focus on the next season. Apple was building the foundation for its next decade. The OS X demo I'd seen at Macworld a few weeks earlier was one of the coolest things I'd ever seen, and what Steve shared at the Top 100 *blew it away.* What would become iMovie 2, yes, and more updates to OS X. But also, new applications the likes of which the world had never seen, including a digital jukebox—iTunes. And with our store, *I would get to bring these things to market.*

My first reaction to this realization was simple: I needed to better understand what everyone was talking about. So I filled a notebook with terms I'd never heard (and didn't think most Americans would've heard, either)—*bits, megabytes, random access memory*—and figured I could ask Steve what they meant later. Then, when I ran into him in the hallway during a break and he asked how I was doing, I said "Great," explained that it was "like drinking from a fire hose," and told him I was taking a ton of notes. I thought he'd be impressed. But given his previous emphasis on secrecy, maybe I shouldn't be surprised that he wasn't.

I returned from break to find my notebook missing and Steve back at the front of the room.

"Just a quick housekeeping item," he said. "Everything we discuss here is confidential."

I felt my eyes narrow.

"Also," he said. "You hundred are the smartest people at Apple. You can remember what's important. If you can't, you shouldn't be here. No note-taking."

A lump formed in my throat.

I'm John Bruce.

I'm nobody.

I shouldn't be here.

But for as small as I felt in that *moment,* I felt even more inspired in that *room*. I could feel what the store had the potential to be amid a team who cared about user experience as much as this one did. I knew that I was working with the smartest people in the world and that I had a profound responsibility in bringing their products to market. I knew the store would outlive every product Apple developed, too, and be the place where people discovered the next one. We would thus have to win in the same way Apple was going to win—on *innovation*.

I had another realization in that room, too. If we were going after everyone with the store, eventually, it wouldn't be Apple's products that were people's first experience with the brand, as had been the case since 1976. Instead, it would be *the Apple Store itself.* And this meant that we could embody everything Apple's brand stood for. We could win on experience because *Apple* was going to win on experience. Our store could feel simple and intuitive and human because Apple's *products* would feel simple and intuitive and human. Our spaces could be beautiful because Apple's *products* were going to be beautiful. It was so clear, so obvious, so interesting and inspiring and inevitable. The store wouldn't just sell Apple's products. The store would *be* an Apple product. This project, this *nexus* . . . if we got it right, we could become the face of Apple's brand.

Not long after the Top 100, I brought this thinking to Steve.

"Apple already *has* a great brand," Steve said. "I don't need stores to build the brand. I need stores to build the business."

"I understand that," I said. "I respect that." The words were coming out quickly, too quickly, and I tried to slow them down.

"But, *but*—most of our future customers will be introduced to Apple through the store," I said. "So, eventually, it will become the most powerful physical expression of the brand."

Steve paused, digesting. I watched. Was he getting it? How could I make it clearer? A visual?

I explained that it was like Ralph Lauren or Gap.

"Whenever I buy a Polo shirt, I'm reminded of the wood-paneled, art-filled mansion that Ralph Lauren created at Seventy-Second and Madison in Manhattan," I said. "With Gap, I can't put on one of their T-shirts without being reminded of clean spaces, wood floors, white walls, and folded merchandise. *That's* our opportunity. *That's* the store's future."

Steve could process things quickly, but he took time with this.

Then, the following day—at the end of which I'd be traveling back to Minneapolis—Steve called me into his office.

"What time do your kids go to bed?" he asked.

"Uh—eight p.m."

"Great," he said. "Can I call you?"

"Tonight?"

"Every night."

"Sure!" I exclaimed, surprised. Perhaps sensing my confusion—or was it excitement?—Steve clarified.

"If this store is going to be people's introduction to Apple's brand," Steve said, "then you have to understand how I think."

Makes sense, I thought. I'd never been a part of a company whose brand seemed more tied to its founder.

"The only way for you to understand how I think," Steve continued, "is for me to go deep with you on every aspect of my life and your life. And we don't always have to talk about Apple. We'll just talk. After about a year, you will know how I would think about almost everything. You will be free as a bird to do what *you* think is right, unless you don't know what I'd think about it, in which case you can come ask me."

That afternoon, I traveled back to Minneapolis. Then a few minutes after I'd put Lizzey to bed, Steve called our landline. We spoke. Then, the next night, we spoke again. And the next night, and the next. To that point, Karen had always been the one answering Steve's phone call. Then, after a few weeks of his calls, I heard the phone ring once, twice, three times.

"Are you going to get it?!" I asked.

"*You* get it," she said. "It's probably your boyfriend."

Years on, I would be exceedingly grateful for the time Steve invested to help me get to know him and Apple. In the moment, all I sensed was that he understood the stakes. If the store was going to be the most powerful physical expression of Apple's brand, Steve and I had to really get to know each other. So, for the next six months, that's what we did.

□

In one of our first nightly calls, Steve asked me to create a list of ten things required for a great retail store. A list of ten would invariably understate it, but asking for it was a quirk of Steve's; he knew that constraining someone's thinking tended to sharpen it.

I came up with a list.

1. Great real estate
2. Engaging marketing
3. Expert support
4. Fast-turning inventory
5. Must-have products
6. Ability to engage with products
7. Inviting store design
8. Appropriate funding
9. World-class execution
10. Friendly employees

"Dividing and conquering will simplify your work," Steve said. "Phil will help with marketing. Ruby and Jony will get you the products. Fred will handle funding. And Tim will take care of inventory. All I want you to focus on is finding great real estate, creating world-class support, and hiring great people."

The one thing missing was store design, and Steve said we'd handle that together—and that he'd want to be involved with some real estate decisions, too. And that was fine. In fact, it was *more* than fine.

If I'd learned anything about Steve from Macworld a few months earlier, it was the quality of his design sensibilities.

In the meantime, I began having conversations with everyone Steve had hired to manage everything I wouldn't have to worry about. I spoke to Phil about marketing, to Tim about operations, to Fred about finance. I was introduced to several people who would become critical to our success: Deirdre O'Brien in operations, Sandy Buescher in inventory, Mary Demby in IT (who liaised between us and Apple's head of IT, Niall O'Connor), and Bill Frederick in technical support. Also, Eddy Cue, who had launched Apple's first online store a few years earlier in 1997.

Apple's "A players" would make my life easy.

Now, I needed to find some of my own.

□

On a cool spring morning in 2000, I drove north on 101 from Cupertino to San Francisco to check out an updated version of CompUSA's store-within-a-store concept. It was there that I met the guy I'd hire as my first store manager: Steve Cano.

Cano was smart, engaging, and seemingly fearless, and I liked him immediately. He paired everything I didn't know about technology with the demeanor of a Boy Scout, and I could've talked to him forever. He had the "sparkle" I loved seeing in people and wanted in those I'd hire. I introduced him to Dan Walker, who had recruited me and was now leading HR for Apple, and Sue Webb, who Dan had hired to lead all recruiting for Apple Retail. A week later, Cano joined Apple.

Part of what drew me to Cano was his tech expertise. Steve and I had been discussing a store in Palo Alto, and I had known from the get-go that whoever I hired to lead that store would need to know technology at least as well as Steve did, because he would be visiting the store often. But Cano's tech expertise would be the exception, not the rule; it would be *nice* to have managers who understood technology, but to create stores that would win on experience, we needed managers who cared about people first, and products second.

Over the next few months, Sue and I worked together to bring in candidates not from Best Buy or Circuit City, but from retailers you might find in the same malls I imagined us in. We hired Stacey Brown from Banana Republic, Linda Turner from Williams Sonoma, and Laura Wynne from the Nature Company. The three of them began working with Sue to find more store managers. Stacey would oversee all West Coast stores, Linda would take the East Coast, and Laura would take the Northwest. I encouraged each of them to bring their own unique experience—their own geography—to their portion of the field. Steve had always said that he didn't hire smart people so he could tell them what to do but so they could tell him what to do. This would be true of our store employees, too.

The next question I found myself having to answer was simple: How would the stores win on innovation? It couldn't be top down. Steve could control Apple's products, but every retail store would have its own unique interactions with people, and those interactions would reveal different things we could do in those stores. I came up with a simple question to ask the store leaders, which I encouraged them to ask their teams.

"What's your store going to be *famous* for?"

The point of the question was to inspire store leaders to observe and act on what customers needed in their store, and I structured the organization such that we could act quickly on new information. I didn't want Apple to feel like a traditional retailer, where if a store manager saw something that needed to be done, they had to tell their district leader, who would then report it to the regional manager, who would then report it to the COO . . . and on and on and on. I wanted anyone who had an idea to be able to share it with their manager who would share it with me. This would keep us small and nimble no matter how big we grew.

As for who the *stores* would hire, Steve had made that clear.

"I want you to hire interesting people," he said.

This was different from, say, an apparel retailer, who would've hired employees who looked like the pictures in their ads. Interesting people "thought different," Steve said, and they were fun to talk to.

I agreed with Steve, but I knew that interesting wasn't enough. To make the contributions I imagined them making, they needed to be fearless like Cano was fearless, and they needed to be able to go toe-to-toe with Steve on technology. Also, because our target customer could be anyone, we would need each store's employees to represent as broad of a range of people as possible. Technology was intimidating for people (including me); being able to talk to someone who looked like them would make it less intimidating. I thought of my dad, and I knew that he would feel more comfortable talking to someone his age about a computer.

Still, the obvious question remained: Where would we find people like this? Where did eighty-year-olds who understood technology hang out? I wasn't sure, and Steve wasn't, either. And we couldn't really answer that question until we knew where we were putting stores, and we couldn't know *that* until we had someone to handle our real estate. It was time to hire another A player, and as it turned out, Dan and Mickey knew one from Gap.

George Blankenship.

One of the most experienced real estate guys in the world.

A few weeks later, Steve and I met with George in the same conference room I'd interviewed in. Steve, perhaps understanding through conversations with me how most Americans at the time might look at computers, asked George where we would need to go if we were trying to attract an alien. George wasted no time trying to interpret the question.

"Well, you go to the shopping center to go shopping," he said.

"I *knew* you were going to say that," Steve said.

"You asked a question," George said. "That's the answer."

"Well, I want to do three hundred stores in three years," Steve said.

"No, you don't," George said.

The two men stared at each other for a moment.

"Why not?" Steve asked.

"Because," George said, "you're *really* not going to like where they are."

George was right. We'd need to move fast if we wanted three hundred stores in three years, and that speed would mean accepting locations for which demand was lower, like B and C malls, or the wings of A malls with less important stores. The question that revealed itself through that debate was simple: How many stores could we conceivably open per year such that each would be in a great location for Apple?

Steve said a hundred.

I said fifty.

George shook his head. "Twenty-five," he said.

At first, Steve pushed back. We were launching ourselves into a battle with Windows for the PC user, which meant we needed not only coverage but we also needed it *fast.* Credit to George, though, for standing his ground; he insisted we not rush, and Steve respected him for it. Finally, we decided he was right. Twenty-five stores a year it was. And to do it, George would create a list of the best three hundred locations in the US for Apple, then negotiate with landlords to get them when—and if—they became available.

If I'm making real estate sound easy, let me clarify: It's not. You don't pop a quarter into a vending machine, press a button, and get a great spot. George knew from experience that the locations we wanted didn't come around often, and when they did, their landlords would be inundated with interest from proven retail concepts—Gap, The Limited, Pottery Barn. The Apple Store, in contrast, was not only an unproven retail concept but also one whose closest comparison—the Gateway Country Store—was struggling. This didn't mean George couldn't convince those who managed great locations to let us have them—say, for less favorable terms than a proven retail concept might get—but it did mean that he would have to use all the rapport he'd earned from fifteen years in the industry to get us into the locations we wanted. And even then, it often wasn't enough.

George joined Apple a week into June 2000, and hired Angela King, who had been overseeing special projects and real estate strategy at Gap, to work with him. One of the first landlords they approached was David Simon, the late CEO of Simon Properties, who oversaw dozens of the best malls in the country, including Roosevelt Field in New York and the Forum Shops at Caesars in Las Vegas. As a landlord, David was naturally conscious of his own interests. But so was George. And game, as it's said, recognized game.

Kind of.

George called me after his first conversation with David to give me an update. I was excited to hear what he'd learned and was hopeful it was something good. We needed great locations, and Simon's were some of the best. I asked George how it went, and what David had said.

"He said he loved me," George replied.

Okay, I thought. Good start.

"But . . ."

But?

"He's not putting a six-thousand-square-foot Radio Shack at center court in his malls."

"What did you say?" I asked.

"The truth."

"Which is?"

"That when we're successful, it's going to cost him a lot more to get us."

I smiled. George's confidence was contagious. I liked that about him, and so did Steve.

Over the next couple of weeks, George had similar conversations with landlords around the country. David didn't come around—at least, not at first. But another landlord did, and her mall was the same one I'd cut my teeth in at Mervyn's over a decade earlier: the Glendale Galleria. The location was at center court. Its lease began in November—only four months away. Still, our problems were far from over. The first was that we still hadn't designed the store. The second was that we hadn't yet hired anyone to staff it.

□

Before we could design the store—or hire people to work in it—we had to design the customer experience. I had been imagining it now for months. But I also knew the store would be catering to everyone, so I wanted input from all types of people. So I hosted an offsite and invited a diverse group.

Eighteen people attended the offsite. Lee Clow—the head of Chiat\Day and architect of the "Think Different" campaign—was there. So was Dan Walker, who had led people for Gap as Mickey Drexler transformed them into the best specialty store in the world. We also invited a sixteen-year-old, Chris Angelotti (to get the younger generation's perspective); Pat Mene, the head of HR for one of the most well-respected hotel chains in the world in the Ritz-Carlton; Cano; and several others. They would help us think different.

The biggest conclusion that emerged from the offsite was that we would base our customer experience on that of a five-star hotel—the Ritz-Carlton—instead of a store. Winning on experience would require us to deliver exceptional service, and no one offered a better service experience than the Ritz. Pat explained that their employees greeted customers with warm welcomes, probed to understand their needs, and finished with a fond farewell. I liked the simplicity of these steps, but more than that, I liked the idea of a store that served people instead of selling them. This would help us create a place where people felt comfortable, which would in turn give us a chance to reveal customers' unmet needs. But it would also require us to think different about everything.

To that point, most computer stores were thinking transactionally. But even in my write-up to Steve, I'd been expressing a simple idea: that people appreciated relationships, and that in a high-tech world, relationships were only going to become more important. In any relationship, I told Steve, people should be doing one of three things: launching, deepening, or restoring. I imagined the front half of the store being where customers launched their relationship with Apple, and the back half of the store being where they deepened and restored it. Then I imagined how to actually get customers in the mall—who wouldn't have come looking for our store—to turn their heads toward us.

The logic of our real estate was instructive here. Steve hadn't immediately liked the idea of malls, but he came around when he realized that the Windows user wasn't going to go out of their way to visit an Apple Store. Still, even once they were in the mall, we needed a way to capture their attention. We talked about winning the Windows user over with window displays. We wondered if this might attract women, too—the window displays of iconic department stores like Harrods and Bloomingdale's certainly had—and broaden the perception of who, exactly, could use computers. Then we discussed what people would do when they came into the store. First, they would be greeted warmly. But then what?

We talked about what could make a customer's experience fun in the store. Amusement parks came up. *Rides* came up. I asked what a ride would look like in the store. Someone volunteered that we could merchandise camcorders and allow customers to experience shooting a video, uploading the footage to a computer, editing it, and making a movie in our stores. I knew Steve was working on other applications internally with Sina, too. Rides would enable us to consistently adapt our experience around what people could do with our computers *and* technology itself. They would also make employees' jobs more fun, replacing the pressure to discuss products with the joy of showing people what they could do with them.

A few other ideas emerged from that offsite. We decided that the back half of each store would be dedicated to service and support. Each store would have a theater, like Macworld, where we could run classes that helped people better understand what they could do with Apple's products. Classes would deepen our customers' relationships with technology. We also needed a clear and obvious place where customers could go when products broke.

Except, did we?

Some thought we should hide support. Gateway had done that. So had CompUSA. We had two options: either leave it out or stick it out. But if we were going to stick it out, the idea needed to be truly great.

Or, dare I say it, genius.

□

I wasn't a tech guy. I was a retailer from Minnesota.

When I walked into the interview with Steve for the first time, my relationship with technology was . . . *underdeveloped.* I grew up in a house with a single rotary phone. As of 1999, I owned four pieces of technology: a television set, a VHS player for the movies I'd rent at Blockbuster, a calculator (the HP 12C, standard issue at Harvard Business School), and a CD player. Karen and I shared an SLR camera, but I had largely stopped using it because I'd accidentally exposed the film and lost a week's worth of photos of Karen and the kids. From that point on, I was afraid to even *touch* that camera. It was intimidating. And I thought that a lot of people probably felt the same way about computers.

This is why I didn't agree that a computer could sell itself. There were all kinds of preexisting assumptions that we would be battling in our effort to establish people's relationships with technology. People might be *afraid* of computers. They might not understand *what* computers—or, specifically, the Mac—could do for them. And because a significant portion of these people wouldn't yet *have* computers, they wouldn't have access to a search engine (let alone ChatGPT) to get help. The best option for most people was a friend or family member, but even then, most of those who understood computers understood *Windows.* Apple had less than 5 percent of the PC market. There just weren't that many people, I thought, who would know Macs well enough to be able to help someone transition to them. But that didn't mean there *couldn't* be.

My experiences with all of Apple's resellers contributed in their own way to this idea that was now emerging in my imagination. CompUSA and Gateway, it seemed to me, had both grasped what was true—that people were intimidated by technology—but they had come to the wrong conclusion as a result. Those stores kept their repairs teams behind closed doors, as if trying to hide one reason people might find computers intimidating. But if this was the truth, it didn't make sense to hide it. It made sense to embrace it. People wouldn't forget what they knew to be true because we tried to avoid sharing it with them. People would wonder why we were trying to avoid telling them the truth, then doubt everything else we said as a result. Our job as a store wasn't to convince people that computers *weren't* intimidating. It was to acknowledge that they *could* be intimidating, and to offer a place for people to get their concerns addressed and questions answered for free.

I came into the morning of the second day of the offsite with a crazy idea. We needed to put support on display, and we needed to make it fun. And the crazy idea that had struck me as I'd woken up that morning was that we could offer support, perhaps, at a place I'd always found fun.

The bar.

I'd frequented my fair share of good bars in Minnesota, especially with my brother, Dwight. I'd been to a few more on buyers' trips to Europe—and specifically, at hotels. It had been the bartender at the Shangri-La Hotel who suggested the running path that led me into the Singapore Botanic Gardens. The most knowledgeable person in any city I visited—and the person who both showed me what I could do in those cities and gave me the confidence to explore them—was *always behind the hotel bar.*

Now, the idea of a "support bar" was not immediately popular with the team at the offsite. We wanted to model our service philosophy on that of the Ritz, but we also knew that the Ritz had a policy of owning every customer issue to completion. The problem with offering support in our stores, period—bar or not—was that we were opening ourselves up to tech issues that we might not be able to solve, like a bug. But if we had a way to relay that problem to Apple headquarters, we could not only own a customer's issue to completion but also help Apple itself identify and solve a customer problem faster than they had been able to before. We just needed a hotline to Cupertino—a way to reach someone who could save the customer when no one else could. We called it the "bat phone." It would be the final touch on a bar where, after customers had launched their relationships with technology and deepened them through classes in our theater, they could come back—if needed—to restore them.

After the offsite, I called Steve.

"I've got how we're going to offer support," I said.

"Oh?"

"Yeah."

"How?"

"A bar."

"A what?"

"A bar," I repeated. "Customers can belly up and ask the person behind it any question about technology. Or get help with their computer!"

"I like it," Steve said. "What are you going to call it?"

"I'm not sure."

"Come back to me when you do," he said. And he hung up.

I thought about it. Whatever we called those staffing the bar, I knew it would matter. Names always did. I went back to my brother, Dwight, or my being named captain of my soccer team and believing that the title imbued the position with meaning. As a captain, I was a leader; I was responsible for determining where the team could go. As much as names and titles signified who people were, they also demonstrated who people could be.

Anyone who staffed the bar would need to be capable of answering any question anyone who came into the store had about technology. They would fill the role of trusted friend or family member who everyone could come in and talk to. If I was going to find someone—anyone—like that, I needed to attach a level of meaning to the position that would attract the right type of person.

Before I'd gotten to Apple, I'd heard the ad that Steve came up with not long after his return: "Think Different." I remembered his celebration of "the crazy ones": misfits, rebels, and troublemakers. And then I remembered what Steve said he'd seen in them.

Genius.

That's it, I thought.

I dialed Steve, my heart racing.

"Hello?"

"I've got it," I said.

"Got what?"

"The name."

"For?"

"The bar!"

"What is it?"

"Genius."

A long pause.

"Genius?"

"Yes."

"The *Genius* Bar?"

"Yes!"

"Try again," he said. And he hung up.

I stood there, looking at the phone. Then, I dialed him back. Steve picked up on the first ring.

"You can't call them Geniuses!" he exclaimed.

"Why?"

"You've met them, right?"

"Who?"

"The people who *really* know Macs."

I had—at Apple's reseller, FirstTech. And no sooner had I tried to answer the question than I realized Steve had asked it rhetorically.

"They're *geeks*!" he said.

Another long pause.

"You could call it the 'Geek' Bar," he said.

We absolutely *cannot* call it the Geek Bar, I thought.

"I'll keep thinking about it," I said. And we hung up again.

There were times when Steve would kick ideas to the curb and I'd let them sit there.

This was not one of those times.

I was back in my dad's letter, back in my marketing posture. I was about to do to Steve what he so often did to others. I was going to market the living *heck* out of the Genius Bar.

It wasn't hard. I thought about the malls I'd walked through for years—about stores like GameStop, which had opened in 1999 after being rebranded from Babbage's and quickly became one of the busiest places in the mall. I thought about EB Games, which had locations in all the malls I knew so well: Southdale Center, Rosedale Center, Mall of America. I thought about the computer games that Target sold and the people who bought them.

Young people.

And young people also worked retail.

In Minneapolis, too, we needed only three of them. Three Geniuses in a city (including St. Paul) of nearly three *million* people. If we looked hard enough, I knew we could find them. But if we called them Geniuses, perhaps they would find us! The "Think Different" ad had been playing for years. There would be status to being a "Genius" at Apple. Anyone who could do that job would want it, and we would want them: these people who would fit in by standing out, these people who would eventually make a crazy idea look genius.

That night, Steve and I spoke again. I explained my thinking on the Genius Bar, why I thought the name was necessary, and probably did just a little more seeking to be understood than seeking to understand. But I knew that Steve didn't have an ego about these things; I knew he wanted the best idea to win. I did, too.

The next morning, I got up, showered, and drove to work. I'm sure I called my dad, told him about the Genius Bar, explained that I wasn't sure, based on the firmness of Steve's initial position, that it would ever get its chance. My dad probably said something wise, something like "What will be, will be."

We hung up. I parked at 1 Infinite Loop, walked in, greeted the security guard, and proceeded up to my office.

Then I ran into Apple's general counsel, Nancy Heinen, in the hallway.

"What's a 'Genius Bar'?" she asked.

"Support," I said. "Why?"

"Steve just told me to trademark it."

I smiled.

A big victory, then.

An even bigger victory in retrospect.

It was time to start building.

□

Most retailers would design a store on paper, in two dimensions. But when Mickey Drexler joined the Apple board in early 1999, he gave Steve a good piece of advice.

"Get a warehouse," he told Steve, "then design the store there and hang out in it until *you* like it."

We rented a warehouse in Cupertino, ten minutes from 1 Infinite Loop, and named it after the street it was on: Bubb Road. We had our first design meeting there in early July. I shared the high-level concept that we had developed at the offsite, explaining to the team that we needed an inviting storefront with interactive windows that made people want to enter, and that once customers were in the store, the front half would be dedicated to launching customers' relationships with Apple and would have four bays, each of which would house one of our four computers: the iBook, iMac, PowerBook, and Power Mac G4. The back half would then be devoted to training in the theater and support at the Genius Bar. That was where we would deepen and restore customers' relationships with Apple.

In the meantime, I sent Cano to our first store in Glendale (and a second that George had managed to secure in Tysons Corner, Virginia) to find the people I'd imagined us hiring—those who loved technology and loved people—and added one more line to the ideal employee profile: that whoever we needed to hire would also have to be someone the Ritz would want to hire to work in their hotels. And lo and behold, Cano found them . . . albeit in a *very* different place than I ever would've expected.

Bookstores.

We didn't hire people from only bookstores; we also brought on teachers, firefighters, and nurses. But at first, a nontrivial portion of our hires were booksellers. There was a correlation between people who found themselves in books and those who could help others find themselves in technology. If there was anything reading tended to show people, it was how *other* people might experience the world.

As Cano was finding people to work in the stores, we continued designing them. Our deadline was tight from the beginning; we hoped to launch our first store at the Glendale Galleria in time for the holidays. Eight Inc., led by two designers who Steve had worked with on Macworld, Wilhelm Oehl and Tim Kobe, offered their expertise on the store's design. They were also responsible for putting the plans on paper so a construction team could build them out each week in the warehouse. We met there every week to discuss, and our first meeting was about floors. We debated materials. Wood, matte, stone. Gap had wood. But what type of wood? Should we use the same one? And how wide should the planks be? And how should we orient them—lengthwise, or crosswise? And how should we fasten them together? Nail down? Glue down? Tongue and groove? The questions were endless, but the benefit of the warehouse was that we didn't have to imagine the answers. We could see them. We could feel them. And once we felt them, we could tweak them.

Some tweaks were obvious. Others were not. But week after week, we kept making them. We'd ideate, then Tim and Wilhelm would outline new layouts on paper. Every change in product placement required moving the light fixtures, too, since lighting would make the products shine—literally. Then, a different team would do the physical buildouts, which we'd feel our way through the following Tuesday. We'd compare 2.25-inch planks of birch in one corner with 7-inch planks of European white oak in another. We'd pick one, then we'd change it. Steve would catch every change we made. You never knew what he would see—what he would notice that no one else could possibly have noticed. One day, he spent thirty minutes debating us over the hue of gray for the bathroom signs. Another day, he remarked that our suspended ceiling was too close to the wall and insisted that we move it a *quarter of an inch* farther away. His impossibly high standards were why so many within Apple had been convinced that we'd never open a store, let alone meet a target opening date. But despite the skeptics, we kept pushing, meeting, talking, tweaking, building. What would become a revolutionary retail concept began with an evolutionary process. And like any evolutionary process, stress—and the opportunity to imagine our way through it—often led to innovation.

We'd known that customers needed to be able to use the products in the store. The conclusion we'd landed on almost by default was to create four bays in the front half of the store, each of which would be dedicated to one of Apple's computers, then have the products sitting on those tables at a usable height. We settled on thirty inches for the tabletop fixtures, with the only exception being our kids' area, where a curved wooden table surrounded by cushy, orb-shaped seats was a foot off the ground. But putting products *only* at usable heights left us with blank spaces on the walls between our computers and our ceiling.

What *could* we fill those spaces with?

As a retailer, I knew the power of vertical merchandising. In 1984, Gap had created dominance with a beautiful "sweatshirt wall" that articulated the brand's transition back to basics. In 1999, my team working on design at Target had created artwork with boxes and graphics panels that made design approachable for the masses. Our window displays would do this in three dimensions to draw customers into the store, but I soon realized that two-dimensional graphics panels could help us get customers onto computers. We created eighty-square-foot graphics which, when several were lined up side-by-side, would run the entire length of the store. Resellers used their walls to display products. We used ours to tell stories.

The blank spaces between our computers and ceiling would become canvases on which Apple's graphic design team, long used to seeing their work in magazines, newspapers, and on twenty-four-inch screens, could witness it blown up in physical space. We could also match the panels with the window displays to create a cohesive brand statement. Just one problem: We needed a windows guy.

Enter: Mike.

Mike Fisher—or "Fish"—had been at Bloomingdale's for a decade doing windows when I found him. He was the best window designer in the world. I explained what Steve had explained to me: that Apple's computers were going to be the tools that helped people change the world for the better, and Mike would be responsible for pulling people into the store that would put those computers in people's hands. It was a mission. And maybe Mike bought into it. What he really bought into was the idea of working with Steve. The two of them became exceedingly close in the years that followed, and I got to enjoy the fruits of what they created together.

□

Before we could open, I had to make one final hire. This person would be overseeing store operations, navigating debates with Tim over how much inventory we'd get, and critically, going toe-to-toe with Phil over what third-party products we could display so people could take "rides." We needed someone good.

We found someone great.

Jerry McDougal had spent the past few years overseeing merchandising at PC Connection—then one of the major PC resellers in the United States. He hadn't been a fan of Apple; the company's products commanded lower margins than PCs, and his stores had numbers to hit. But I told him that Apple was creating a human future for technology, that the store would be at the center of that future, and that he—Jerry—could be the face of that store internally. And he was intrigued—or, at the very least, intrigued enough to come back out and meet Steve.

Jerry returned a few weeks later with his wife. After his interview, I called Steve to learn how it went.

"It was okay," Steve said.

I waited.

"I asked him why he wanted Apple in his life," Steve said.

"And?"

"He said he'd been trying to get Apple *out* of his life."

"He had been," I said. "The margins are lower, and he has numbers to hit. He's a sales guy!"

"That's what I told him," Steve said.

"You *told* him he was a sales guy?"

"I told him he was *just* a sales guy."

Steve . . .

"What did *he* say?"

"That I was 'just a sales guy,' too," Steve said. "Out there on the stage at Macworld, shilling all my products."

I couldn't help smiling through the phone.

"Is he wrong?"

A long pause.

"No," Steve said.

"So?"

"Hire him."

I got off the phone with Steve, gathered myself, and dialed Jerry.

Straight to voicemail.

I called him again.

Again, voicemail.

That night, I tried Jerry a third time. When he answered, the background noise was deafening.

"Where *are* you?" I asked.

"O'Hare," Jerry said.

"O'Ha—" I started. "Why?"

"Did Steve tell you how the interview went?"

"He did," I said. "He liked you! And I want to make you an offer."

"He, you—*What?*"

"Yeah," I said. "Steve's on a plane to New York, and I'll be working out the details with him, but is there anything you need to know?"

"Yeah," Jerry said. "Can he stop in Chicago and pick me up?"

I laughed. Jerry was funny—and funny usually means smart. Humor would also lighten the inevitable debates over what products and software we could display, or how much inventory we could get.

There had been a question, too, about whether we would even have inventory for purchase in the stores. Tim's team had presented the option to leave it out, wondering if it wouldn't make more sense to have customers come in, buy a product, then have it shipped to their home like an online order. But Steve, whose son Reed was getting to the age where he might be using a computer, immediately pushed back.

"If I buy Reed a computer, I don't want the *mailman* to get the credit," he said. "I want to give it to him myself!"

With that, we decided that the stores would carry inventory.

Crazy though it may seem now, there had been a few debates, too, about if we even needed salespeople (specialists) in the stores. Some at Apple thought that the products were so easy to use that if you just improved the physical environment, they would sell themselves. But coming from a low-tech background, I didn't agree, and Jerry didn't, either. He knew from his time at PC Connection that for a PC user, the Mac would feel foreign, even alien. Remember: Most people who knew anything about computers to that point were using PCs. New Mac users wouldn't be able to go to a friend or neighbor for help with the software, or with the transfer of the data from their PC. The transition *would* be scary. That was but another reason we needed to keep employees off commission and ensure that the stores were not just beautiful showrooms but also places with people who could make customers feel comfortable and at ease.

Over the coming weeks, the team moved at a speed the likes of which I'd never seen. Jerry worked with Mary and Niall to get our POS systems ready, then with Phil and Steve to get software titles and third-party products approved for the stores. Bill nailed down technical support protocols for the Genius Bar (and would later coordinate Geniuses' travel out to Cupertino for training). Sandy got us iBooks and PowerBooks and iMacs and Power Macs. George got more real estate—Mall of America in my home state, University Avenue in Palo Alto, Northshore Mall in Boston. Deirdre operationalized . . . everything. Meanwhile, I was speaking to everyone, all the time, and worked to ensure that each store got the content it needed to encourage customers to attend classes. The collaboration's scale could be summed up by three words that we would later emblazon in the back of our first store in Tysons Corner.

Retail is hard.

□

As August turned to September, store design continued. Tuesday meetings started at 8:00 a.m. and went as long as necessary for everything to get done.

Who would present first in those Tuesday meetings was always a subject of debate. No one wanted to go first because no one wanted to risk Steve's mood. He was always intense, but in the mornings, he could seem downright tortured. I was never entirely sure why. I just tried my best to help him go easier on people, modeling encouragement, kindness, compassion. And as the meetings continued, Steve would lighten up. The more time he spent with us, the gentler he got.

On our drives over to Bubb Road, I'd update him on anything we hadn't already discussed on our nightly calls. I'd tell him who would be at the warehouse when we got there, share something nice about them, try to frame their presence as a positive because I knew that helped Steve see it similarly. Then, when we got to the warehouse,

I'd introduce him to whoever was there. And it was always different people. Many were those he knew—Peter Bohlin, who had designed Pixar's Emeryville headquarters for Steve and provided our reflective suspended ceiling, or Kenji Ouecki, a designer he brought in from Japan who created the white kidney fixtures on which we presented the products. But many more were unfamiliar. The store's design emerged and evolved through conversation, and conversations went better when people were nice to each other. Also, if there was anything I'd learned growing up in Minnesota, it was that familiarity bred kindness.

As the Tuesday meetings progressed, Steve's mood would improve. He would crack smiles, laugh, imagine. He would summarize.

"So, what I'm hearing is . . ."

Then he would use his logic tree.

It was, for Steve, a tool to assess the quality of his thinking. The ideas that revealed themselves in conversation needed to be rooted in a purpose: Locating in malls, for instance, was rooted in the need to reach everyone. Still, the risk of letting ideas emerge like seeds at the ends of branches is that sometimes when they fall and take root, they begin to grow into a different—and better—idea. And more often than not, they do it at the least convenient possible time.

This was the double-edged sword of working with Steve. Nothing was ever done. Things could always change. A new and better idea could always punt a deadline, kill an initiative, upend a project. But ask anyone who worked with Steve for a long period of time, and they'll tell you: This was also what made creating with him so damn *fun*. The best idea could always win. And now, literally standing on top of our design deadline, one such idea was about to reveal itself to me.

CHAPTER 6

Genius Is Revealed

Up until August 2000, when Karen and I moved Lizzey and Will out to Atherton to start school, I had been commuting between Cupertino and Minneapolis weekly. On Saturdays back in Minnesota, Karen would document Will and Lizzey's childhoods by taking photos with her film camera, then drop the canisters at Lunds grocery store and return days later to pick up the prints. She would then spend hours scrapbooking—a big deal in Minnesota at the time, with entire stores dedicated to it. Then on Sunday, I'd return to Cupertino, where all of this seemed downright insane. People used digital cameras in Cupertino because Cupertino was the digital world. But Minneapolis was the *analog* world. Back and forth, back and forth.

I was getting whiplash.

Of course, it wasn't like I had nothing digital in Minneapolis. I did. The iMac Steve had sent me. I used it for work, and the kids toyed with it, but Karen had largely kept her hands off the computer. I kept encouraging her to get to know it; it would offer her an easy way to manage photos once we moved to California, where she wouldn't have Lunds. But for her, that wasn't the point; she was an incredible scrapbooker, and that was a creative outlet that was hard to give up. Watching her create what would become our kids' most prized heirlooms, it occurred to me that she found meaning in an analog life. And then it hit me that maybe others could find meaning in a digital one.

On a Friday in the fall of 2000, I mentioned that thought to Steve.

"The more I think about the Mac," I said, "the more I realize it's really the center of our digital life."

He asked what I meant. I explained. I told him that the Mac could be the connection between the photos people took on a digital camera and their ability to enjoy them. Karen wasn't there yet, but others could be. With videos, too, or music. Without the Mac, I told Steve, people didn't really have a digital life they could enjoy.

"Send me an email on that," Steve said.

I did and thought little of it. But Steve thought a *lot* of it. And he thought a lot of it because in April 2000—just a few months after the January 2000 Macworld—the dot-com bubble burst, and questions emerged about the PC's future. More interesting now than the world's migration online was its move from analog devices to digital devices, and the most interesting digital devices were those Jerry had been debating with Phil since he'd joined in August: camcorders, cameras, and MP3 players. Compared to what they could do, the PC had become, in the immortal words of the *Wall Street Journal*'s Walt Mossberg, "boring."

Looking back, I think this is part of what was torturing Steve in his store design meetings with us throughout 2000. He knew Walt had a point, and he knew he had one about the *Mac*. As far back as the iMac's launch in 1998, Steve had been positioning it as a device that would help people get on the internet, and he had discussed its success in serving that need at the Macworld I attended in January 2000. The problem was that with excitement around the internet waning—by fall of 2000, the Nasdaq had fallen *50 percent* from its peak—the story of the world's migration online was no longer enough to give the Mac's existence meaning. Steve needed a new way to describe its value proposition—a way to position it at the center of an increasingly digital world. And without even realizing it, I'd just contributed to one.

The following Monday, Steve showed up at our ET meeting late, as per usual. But there was an excitement I'd come to know—an energy that I could feel in Steve whenever something inspired him.

"I've got the future of the Mac!" he exclaimed. "We're going to position it as the *digital hub*."

He outlined the idea on the whiteboard, presenting the Mac as the one device that would coordinate all the *other* devices that pundits seemed to think would supplant it. The FireWire port could make the Mac a "hub" for camcorders, MP3 players, DVD players, and digital cameras. The apps Steve and Sina had been developing would unlock the magic of those corresponding devices on a bigger, brighter screen. I smiled, thinking it funny that my observations as a naive outsider might have had some hand in Steve's now describing the Mac as the center of the digital world. I smiled through the end of the day, back home that evening, into bed that night. Then, the following morning, I stopped smiling. Something was wrong.

Really wrong.

I didn't know what it was at first, so I lay in bed, turning the store's design over in my head. It had seemed right only the day before. But there was that inner voice again—quiet but persistent. In light of the digital hub, it whispered, we were going to have to design the store differently.

□

When we say that our minds change "in light of" new thinking, or a new idea, we're describing a new way of seeing reality. Steve had a term for what kept people from seeing things in new ways. He called it a "reality filter."

I don't know where that term came from, but that day, I learned what it meant. Reality filters are just people. We can all shed light on new thinking or obscure it. Karen had shone light on there being an analog world and a digital world. I had shone light on that idea for Steve, revealing the idea of a digital life. And now, by describing the Mac as the digital hub, Steve had shone light on an idea in my imagination—that the store couldn't be designed around our computers but around what people could *do* with our computers. What was a life, after all, if not the things people did?

I lay awake at 4:00 a.m. torn between the urgent need to answer that question with our store and the risk of sharing the news with Steve. *Everything* would have to change. Graphics panels, displays, merchandising. The way we thought about inventory, the way we had our computers positioned, even the products we would offer for purchase. If the Mac was the digital hub, customers in each store would expect the complete solution, which meant we had to offer digital camcorders, digital cameras, and products from the emerging MP3 category. I shook my head. But I also knew we had to do it. Organizing the store around what people could do would improve all our existing ideas. Rides were *based* on what people could do. Mike's window displays would be infinitely more compelling if they *showed* what people could do. Our graphics panels would be more fun to create if they *illustrated* what people could do.

All of this was great.

None of it was comforting.

When I got to Steve's office that morning, he could tell something was off.

"What's up?" he asked.

"I didn't really sleep last night."

"Why?"

I took a deep breath, preparing myself, the reality filter, to open. Then I let the light shine through. I explained how I saw the store working if the Mac was, in fact, the digital hub. I tried to make it palatable, to shape it like an opportunity. Oftentimes, that worked.

This was not one of those times.

"Do you have *any* fucking idea how big of a change this is?!" Steve shouted.

Yes.

"I've been working my ass off on this store for months," he said. "And now you want to change *everything*!"

Not . . . everything. I thought. But, yes. A few things. A couple of things.

Okay, yes, I thought. Everything.

Steve rattled on. I let him go. I sat there thinking about what Karen had told me about Steve—that he "fired people in the elevator"—and couldn't help wondering if I'd even *make* it to the elevator. I thought I had Steve's trust, but up until now, I hadn't really put that belief to the test. And Steve, for whom this store would be the path to everyone, was now realizing there was a different—and better—way to build it.

"I'm tired," Steve finally said. "I don't know if I have the energy to design another store from scratch."

I remained silent.

"You might be right," he continued. "You *might* be. But don't say anything about it when we get to the warehouse. Because I don't know if you are."

Steve got up out of his chair. I followed. We left his office, walked to the elevator, and took it downstairs. Then we got in his car and exited 1 Infinite Loop. Typically, we passed the ten-minute drive in animated conversation.

This one passed in silence.

But as we drove, I knew one thing. That with Steve, the best idea won. And the more I thought about it, the more convinced I was that this was the best idea—that to truly "think different," this is what we had to do. It probably would have been easier to leave good enough alone. But "good enough" wasn't good enough—for me or for Steve.

When we got to the warehouse, Steve gathered the team.

"Well, this is going to be an interesting meeting," he said. "Ron thinks we've got it all wrong. He thinks the store should be organized not around products but around what people do."

There was a long pause before he continued.

"And you know, he's right."

Steve went on for a moment, explaining how everything he had done correctly over the course of his career had required a moment of hitting the rewind button. He'd hit it with *Toy Story* after reading the script and realizing that Woody had become a jerk, and another few times as he'd created the original Macintosh. But with landlords breathing down our necks, we'd have only one chance to get it right.

"I'm going to leave now," Steve finally said. "And Ron's going to tell you how you're going to redesign the store."

I explained everything I'd shared with Steve to the team. We developed a new plan. A November launch was pushed out indefinitely. It was George, actually, who all but forced us to set an opening date; the landlord of the Glendale Galleria had kicked out a tenant to get us in, and by January 2001, she had been staring at a black hole in her best location for several months. With his reputation firmly on the line, George threatened to quit unless we locked in a launch date, and we settled on May 19, 2001.

With the store now delayed until May, Steve took a back seat in the design process we'd been driving together. Macworld was coming up in January, and he was spending most of his time with Apple's hardware and software teams to understand what elements he could include in this new story he would tell at the conference. In the meantime, we would press forward with the redesign, and Steve would formalize the strategy that would guide Apple for the next decade.

□

On January 9, 2001, Steve stood onstage at the Moscone Center in San Francisco for Macworld with a new story. He broke the PC's history into two "golden ages." The first went from 1980 to the mid-1990s, and was an age of productivity—word processing, spreadsheets, desktop publishing. By the mid-1990s, though, Steve said, the PC entered its second golden age with the internet, which propelled both business and personal usage to new highs. But now, Steve explained, the internet had matured, and people were wondering about the PC's future.

"People are again asking: 'Is the PC waning?'" Steve said. "'What's going to happen to the PC?'"

He paused, staring out at the audience.

"We think the PC is on the threshold of entering its third great age," Steve said. "And that age is the age of *digital lifestyle*."

He continued.

"And that's being driven by an explosion of new digital devices," Steve said. "We have cell phones *everywhere*. We have portable music players—CDs and their cousins, the new solid-state MP3 players now everywhere. We have digital *camcorders* everywhere. We have DVD players *exploding* in consumers' homes and in business as well, even *portable* DVD players. Digital *cameras* now constitute fifteen percent of all cameras sold in the US. Fifteen percent! It'll be *fifty* percent in a few years. And handheld organizers are everywhere as well."

Then Steve outlined for the audience what he'd shared in our ET meeting in October.

"We believe the PC—or more importantly, the Mac—can become the digital hub of our new, emerging digital lifestyle, with the ability to add tremendous value to our digital devices."

For the next thirty minutes or so, Steve went into detail on why, exactly, he believed the Mac had the chance to be the digital hub. He spoke about its ability to run complex applications, to display what would appear on a tiny camcorder screen on a huge, beautiful display, to take advantage of the Mac's inexpensive storage, and to burn disks and edit footage and make amazing, personal content.

"We first began to understand this with the camcorder," Steve said. "If you've used iMovie, it makes your digital camcorder worth *ten times* as much. Because you convert raw footage into an incredible movie with transitions, cross-dissolves, credits, soundtracks. You can convert raw footage that you'd normally never look at again on your camcorder into an incredibly emotional piece of communication."

It was the combination of owning the hardware (Mac), operating system (OS X), the application (iMovie), and marketing that made this possible, Steve said, along with FireWire and QuickTime. And people could also use the internet—and one of Apple's iTools, HomePage—to publish videos on their personal website. The only question now, Steve said, was what Apple would do *next*.

The audience didn't have to wait long for an answer. A Walkman appeared on the screen behind him.

"Audio," Steve said.

Then he unveiled iTunes.

Once Macworld ended, the reaction was immediate and profound. Downloads of iTunes shattered expectations. People loved the ability to rip music from their favorite CDs, mix playlists on their Macs, and burn their own discs. And although I didn't know it at the time, Steve and Ruby had also been discussing another idea for months: pairing Apple's music software with an Apple music device. Both agreed the idea made sense—existing MP3 players had poor user experiences, unlike existing camcorders and digital cameras—but the problem was storage: the technology to store more than a few dozen songs didn't yet exist. Then, a month after Macworld 2001, Ruby would take a routine supplier trip to Toshiba only to have them show him a 1.8-inch storage drive that could hold five gigabytes of storage—or approximately one thousand songs. Thus began in earnest the development of the iPod.

In the meantime, Steve had rejoined our meetings energized by the reaction to iTunes and was thrilled by the progress we had made redesigning the store around the digital hub. The front 25 percent was separated into two sections: "Home," with the iMac and iBook, and "Pro," with our PowerBook and Power Mac G4. In the middle of that section was a table where specialists would greet customers and check them out. The middle 50 percent of the store was then broken into four areas, each corresponding with one of the "solutions" enabled by the Mac as the digital hub: movies, with camcorders from Sony and Canon; photos, with digital cameras from Canon and Nikon; music, with MP3 players that Ruby would soon replace; and kids, with all the great educational software (and games) that would make the Mac useful, fun, and safe for them. Then, in the back 25 percent of the store, there was a theater, an "etc." section with merchandise that didn't fit neatly into the product bays (cables, printers, scanners, "*etc.*")—and, of course, the Genius Bar and its bright red bat phone. And on the back wall, visible from every corner of the store, was a huge, eight-by-twelve photo taken by Annie Leibovitz of John Lennon and Yoko Ono in bed.

"Think Different," it read.

Steve once described the "Think Different" idea as having a "purity" to it, meaning it contained nothing more than the essential. But the way Steve achieved purity was always through doing and thinking, through debate and conversation. *That's* why better ways to do things so often revealed themselves to him—whether with a movie at Pixar or with a store at Apple. The need to rewind wasn't a result of wondering *how* something was being done. It was a result of Steve's constantly asking *why.*

The lesson I learned from this is simple: Genius ideas reveal themselves through action, because action inspires conversation. It was the conversation I had with myself as I commuted between Cupertino and Minneapolis that revealed the idea of a digital life, which led Steve to the digital hub, which led us to redesign the store. It was then everyone else who brought that decision to life—Eight Inc., yes, but also all the attendees of the offsite and everyone involved with the store design meetings. Today, countless people claim credit for designing the Apple Store, and all of them deserve it. We designed it together. We *did* it together. There was no singular architect or mastermind. There was just conversation—and doing—that kept us all on the frontier.

Still, perhaps the most important thing the need to redesign the store revealed was also the simplest: We needed more time. Now, with the months it would take to redesign the store, we had it. And with it, we would be able to formalize what had now been emerging for weeks and months, through all the trials and tribulations and action and conversation: our culture. The Apple Store was always going to look beautiful. Our culture is what would make us feel different.

□

A lot of people talk about culture like it's something you build, and there's probably some truth to that. But in my experience, culture is more like the soil of a garden. If you want a garden to thrive, you must plant seeds, tend to the soil, and give it a light to grow toward. If that sounds esoteric, it's because, well, it is. As a prescription for how someone *else* can create a great culture, I can't be any more specific.

Still, I can be clear about what I did in my efforts to create a great culture within Apple Retail. As the months had continued in 2000 and into 2001, I had been describing how I wanted our culture to *feel* to Steve. He knew from our nightly calls and Tuesday drives that kindness mattered to me, and that I wanted people within Apple Retail to communicate with a desire to support customers and each other. That would be different from other organizations within Apple. But this was my organization to lead, and that was how I wanted to lead it.

Steve had kept calling me every night. We spoke about everything: past, present, future. We talked about things it felt a little weird to talk about, like money, which Steve said had never particularly mattered to him. Still, for as personal as we got, there was one topic I was sure we wouldn't touch. Then, in late 2000, Steve asked me an unexpected question.

"You go to church, right?"

"I . . . do," I said. I had no idea how he knew.

"Will you tell me about your faith?"

I was surprised by Steve's invitation to speak about it, and I kept it simple.

I explained to him that my relationship with faith had been stronger at times and weaker at others. I grew up attending church every week with my family, went to church camp in the summers, and volunteered with our church in high school. Still, I rarely attended church at Stanford, and never at Harvard. I went a bit more during my time at Mervyn's, but even then, I didn't talk about it. It was only once I returned to Minnesota in my thirties that I reengaged with my faith. I believed that it might help me with leadership, but it would also reveal to me if I really believed, or if I'd simply inherited my belief—like we inherit our genes—from my parents.

"So, what did you decide?" Steve asked. "Is there a guy in the sky?"

"I believe there is."

"Where's the evidence?"

"All around us," I said. "It seems to me that science is uncovering the order something greater than us created."

"You don't believe in evolution?" Steve asked.

"I do, but something had to have started the process," I said. "Wouldn't you agree?"

"Maybe."

"I believe in intelligent design," I said to Steve. "I don't think we're here by accident."

We revisited the topic a few times in the weeks that followed. Steve asked me how my faith manifested at work, and I told him it was simple—I tried to do what Jesus preached and love my neighbor.

"Who's your neighbor?" he asked.

"Everyone that comes into my path," I said. "Friends, family, customers, colleagues. You. Our work as believers is to secure their good. That's the definition of agape love. It's what I've been trying to do for my entire career."

A few days later, Steve called me into his office and handed me a copy of the movie *Brother Sun, Sister Moon*. It was the story of the founder of the Franciscan order, he told me—St. Francis of Assisi.

"This movie had a profound effect on my life," he said.

"Why?"

"I see myself in St. Francis," Steve said. "When he was twenty-four, he renounced his wealth and dedicated his life to the poor."

"But when Apple went public . . ." I trailed off.

"Well, sure," he said. "I didn't renounce my wealth. But St. Francis built a community of people who served the poor, and I built a community of people who use technology to improve the world."

I nodded. And I believed him—and believed that he believed what he was saying. I'd seen the reaction people had to using computers that felt human, to making beautiful memories of their kids with iMovie. I'd heard so much about Steve the tyrant, Steve the dictator. And sure, there was a darkness in him. But there was a light, too. Steve was a creator. All he wanted to do was create great things for people.

Of course, to that point, I hadn't thought that I could bring my faith to work in a meaningful way. But I took Steve's sharing about the story of St. Francis as permission to bring my faith to work. I thought about loving my neighbor at home, about loving my employees at work, about securing the good of everyone who crossed my path.

And then I thought about something else.

The Apple Store needed something to differentiate it from our resellers. I knew that. I also knew that it couldn't be the products: All our resellers sold them, and we'd need them to keep doing so as we built out our retail footprint. I had believed since the offsite that our differentiator was going to be the quality of our service, like the Ritz, but I also knew that while Steve understood this differentiator in principle, he had wanted me to come up with a simple way to articulate it.

"If you can't articulate your vision in four words or less," he said, "you haven't thought it through."

Words had come to me immediately. But I'd pushed them down, unclear on whether Steve—who had not yet revealed his thoughts on faith—would accept them. But once he spoke about St. Francis, I had confidence that the words I *wanted* to use were the words I *could* use, that the person I'd always been was the person he'd hired me to be.

Four words, eh, Steve? I thought. How about two?

Love customers.

I called him.

"I've got it," I said.

"What?"

"Our service philosophy."

"What is it?"

"We're going to love customers," I said.

There was a long pause.

"*Love* . . . ?" Steve asked.

"Yes," I said. "That's what you've been doing at Apple with your products, with the iMac. You're creating products that secure people's good—their creativity, their potential."

For Steve, this was . . . a bit of a leap.

"I wouldn't call it 'love,'" he said. "We design great products."

"But that *is* love," I said, my momentum building. I reiterated the concept of agape love to him as an act of securing someone's good. I told Steve that he'd spent twenty-five years creating a computer that would humanize people's relationship with technology and amplify their innate creative potential, then help them channel it as a force for good. The features of the iMac, too—the handle that invited people to touch it, the egg-shaped design that made it fun and approachable, the simple, intuitive user experience and apps that encouraged people to create—all these were acts of love, because they secured people's good.

"Okay," Steve finally said. "Okay. But Cupertino is the most secular zip code in the world."

"So?"

"So . . . *love*?" he asked. "Can you find a different word?"

□

I would find a different word . . . eventually. But I didn't let my thinking about how Apple Retail's culture would feel go. I wanted a culture of love, a culture of kindness, a culture in which people communicated and collaborated and *cared*. We would be a garden like the one I'd seen in Singapore so many years earlier: one in which the plants wouldn't just grow alongside one another but would grow healthier *because* of one another. I explained this to Dan, focusing on the tactical benefits of a team that constantly looked out for its members. And Dan got it. Then he introduced me to Denise.

Denise Young had been at Apple for two years when I met her. She was exactly what I was looking for. And we were exactly what *she* was looking for. She was a Christian woman—the daughter of a pastor who was also the mayor of a small town in Colorado. No one, I thought, would better understand my vision for a culture of love and kindness. Denise was also a Black woman and a former Broadway singer. Her personal geography was rich, and the diversity of her experiences would enable her to truly "see" people—to recognize what they were experiencing because she had seen something like it before. We were hiring people to build relationships with customers, and for those relationships to feel authentic, we needed people who not only had diverse emotional geographies but also were unafraid of bringing those geographies to work. For them to truly serve customers, their souls had to be unlocked.

I empowered Denise to create this type of culture, and for the next several months, working closely with Linda, Stacey, Laura, and the first store managers we hired, we completed the training program for our store managers, specialists, and Geniuses. One of the biggest questions we grappled with was how to help specialists deliver the type of service that we had committed to offering in the store. It wasn't enough to standardize it; we also had to create room for employees to be creative.

It was here that we turned back to the same hotel that had inspired the service we aspired to offer: the Ritz.

□

People like to say that brands are built on trust. And that's true. But if it's true, it's because trust exists between people. Brands are people. Walmart *was* Sam Walton. JCPenney *was* James Cash Penney. If someone is chronically late, that's their brand. *Great* brands are thus *great* people. And great people are those who you can always count on to do the right thing.

How do you become someone who someone else can trust to do the right thing? To my mind—and to that of the Ritz—the answer was simple: become someone who *you* can trust to do the right thing. How do you do that? Also simple. Do the right things repeatedly, for years, no matter what's going on around you. How do you know what the right thing is? That is the million-dollar question.

It was also the question that the Ritz had managed to answer.

The Ritz offered exceptional service because they could define what it looked like, yes, but also because they knew the steps to create it and took those steps daily. In the months leading up to our originally scheduled November opening, Denise and I had been working with Pat Mene of the Ritz to translate the hotel's steps of service into ones that our store's employees could take, and we had hired our first few store managers and been training them. Then, when my digital hub epiphany pushed our opening into 2001, Pat asked if the leaders I'd hired—Laura, Stacey, Linda, Cano, and several others—would want to come and *train* at the Ritz.

This was a great opportunity. Training at the Ritz meant my team witnessed firsthand how the Ritz executed, but also how they brought on and trained *their* teams. When they returned, they explained that we needed what the Ritz-Carlton had developed: a credo. This was a collection of the Ritz's steps of service, their daily standards, and their mission. When adhered to, a credo would ensure consistent, excellent service and would make it easier to onboard and train new Apple employees. That's what we wanted, including the Ritz's anticipation of unspoken needs or concerns. There were a lot of reasons people might be afraid of computers, and part of our specialists' job would be to anticipate those concerns and address them. So, Denise and I—along with the field leaders and store managers I'd hired—began working on a credo for Apple Retail.

Together, we designed a set of guiding steps that would frame our customer interactions. First, a specialist would approach the customer with a personalized warm welcome. Then they would probe to understand all the customer's needs. Once the specialist understood those needs, they would present a solution for the customer to take home that day, listen for (and resolve) any issues or concerns, and end with a fond farewell and an invitation to return.

Along with these steps, we also made a list of promises. The first few aligned with Steve's vision for a creative, collaborative relationship between humans and technology; we would showcase technology in ways that engaged people's imaginations and invigorated their creative spirit, deliver expert advice from knowledgeable, passionate Mac enthusiasts, and build honest, respectful, and individual relationships with customers while respecting people's right to privacy. With help from Bill, Sandy, and Niall, we aimed to get the operational details right, too, like maintaining key items in stock, executing fast and accurate transactions, and providing an integrated web and retail store. And as we expanded outside the US, we would find a way to serve our global customers.

The final promise we made was about support. When I'd first thought about the Genius Bar, it had occurred to me that people coming to us for help wouldn't have an alternative computer waiting around. It wasn't like when I got my shirts dry-cleaned and had a few at home I could use in the interim. One computer was *all people had*. So we didn't just need to repair it. We needed to repair it *quickly*. This led to a simple question.

"What if we could repair a computer as fast as someone can dry-clean a shirt?"

Of course, I had no idea what this would take. I'm not sure anyone else did, either. And perhaps that's why our promise wasn't that we would offer fast repair but fast diagnosis and *reliable* repair. But that was okay. The vision was aspirational. We would aspire to fixing customers' computers quickly, and we eventually would.

Finally, we developed our mission. It would evolve over the years, but its essence would remain the same.

"The soul of our store is our people," we wrote. "And we exist to enrich lives."

That was our purpose, our reason for existing. And, harkening back to Steve's ask for a "different word" than *love* to describe our service philosophy, *that* word—*enrich*—ended up being the one I used. What did love do, I thought, if not enrich lives? Tolstoy once described love as a life-giving, *enriching* force. So, yes—love was what we would *offer.* But enriching lives is what Apple's products—and our store—would *do.* Enriching lives is what love did. Enriching lives is what love had always done.

We wrote down our mission as part of the credo, then had employees wear the credo card behind their name tag, over their heart. This was a constant reminder that it was sacred, that it was something to honor, that it was something bigger than themselves. Being a part of the Apple Store was always going to be about something bigger than selling products because Steve's vision for Apple went *beyond* selling products. He was on a mission to create the type of relationship between people and technology that would enrich lives, and we were creating the store in which those relationships would be launched, deepened, and restored.

Now *that,* I thought, was a mission.

Ultimately, I believed that a mission like this was what everyone sought. It was certainly what *I* had always sought. Meaning, significance. A team was coming together over a mission to love customers and be loved in return. We were almost ready.

Almost.

□

By May 2001, all that was left to do was put the finishing touches on the stores and prepare them for the press, much like I'd done at Target with design. We would host one press event at our store in Tysons Corner. Our locations would drive traffic, and they would be our marketing—nothing else. I had explained this to Steve, and he'd accepted it.

I thought.

A few days before our first two stores were scheduled to open—one in the Glendale Galleria, and the other in Tysons Corner, Virginia—I was in my office discussing slides for press events with Angela when Steve barged in.

"Open your email!" he exclaimed.

"Hi, Steve," I said.

"Hi," he said. Then he turned to Angela.

"Hi."

Then, he turned back to me.

"Your email," he repeated, rounding my desk to look at my screen.

I noticed as Angela shifted in her seat, then began gathering her things. Steve noticed, too.

"Should I—" she asked.

"No," Steve said. "You can stay."

I opened my email. At the top was a message from Steve.

"5 down. 95 to go," its subject line read.

Steve had created an ad for the stores.

Angela and I listened as Steve read it out loud. He explained that Apple had around 5 percent market share in personal computers, which was equivalent to about twenty-five million customers using Macs. It was a lot, he seemed to say.

It also wasn't enough.

We wanted the other 95 percent, too. We wanted to show them, with the stores, that the Mac offered a better, simpler, more human experience than anything they'd seen before. We wanted to help people understand what *they* could do with computers: burn CDs, create movies, take photos and upload them to personal websites.

And we wanted to be *there* for people—in their neighborhoods, with Geniuses who could help and trainers who could teach and a theater where they could learn. We even had three hundred software titles, including many of the best educational titles for kids. Still, Steve finished the ad by saying that if only 5 percent of the remaining 95 switched to Mac, we'd double our market share and earn the chance to delight another twenty-five million customers. It was as if he were hedging his bet on me; yes, he seemed to say, he wanted everyone, like I did, but he'd be happy with "some."

I think this reflected a maturation for Steve: an experience-driven understanding that bold visions couldn't be forced, or rushed, and would need time to reveal themselves—if they revealed themselves at all. At that point in my career, I did not share his experience; coming off design at Target, I was utterly convinced that we could reach everyone, and I'd heard in my conversations with Steve exactly what my dad said I always heard: exactly what I wanted to hear. We wanted to convince everyone that the Mac could create a better lived experience than they'd ever known, so we'd created a shopping experience unlike any they'd ever seen. And at the bottom of the ad in *The Wall Street Journal*, Steve had articulated that with two words.

Shop different.

Eighteen months of creating had led to this moment; eighteen years of retail experience had led to this store. Steve believed it *could* be Apple's path to everyone; I was certain that it would be.

Now, it was time to see if "everyone"—or even, *anyone*—agreed.

CHAPTER 7

The Difficult Early Years

As I got ready for bed the night before our opening, I knew the next day would be important both for Apple and for me personally. This would be the first time I had led the development of a retail store from scratch to a store opening.

Steve called to wish me luck.

"Are you nervous?" he asked.

"A little bit," I said.

"Don't be," he said. "With all those Pixar movies—we never know how they're going to do. All you can ever know is that you've done your best. That's what makes it fun. You work really, *really* hard, then you get to see what everyone else thinks."

"Thanks," I said. "I'll call you in the morning with an update."

□

The following morning, I woke up early, caught up on email, exercised, and ate breakfast. I had been getting calls all morning—from

Jerry, Cano, and others—telling me about the line that had formed outside of Tysons. By 6:00 a.m., I was out in Glendale's cool morning air walking to my car.

Steve called.

"Have you seen what's going on in Tysons?" he asked.

"Yes," I said, fumbling with my keys as I reached for my door handle.

"It's packed!" he said. "You did it."

"*We* did it," I said.

It was all I could do to stay under the speed limit as I drove across town to Glendale. I got there and told the team about the good news from Tysons. But as the hours leading up to our opening passed and the line Steve had described to me didn't materialize outside our store, we got nervous.

Did we pick the wrong mall? I wondered. Should we have marketed the stores?

And then the big one.

What if this just doesn't work?

Finally, around 9:40 a.m., I pulled my phone out of my pocket and dialed Steve.

"Hello?" Steve said.

His voice came through loud and clear. Mine was stuck somewhere in my windpipe.

"*Ron?*" Steve emphasized.

"I think I blew it," I finally managed.

"What are you talking about?" Steve asked.

"Glendale," I said. "There's no one here."

"Just give it time," he said. "People *will* come."

And come they did.

□

On the morning of May 19, 2001, more than *seven thousand people* found what they were looking for at our Glendale store. Some who attended were local. Many more were not. One couple had flown in from Seattle. Another had driven in from Kansas. Two men had flown in from Austria and Italy.

"I wouldn't have missed this for the world," one said. It was a figure of speech, but it also didn't seem to be. These people had crossed mountains for us, and now, I wanted to move mountains for them. At 10:00 a.m., I told them so.

"On behalf of everyone at Apple, this store has been created for you, our great customers," I said. "It's my pleasure to welcome you to Apple. Thank you."

Cheers erupted around me. High fives, too. Employees approached customers with warm welcomes, probed politely to grasp their needs, then guided them through the "rides" they'd been empowered to create. The love I'd wanted to share with customers became visible. I could see it in the interactions between customers and employees in the store, yes, but also in the line—the *line*!—that had, without our realizing it, grown outside the store.

I'd seen plenty of lines—checkout lines, support lines—inside of retail stores. What I had never seen was a line *outside* of a retail store. I figured its end would be around the corner, roughly forty yards from our doors. It wasn't. And it wasn't around the next corner, or the one after that. Instead, it snaked down the hall, past JCPenney, then across the bridge and into the Glendale Galleria's parking garage. And it wasn't just the length of the line that surprised me. It was the *energy*. I'd always seen lines as symptoms of problems. But there was nothing going wrong in this line. There were just camped-out customers clad in Apple garb chattering excitedly. For twenty-five years, their only connection to Apple had been the company's products. Now, their passion had a place to go.

□

My partner at Target with design, Michael Graves, used to say that everyone has ten great days in their life.

May 19, 2001, was one of mine.

When the books closed on our opening weekend, we had processed $600,000 in sales. It was a blowout by any measure. The Apple Stores had worked. Then, on Monday, *Businessweek* ran an article.

"Sorry, Steve," the headline read, "Here's Why Apple Stores Won't Work."

"I give them two years before they're turning the lights off on a very painful and expensive mistake," commented retail consultant David Goldstein.

I didn't see the article when it came out, and even if I had, I would've shrugged it off. Our opening weekend numbers were more than enough to justify our expenses. Steve also hadn't mandated profitability at the beginning because he'd come to accept what I'd told him: that the stores would build Apple's brand *and* business. But I knew our expenses were higher than they needed to be and could probably be managed more thoughtfully, so I hired a CFO to help us: Mike Kramer.

Kramer was a perfect fit for us. He was smart, confident, and strategic, and he had proven he could go toe-to-toe with visionaries like Steve through his success under Les Wexner at The Limited. But more important, he had proven himself to be an effective intermediary between visionary retailers and those whose purse strings would need to be loosened to support their visions. Fred Anderson had recently assigned Peter Oppenheimer, Apple's controller, to work with Kramer and oversee the stores. Most controllers would challenge the idea of a store without commissions, and almost all would challenge the idea of giving up 50 percent of selling space to training and support. I needed someone in finance who wouldn't try to obscure the vision but could understand and articulate it. And in Kramer, I found him.

One of the things I liked about Kramer was that he was a believer, not a skeptic. He looked at initiatives like the Genius Bar and theater that required giving up half of a store's selling space and, instead of telling me why they couldn't work, asked me why *I* thought they would. I explained it to Kramer—that the focus on training and support dovetailed with getting rid of commissions to create an environment that people would want to spend time in, and that it was only by spending time in our stores that customers would realize technology didn't have to be scary, and that the Mac was better than a PC. This might not have been the *only* way for Apple to get its computers to everyone, I told Kramer, but it was the only way that I knew to give the company a chance. Building creative, collaborative relationships between people and technology would require a store dedicated to giving those relationships a safe place to launch. Deepening and restoring those relationships would require structure and guidance (training) as they grew, and a place (the Genius Bar) where customers could get help. With that in mind, no commissions—and half of the store dedicated to training and support—made perfect sense. And Kramer agreed.

Of course, Kramer would also be responsible for trying to understand if—and how—things could be done better, and perhaps just *slightly* more economically. But with a $600,000 opening weekend, our numbers were good. Right?

Wrong.

The plan for our first year had been to open a store every week after our launch in May. So, every week, operational costs continued to grow: rent, payroll. If the revenue that had come with our Tysons and Glendale openings had accompanied every store opening, none of this would have been a problem. But the numbers weren't there.

Kramer and I quickly found the culprit. A few weeks before we'd opened Tysons and Glendale, Apple had announced its new iBook. When it went on sale, it was only available at Glendale and Tysons, and loyal customers came to buy it. Our $600,000 opening weekend wasn't, as I'd originally thought, proof of concept. It was proof that the Apple faithful would show up at a store opening and that customers in the mall would check out a new store, but it wasn't proof that we could convert anyone to buy a Mac. Evaporating sales left only growing expenses, and pressure began building again.

On a Monday in August, I walked into ET. The look I caught from Steve was like having daggers shot through me.

"What's up?" I asked.

"What are you doing here?" Steve asked, not even remotely curious.

"I'm here for E—"

"You opened a store this weekend that hasn't sold a computer!" he shouted. The words cut through the air like a knife. The message was simple.

Fix it.

Now.

Sales commissions came up the following day at our weekly retail leadership meeting, but I remained resolute. I knew Steve cared about selling computers, but I also knew he cared *more* about creating an experience. And as I watched customers flood our stores, I could tell just how good ours was. I knew that our free Wi-Fi was driving traffic. Phil pressed me, arguing that we couldn't let customers just come in and browse the internet because it was keeping those who wanted to buy Macs from being able to use them, but I insisted that people would wait, that customers were doing stuff on the computers—emailing photos, watching videos.

"It's not just videos," Jerry told me one day.

"What is it?"

A long pause.

"Porn," Jerry replied. I laughed out loud before catching myself.

We eventually updated safety preferences to fix the issue. But the occasional misuse of computers was a price worth paying for a store that showed people how they could use technology. Yes, if you gave people freedom, some would misuse it. But most people capitalized on it. They took rides. They snapped photos with our digital cameras, uploaded them to our computers, then sent them—via email—to their friends. Our traffic was also proving to be a pleasant surprise for the landlords that had bet on us—and a much less pleasant surprise for those who hadn't.

In August, George called me.

"I just got off the phone with one of David's leasing agents," he said.

"And?"

"He told me that David just barged into a meeting and asked why he didn't have 'more fucking Apple Stores.'"

I smiled.

I knew that our store meant something to people, and that it was generating the type of brand affinity that, when the products came, would allow us to capitalize. But, as I would continue to learn, when an initiative meant something to people, it also meant something to Steve. And when it meant something to Steve, it had to be perfect. I hadn't yet truly learned what happened when it wasn't.

In early fall of 2001, I did.

□

When you're trying to execute an ambitious strategy at high speed, you make decisions constantly. Ideally, you get them all right. Realistically, you get some wrong. That's okay. Make mistakes, then learn from them. Still, if you know there's something you need to do and someone above you who will lose it if you do it, it's *always* better to err on the side of transparency. I never liked getting bad news (one of my biggest shortfalls as a leader), and I especially didn't like breaking it. But, as I was about to learn the hard way, it was always better to break bad news than trust.

Opportunities to break trust—or build it—typically emerge from two conflicting certainties. As of 2001, one such certainty was that many malls were physically supported by columns. Another such certainty was that Steve absolutely *hated* columns. In the first five stores we built, we got lucky; the columns were built into the walls, so they mostly blended in. But in our sixth location, in Boston's Northshore Mall, the columns were in the middle of the store.

I remember staring at the renderings of the Northshore Mall space with George and scratching my head.

"Steve's going to *hate* these," I said, referring to the columns.

"He'll have to deal with them," George said.

"They can't remove them?" I asked. George shook his head.

"Okay," I said. It was our sixth store of twenty-seven planned for that year, and it was September. I needed to believe that this was going to be okay, so I told myself it would be. But I never really believed it. In fact, I knew that absent an act of God, it would be anything but okay.

On the Saturday morning of Northshore Mall's opening, I was in Menlo Park coaching Will's soccer game when my phone rang.

You know who it is, I thought. Don't pick up.

I picked up.

"What's with the forest?" Steve asked.

"The *forest?*" I asked. I'd heard him correctly, but I wasn't sure what he meant.

"Northshore Mall!" Steve shouted. "The *fucking* columns!"

"Ohh," I said. "Yeah. They—"

"You broke my trust," he said. And then he hung up.

Fuck.

I tried him back.

No answer.

I tried him again.

Nothing.

Thoughts flew through my head. It was like I was going through the five stages of grief all at once.

First, denial.

He's not upset, I thought. How could he be upset? Malls have columns. Malls *have* to have columns.

But then, anger.

Why did you approve a store with columns? You *knew* he'd hate them.

Then, a question.

How did he even *see* the columns?

Then, more anger as I answered my own question.

The internet, you *idiot*. You know, the *i* in those iMacs you aren't selling.

Anger quickly gave way to bargaining—a futile effort to convince myself that all I needed was to explain the columns to Steve, that he'd understand. But I knew that wasn't the point. The point was that I hadn't told him, that I'd broken his trust. And as a result of that, well, depression, and eventually, acceptance.

At least I didn't get fired in the elevator.

It was the worst day of my tenure at Apple. Later that night, I spoke to Fred Anderson, Apple's CFO—someone Steve often called when things were going sideways.

"Is it over?" I asked.

"No," he said. "Dan and I talked Steve off the ledge. He's fine."

I believed Fred, but I wondered about that word.

"Fine."

That wasn't how Steve had sounded to me.

Of course, it wasn't hard to grasp why he was so upset. He'd bet massively *on* me, then invested significantly *in* me. Money, yes, but also time. What had our nightly calls been about if not getting to know who each of us truly was? For Steve, my approving the columns felt like an indication that, when things got hard, I wouldn't speak in his voice.

Fortunately, Fred convinced Steve that I deserved a chance to earn his trust back. In the meantime, Steve established a new protocol: I'd now be required to get his sign-off on any store with columns. This included several stores for which we'd already signed leases. When we told Steve we couldn't get out of the leases, Steve told us to get rid of the columns. George explained, surprisingly calmly, that columns weren't a matter of aesthetics, but physics. But Steve had a way of making the impossible seem possible, and we eventually managed to move a few of them. The rest, we kept. Luckily, none of this affected the one thing we could point to as a signal of early success—traffic. And then, a little over a week after our Northshore Mall store opened, we lost that, too.

□

On a cool fall Tuesday morning, I received an email from Steve.

"Today," the subject line read.

"Given today's events, if you'd like to stay home, please feel free to do so," the email said. Steve then followed up with a note to me saying he would still be going in and would love the opportunity to spend time with the group. I looked up at Karen, who was making coffee in the kitchen.

"Did something happen?" I asked.

"What do you mean?" she asked. "Today?"

"Yeah," I said. I shared the email from Steve. She turned on the TV. And then the air left the room.

September 11, 2001. That day was marked by horror and uncertainty. As I drove Will and Lizzey to school, everything seemed to be moving slower. The streets were quieter. Apple's headquarters was only a few miles from the San Jose airport, so I'd gotten used to hearing planes flying over me on the way in. That day, not one did. The sky was quiet, cloudless, and empty.

When I got to Bubb Road, the conversations were different than they'd been. Steve asked us how we felt, what we thought it all meant. Some of us spoke, wondering out loud about the people we knew in New York, the people we *had* in New York. It was a dark day with no certainty. No one knew what to do. All we could do was be there for each other. And in the days that followed, all the stores could do was remain open and ready to serve the customers that came in.

And yet, for weeks after the attacks, there weren't many customers to be there for. This was true for every retailer, every mall. Tysons Corner was fifteen miles from the Pentagon, which now had a gaping hole in its southwest wing. The tragedy notwithstanding, this was hard to swallow; we had bet big on malls, and now we didn't know if their traffic would ever be the same. Apple's stock price was also sitting 70 percent off its pre-dot-com-bust high. Nevertheless, we stayed committed to our strategy and continued opening stores.

On October 13, 2001, we opened our most important location yet on University Avenue in Palo Alto. I knew that Steve would be paying particularly close attention to this store; it was why I'd hired Cano to run it. And it had a *huge* crowd for the opening, including other members of Apple's executive team, who had come to see their first Apple Store. I stood there, trying to enjoy the moment. Still, I knew from Tysons and Glendale that this image of success was unlikely to last more than a day. I hoped I was wrong—that given our Palo Alto store's proximity to Apple headquarters and location in Silicon Valley, perhaps it would do just slightly better than our other stores were doing.

It didn't.

A few days after Palo Alto opened, Cano called me.

"Got some good news for me, guy?" I asked.

Silence.

"Ah," he said. "Well, actually, I had a question. But I can ask someone else."

"No!" I said. "How can I help?"

"Well, uh, we had a customer return a computer at Palo Alto today."

"And?"

"And we didn't have anyone *buy* a computer at Palo Alto today."

I grimaced as I realized what Cano was asking me.

"You're wondering how to close the store with a negative till," I said.

"Yeah."

I paused, thinking.

"I have no idea," I finally said. "I never imagined that could happen."

"Neither did I."

I could only hope that Steve wouldn't check the day's sales report.

In the meantime, I was on the phone with store managers like Cano every day to understand what was working, what wasn't working, and what we could be doing better.

A lot, it turned out. There were a *lot* of things we could be doing better.

A few issues had revealed themselves immediately. The first was that we weren't selling computers to first-time Mac users. As a result, the Genius Bar was empty, and after a few weeks, I called Bill Frederick with an idea for something productive it could do. Those who visited Apple Stores in late 2001 might recall there being mini refrigerators at their Genius Bars. Years before Bill would get busy sourcing parts, he was also sourcing Evian waters.

The Genius Bar being a place to hang out did not go over particularly well with some of our Geniuses. I'd imagined them having the people skills to get hired at the Ritz and the technical skills to go toe-to-toe with Steve on technology. But while all those Denise found met the technical standard, and some had the confidence to go toe-to-toe with Steve, unfortunately, many struggled to carry on casual conversations, as Steve had intuited from day one. We tried, mostly in vain, to train them for it, but some of the Geniuses told us it wasn't what they'd signed up for and quit. But my dream of the Genius Bar was too clear to give up on it, so I didn't. I kept outlining my vision to Denise, encouraging her to keep looking for the people who could create it.

In the meantime, we were running into another issue in the theater. The Apple teams had done heroic work coming up with content for the classes we'd offer—Intro to Mac, Mac OS X Basics, Switching from Windows—and those we'd hired to run the classes, including the occasional celebrity, were doing as well as they could. But one-size-fits-all classes, it turned out, did not make sense when some attendees were true creative pros switching over from the PC, and others were so new to computers that they didn't even know how to use a *mouse*. A few days before we'd opened stores, Steve had asked me which I thought would do better: the theater (his pick) or the Genius Bar (my pick). By October 2001, the better question was which was doing *worse*.

□

By the end of October, foot traffic to the stores had returned to a similar level to that which we'd seen pre-9/11. But the revenue still wasn't coming. We needed to be doing $15 million per store annually to break even.

We were pacing for $10 million.

Now, to be clear: this was an objectively great revenue number; with six-thousand-square-foot stores, it meant we were on track to do just shy of $2,000 per square foot, which was more than double what Best Buy and Circuit City were doing. The problem was that our operational and capital costs were significant. We were generating revenue, but we weren't profitable.

Steve hadn't mandated that the stores be profitable immediately, and Wall Street wouldn't, either; it takes time for retailers to figure out a profit formula, and we would be no exception. But the math in my head was simple. If we couldn't find our way to $15 million, it was unlikely we'd survive long enough to get to fifty stores, let alone our target of three hundred. And this meant we would never be able to help Apple—and Steve—reach the 95 percent. Meanwhile, our resellers—who would remain our path to every American as we expanded our own retail footprint—were furious that after over a decade of what they saw as having kept us afloat, we appeared intent on abandoning them by opening our own stores. I had believed that, in their minds, a rising tide would lift all boats, but this hadn't proven true *yet,* and reseller frustration was beginning to boil over.

This put me in a tough spot. I knew that the resellers were struggling. I also knew why. *Apple* was struggling. Sales were down. But I didn't want to tell the resellers this. They would be a critical part of our go-to-market infrastructure as we expanded our retail footprint, and if I told them that Apple was struggling, they might dedicate fewer resources to us in their stores, which would mean even fewer sales for us. Thus, when an important reseller complained to the channel, I would visit them, bring them to the closest Apple Store, and ask them if they saw any of their customers. One Pasadena reseller had been adamant that we would steal business with our Glendale store, but after two hours in it, we hadn't seen *one* of his customers. I explained that this was why we were launching stores—to go after the customers he *didn't* have. But some of the resellers alleged that they were, in fact, losing business from their customers because we were favoring our stores with inventory. We weren't, but it didn't matter. Several resellers took legal action. No wrongdoing was ever found, but their lawsuits would follow us for years.

Legal action and being short of our breakeven number were not our only concerns. Optics was proving to be another. Steve announced in early 2002 that the leaders of most departments—including Tim in operations and Niall in IT, who Jerry and Kramer were working with—would need to cut 10 percent across the board to support the investments Apple was making in Sina's apps and retail. This announcement gave me confidence that Steve still supported what we were trying to do, but it also shone a spotlight on what we were spending to do it. Several of the designers we'd hired had come from Disney, and they believed that you couldn't design a truly game-changing experience within budgetary constraints. There was probably some truth to that, but it wasn't a truth that I had any interest in sharing with those who were cutting costs to support us. In our lack of sales, they already had a good reason to believe we had no idea what we were doing. We didn't need to give them another one.

In early 2002, Fred Anderson came to me with another problem. Apple's revenue in 2001 had been just over $5 billion, and he explained that with stores on track for $10 million in sales, once we hit fifty of them, we would account for more than 10 percent of Apple's revenue. At this point, the SEC would require us to report our financials. In the weeks that followed, I sat down with Kramer, Fred, and Peter to review how our costs were being allocated. There were shared expenses—people, marketing—that supported the stores and Apple as a whole, and as retail grew, we had to decide which costs belonged in each segment. This was standard corporate accounting practice, but reviewing the numbers made it even clearer that we had to get control of our capital costs. So, I made another hire.

Bob Bridger.

Bob came from Nike, where he oversaw real estate design, development, and construction across Europe, the Middle East, and Asia. He'd also worked with Steve at Pixar and earned his trust. Bob helped us understand what it cost to build a store so we could see where we could make cuts. Location and experience weren't on the table, but size was, and we eventually found that we could offer the same experience in the same locations we wanted in a smaller footprint. Our new stores in 2002 would open in four-thousand-square-foot locations (compared to the original six thousand square feet). An added benefit was thirty feet of frontage, which meant no columns. Steve was thrilled, and so were we.

Still, our efforts at cost control would mean nothing without revenue, and it hadn't been coming. Along with lawsuits from resellers and optics-driven pressure from other teams at Apple, I was also starting to deal with pressure within my own organization. We had a sales issue. That much was clear. And it was leading some on my team—including a hard-nosed operator I'd hired at Dan's encouragement—to vocalize doubts they had been keeping to themselves. Still, I had continued to insist on patience because if we did any of what was being suggested—charge for the Genius Bar, turn ourselves into a (paid) Wi-Fi café, or introduce commissions—we would kill the one thing that we truly had going for us: traffic. In my mind, the best thing we could do was ensure that every customer who came in spoke to a specialist, got their hands on a computer, and experienced the digital hub..

"If we can do that," I said, "we've won."

I believed this firmly, but I also knew that work was being finalized on the product Ruby had started developing with Steve over a year earlier: the iPod. I *also* knew that Steve had insisted it only be compatible with the Mac, believing that this would give us a powerful lever to sell a product for which demand had dropped precipitously in the wake of the dot-com bust. This was part of why, as sales remained sluggish throughout the end of 2001, I remained convinced that we couldn't introduce commissions or do anything that would threaten our traffic. Reinforcements were coming. The *iPod* was coming. We just had to be patient.

When the time came to launch the iPod in November 2001, I challenged Jerry to shoot high and ask Tim for a *ton* of them; I knew from our allocation of iBooks at launch how much inventory mattered, and that we'd probably get less than we wanted. Jerry came back with fifty thousand iPods—an astonishing number, given that it meant we'd need to sell eight times more iPods than we'd been selling Macs to keep up with what we'd asked for. Regardless, it was a pleasant surprise. This was our moment; this was the product that would eliminate doubt in a strategy of service, of support, of love; this would prove that the sky was not, in fact, falling, and force those calling for a change in strategy to put down their pitchforks.

I thought.

The next day, Steve barged into our Tuesday meeting, unexpected and unannounced. I looked up. Everyone else did, too, including several team members who had been pushing hard for a change in strategy—some way to sell more computers that wasn't an iPod. I had been insisting on patience, reminding people that these things took time, explaining that our job wasn't to sell computers, but to enrich lives. But I'm certain in retrospect that many of those around me had been wondering what, exactly, Steve thought of this strategy, and now, he had the chance to tell them.

And tell them he did.

"Tim is telling me you all want more iPods," he said. "Well, tell me this. Why should he give you more iPods if you can't even sell a *fucking* computer?"

The words hung in the air.

For many in the room, Steve's words served as confirmation that love was not a strategy, a store without commissions wouldn't work, and maybe it was time not just for a change in strategy, but a change in leadership. Still, Steve hadn't fired me yet. And if he wasn't going to, I'd be damned if I let him strike fear through the heart of my team.

When I got back to 1 Infinite Loop, I walked down a few doors to his office and entered.

"What?" he asked.

"You know I'm trying to build a culture of kindness," I said. "How you spoke to the team earlier . . . that wasn't kindness."

"The highest form of kindness is telling the truth."

"You can tell me whatever truth you want," I said. "I'll tell it to them."

There was a long pause as we stared at each other.

"Okay?" I asked, not having broken eye contact with Steve.

"Okay."

"Okay," I said. And then I walked out.

□

Steve spent less time with my team after that, and he never again spoke to them like he'd spoken to them at Bubb Road earlier that day. But their concerns were real. After addressing Steve, I had to address my team, too.

The next time my field managers visited Cupertino, we talked about the stores' sales issue at a meeting. Several people attended. Kramer and Jerry. My store manager in Minnesota, Duke Zurek, who I'd hired from Target. And of course, my operator. She suggested, once again, charging for the Genius Bar. I had taken to calling the back half of the store the family room because it was a place where I wanted customers to feel like family; it was a place where they could come and talk to a "trusted family member"—i.e., a Genius—about issues with their Mac. I asked the operator I'd hired if she would charge someone who came into her home. I don't recall exactly what her answer was, but it was probably something along the lines of: "It's not a home, Ron. It's a store."

But to me, it was more than a store. That was the difference between my vision for the store and hers: she wanted a place that sold computers; I believed that the only way to sell computers was to create somewhere people felt like they belonged. This, too, was why I kept pushing back on commissions. It didn't make sense to me that people would be more likely to buy a computer because we pressured them. And even if they were, my main emphasis with my team wasn't selling computers, but launching relationships. And no healthy relationship started under duress. Also, if we kept our fixed-cost model and started to generate sales—and I believed that with the right products, we eventually would—our upside was limitless. I'm sure those in the room thought I was crazy to talk about upside when we were $5 million short of our goal (per store), but I wasn't crazy, and I knew it.

Few others did.

Still, as the weeks went on, I did what I always did when times were tough: I reached out to more people. Kramer, Jerry, and my dad. Some of my managers told me they needed time and space to figure things out, but I continued to emphasize the importance of finding solutions through dialogue with their teams, and of demonstrating belief in the mission of enriching lives. I shared multiple conversations with my operator, too, in which I reinforced that mission by making it clear that we were absolutely not going to charge for the Genius Bar. Then, weeks later, I found out that she'd gone ahead and tested charging for it—in a few of our east coast stores—anyway.

As a leader, I knew how critical it was to create a space in which people could play, experiment, and learn. Those are the spaces from which innovation emerges. But the reality I was forced to accept with the operator I'd hired was that how people play is shaped by how they see the world, and sometimes people's views of the world are so different that the effort it takes to reconcile them simply isn't worthwhile. I was always open to debating ideas, but I was done debating the vision.

I had to let her go.

Still, for all our disagreements, she had a point. We were doing a great job with service in the family room, but we had to sell more products to get to $15 million per store. To help us drive sales, I coined a new term for the front half of the store: the red zone. When a customer was in the red zone—named after the space between the end zone and the twenty yard line on a football field—the specialist was empowered to figure out how to get them over the line. It wasn't my job as the leader to tell them how to score. It was my job to help them play, innovate, and figure out what worked best.

In the weeks and months that followed, the stores shared what they learned with our headquarters team, which led to a focus on small business and education. Jerry developed a program called "MacPac" that bundled small-business essentials in with the Mac. (Our channel partners who *weren't* suing us—and, I think, even a few of those who were—later adopted a version of this.) Christy Schrader, who led retail marketing for Apple, worked with Apple's education team and later created "school nights," where we invited local institutions into stores to explore the type of creative, collaborative relationship that Steve had believed possible between people and technology. We created school days, too: field trips for teachers to bring their kids and have them play on computers. Week by week, these initiatives gave customers more reasons to come into the store and more reasons to end up in the red zone, and our specialists began figuring out the types of plays that would get them into the *end* zone. The revenue gap was closing . . . slowly. And most important, it was closing without commissions.

And yet, by late spring 2002, I still had this nagging feeling that I wasn't doing what I'd come to Apple to do. I'd had a dream of loving customers being Apple's path to everyone, and I'd uprooted my life to make it real. But as we closed our revenue gap by focusing on *existing* customers, I couldn't help wondering if a store was just a store and a dream was just a dream.

As it turns out, Steve was simultaneously grappling with a very similar feeling.

CHAPTER 8

Love Works

In 1997, not long after Steve had first returned to Apple, the CEO of Dell Computer, Michael Dell, had been asked what he would do if he were CEO of Apple.

"I would shut it down and give the money back to the shareholders," he said.

Steve seemed to take that personally. But five years later, in 2002, it wasn't inconceivable—at least, to the external observer—that we would do exactly what he'd suggested. Our stock price was down 70 percent from its 2000 high, David Goldstein's prediction about Apple Retail having two years before lights out was beginning to look downright prescient, and Wall Street's perception of Apple—given that our market capitalization was equivalent to the cash on our balance sheet—was that the company had no future. All of this was putting immense pressure on Steve to do something that he really didn't want to do: drive sales of the iPod by making it compatible with Windows.

To that point, Steve had been diametrically opposed to doing anything that would help Windows, and I could understand why. Apple and Microsoft had been locked in a philosophical battle since inception; Steve believed that computers should adapt to people, and Microsoft believed that people should adapt to computers. Both arguments had merit, but after Steve was ousted from Apple in 1985, the company gave in to pressure to compete directly with Microsoft by licensing its software to PC makers. This backfired spectacularly. Apple never got close to the scale necessary to make the paltry licensing fees they earned greater than the hardware margins they'd given up, and the trade they'd made contributed to the company's nearly going bankrupt before Steve returned in 1997. One of the first things he did upon his return was kill the clone program. This—along with everything he did with Tim and Fred with inventory, and the launch of the iMac—helped him save the company.

Still, all "saving" truly meant was rescuing Apple from bankruptcy, and while Apple's balance sheet was better by the time we launched stores in 2001, Windows still had its 95 percent of the PC market. Steve knew that; he also knew that half of Americans did not yet own a PC, and that the stores—even with the iPod—weren't proving to be enough to get them to buy one. Apple's sales in 2000 had been $8 billion, but in 2001, they dropped to just north of $5 billion—and in 2002, they weren't expected to grow much from there. All of this was putting pressure on Steve to start thinking about the iPod as its own business line, and that meant making it compatible with Windows. The problem was that this would render it useless as a lever to sell Macs.

The debate over what to do continued from late 2001 into 2002. Making the iPod compatible with Windows would not only be a philosophical concession for Steve, but an economic one for Apple. In 2002, every prospective PC customer who was interested in a music player would be looking at two computers with which they could use it. One was the Mac, which was $1,500 and—as of early 2002—had only twenty-five stores' worth of Geniuses and trainers who could help them navigate it. The other was literally *any* Windows machine, most of which cost *half* of what a Mac did, and *all* of which would come with a built-in base of people who understood Windows: parents or friends who had been using it for years. If Steve made the iPod compatible with Windows, he believed, he might sell more iPods, but he was handing the battle over the 95 percent to Microsoft on a silver platter.

That logic was sound. But given that the iPod wasn't doing what Steve had imagined it would do, he began to do what he hired smart people to help him do: examine—and stress-test—his own thinking. And he did it, among other places, in the stores.

In the spring of 2002, Cano called me.

"Steve just dropped by the store," he said.

"What did he want?"

"To know when we should make the iPod compatible with Windows."

"What'd you tell him?"

"If he wants to sell iPods, go Windows," Cano said. "But if he wants to sell Macs, stay Mac-only."

Cano's thinking tracked Steve's. But it didn't track mine. My retail experience told me that a customer was more likely to make a big purchase after having made a small purchase. This was true for every shopper. It was also true for *me*. As a young person, I bought a Polo shirt and liked it. So, I bought more Polo shirts. We hadn't tested this theory at Apple, so we didn't know for sure if a customer who bought the iPod would like it so much that they would come back for a Mac—especially if they already had a PC. But it was a possibility, if only Steve would forego his desire for leverage. You only have leverage, after all, if the lever that you're pulling gets people to do what you want. But that's the thing about people: They don't do what *you* want. They do what *they* want. On a long enough time horizon, people who feel "forced" to do anything—customers, yes, but also anyone—come to resent the source of said force. The best "leverage"—in business and in life—comes from finding a way to marry what you want with what other people do.

This was the nature of Apple's creativity. But it also created enormous cognitive dissonance for Steve. He knew that Windows users wanted to use the iPod. He knew it from Cano, from me, from the stores. But he also knew that Apple as he'd founded it—still then legally Apple *Computer*—had always been a computer company, and not *just* a computer company, but one that controlled every aspect of the customer's experience. The projections we'd been running said that in every possible scenario, iPod sales resulting from Windows compatibility would more than offset a corresponding drop in Mac sales. But as much as sales mattered, Steve wanted to be selling *Macs*. And he didn't want to open any device in the Apple ecosystem up to Windows without an extremely good reason. Then, in the summer of 2002, he would reveal that someone had given him one.

The revelation came as part of Steve's keynote address at Macworld New York City in July 2002. A month earlier, Steve had launched Apple's "Switchers" campaign, which took real people and had them share why they had switched to the Mac. Steve opened his presentation by playing three of the best "Switcher" ads. Student Ellen Feiss described losing a paper to a "beeping" PC and consequently switching to a Mac. Another student, Hamilton Morris, shared the pain of carrying around a case of CDs and the consequent joy of owning an iPod. Finally, actor Will Ferrell described a half dozen things people could do with a Mac as he ate a parfait.

"You can make art, send messages, write letters," he said. "Do your bills. Communicate. Play music. Watch movies!"

Then he paused.

"All you can do with the parfait is . . . eat it," he said. "And poop it out."

There was another long silence.

"This computer is better than a parfait," Will said. "And this parfait is *good.*"

Then, finally, he finished with a trademark comedic flourish.

"I'm Will Ferrell," he said. "And I'm a porn actor."

Laughter erupted from the audience, and Steve took the stage.

For the first few minutes, Steve spoke about the Switchers campaign. He explained that there were a lot of people who were interested in switching to the Mac, but were concerned for one reason or another. This had been the origin of initiatives like the Genius Bar and the theater, of course, but the best way to get people over their fear, Steve said, wasn't just to offer them support *as* they switched, but also reasons to *want* to switch—i.e., people just like them telling them what life had been like before the Mac, and what life could be like *with* the Mac. And the performance of that messaging had been good. Steve had set up a website where people could explore what it would be like to "switch," and in a little over a month, he told the audience, that site had seen 1.7 million unique visitors—over 60 percent of whom had been Windows users. But the most visceral reaction to the campaign, he noted, was in the stores.

This was true . . . to a point. We *were* seeing people who came in curious about the ads they'd seen of Ellen, and Hamilton, and Will. A lot of people. We had an average of 100,000 people per week visiting the stores, and some were visiting with physical "Switcher" ads cut from newspapers, torn from magazines, or printed from web pages, then asking us to tell them more. But, as Steve avoided saying explicitly in his presentation, they weren't the only ones buying Macs—nor were they the majority. Instead, most who were buying Macs were business and education customers. Still, that didn't stop Steve from reminding the audience that the Apple Store was the best buying experience in the world—and that the following day, we would make it even better. Ten months after 9/11, we would open our first store in New York City: Apple SoHo.

"It opens tomorrow at 8:00 a.m.," Steve said, the time emblazoned in big white letters on the screen behind him. And, perhaps anticipating what we'd seen in front of Tysons, Glendale, and Palo Alto on opening day, he added one last thing.

"If you really want to get in," he said, "you might want to get there a little early."

The audience chuckled knowingly. Then, Steve moved onto the technology.

For the next ninety minutes, Steve went deep on everything he'd been working on to improve the Mac's user experience. He spoke about updates to OS X, including the launch of the newest version, "Jaguar." He described new ways to communicate in Mail and iChat, and new methods of organizing your contacts in Address Book. He reminded the audience about iPhoto, which he had released six months earlier and positioned as the equivalent of your "shoebox for digital photography." He then revealed a new tool, iSync, which he described as "synchronizing your digital life." He described what a pain it was to input contacts using phones' triple-tap keyboards, and what a disaster it was if, God forbid, you lost your phone. With Address Book, people could input their contacts using a full-size keyboard on the Mac, and see them on a big, bright, colorful screen. Then, when they connected their phone to their Mac, those contacts would sync automatically, including with any changes that had been made—either on the Mac or the phone itself. It worked like magic, and Steve described the tool as "landmark" and "groundbreaking."

"I think this app is going to change a lot of things," Steve said. "We're going to look back on this app as the beginning of something pretty cool and pretty new."

Finally, at the end of the presentation, Steve announced one more thing: a larger, 17-inch version of the iMac G4, which had previously been available only in a 15-inch model. Everything, in other words, was about the Mac—the digital hub.

Everything, except one thing.

Immediately following his hour-long description of the apps that put the Mac at the center of people's digital lives, Steve had pulled up a slide announcing one more *little* thing. It was almost like he didn't want it to be a big deal but simultaneously knew he had to say it. He cited a quote from an article written by Charles Haddad, who—like David Goldstein, interestingly enough—had published in *Businessweek.*

"What if the iPod *did* work with PCs?" Steve quoted on stage. "Could it become a Trojan horse that steals inside fortress Windows and wins over die-hard PC fans?"

Steve stood there for a moment before answering Charles's—and now, his own—question.

"We think yes," Steve said. His words conveyed certainty, but his tone of voice suggested otherwise.

"We're bringing the iPod to Windows users, so they can join this amazing portable digital music revolution," he said. There was scattered applause. And then, when the conference ended, what little energy there had been around the announcement faded away.

Steve, of course, cared deeply about how the press reacted; he knew that what they said would shape how people felt. And while the general reaction to the conference was fine, no one was claiming that Apple had changed the world. Instead, many chose to pick on Apple for not unveiling any real performance improvements to its hardware outside of a larger screen for the iMac G4. More still reacted to Steve's announcement that Apple would be replacing iTools, the free suite of internet services like storage and mail that Steve had unveiled two-and-a-half years earlier, with a paid subscription, .Mac (pronounced "dot-Mac"). Steve referred to that service as a way for customers to expand their digital life, but at $99/year for something that had been free, pundits had a different way of describing it: a money grab. The press's energy, in other words, was muted. And Steve, who fed on it, was despondent.

Still, there was one thing keeping him going: the SoHo store opening. Steve had gone on about the store during his presentation for a few minutes, describing it. He also made a point to clarify where, exactly, it was, pressing the button on his clicker and ushering forth a picture of the signpost at the corner of Prince and Greene Street in SoHo, then reminding people that the closest Subway stop was Broadway-Lafayette.

"In case you might want to go," he said, to laughter from the audience.

And of course, he thought people *would* want to go. We all did. The lines outside of Tysons, Glendale, and Palo Alto had stretched into the thousands, and *this* location—the 100-year-old Station A post office in SoHo, and the very first post office in Manhattan—would put those to shame. Steve loved everything about Station A: the history, the brick, the glass skylight. Peter Bohlin, the architect behind Steve's Pixar headquarters, worked with Karl Backus, a partner at his firm, to redesign and modernize the glass skylight and create a corresponding glass staircase. Bob figured out how to construct the staircase and skylight, turning them into the central architectural features of the store. We also put *two* Genius Bars on SoHo's second floor, and two kids' areas, too, complete with circular red carpets, black orb seats, and iMacs. If there had been any doubt in our commitment to stores, this store—and the line we were certain would form outside of it—would put it to rest. But when Steve arrived for the 8:00 a.m. opening the following morning, the paltry line that had formed was gone within minutes. And then, a few minutes after that, all the customers who had been in that line were gone, too.

Now, I had never known Steve to be a morning person, and getting to SoHo at 5:00 a.m. his time couldn't have helped his mood. But the exhaustion I sensed from him that morning—with our sales lagging, our stock price down, and the press seemingly unenthused by a presentation that he had pumped every ounce of his energy into—wasn't just physical. It was emotional, existential. He said nothing, and that said everything. As articulate as he could be, I'm not sure words could've captured the emotions on his sleeve.

Finally, around 9:00 a.m., Steve turned to me.

"I'm leaving," he said. There was a resignation in his voice that I neither recognized nor liked.

"Why?" I asked.

"*Why?!*" he exclaimed. "Nobody cares! The press has been awful. The store is empty. Nobody gets what we're trying to do. I should just quit."

I stood there as Steve walked out of the store, past the hand-counter, Matt Gluck, who we'd brought in to track store visitors, and went back to his hotel to work. I wasn't a worrier—I never had been, nor had I thought I ever would be. But in that moment, I was worried about Steve.

Of course, someone else's emotional state is not mine to analyze; all I can say is what I know to be true. But what I knew then was that for twenty-five years, and perhaps longer, Steve had been possessed by a vision of a creative, human relationship between humans and technology, and had more recently come to believe that I could help him create the store that would develop those relationships. It had been an honor to be chosen, and I'd done my best. But now, the flagship location of the store that would launch those relationships was empty, as was the theater that would deepen them and the Genius Bar that would restore them. Even at Macworld, Steve had made it clear that the customers we were selling to were in education and business. As much traffic as we had from *prospective* switchers, the stores were not yet switching them. There was no way around this. It was simply true.

I didn't know this at the time, but the internal picture at Apple, too, was even bleaker than I'd imagined. Yes, we were getting sued. Yes, Kramer and Jerry were battling with Tim for allocation, with Phil over what products they could display, and with Niall to get the IT systems support we needed. But with the stores still a long way from profitability, some departments within Apple had been placing bets on how long it would be before Steve killed retail. Jerry and Kramer, knowing that I didn't love hearing bad news, had been trying to keep this from me, but I had a vague idea, and on top of that, concerns about Steve—and whether I was about to lose the ally I'd had since that first conversation in November 1999—had me experiencing an unfamiliar feeling: doubt. I didn't want my team to see it, so I took a walk, and as I made my way along Prince Street, I might've said a prayer. If there was ever a moment for divine intervention, this was it.

But of course, what happened next wasn't an act of God. It was simply another reminder of the same truth I'd learned—and would continue to learn—repeatedly throughout my life: that people in different places do things differently. I returned to the store around 11:00 a.m., just before lunch, and Matt jogged up to me. Both he and I knew that the average store had been seeing five thousand customers per week.

SoHo, Matt told me, had just seen a thousand customers in the last *hour.*

I nodded, watching as more people poured in, individually, then in groups. And as I spoke to them, and they told me where they'd been the night before—at a show, or a restaurant, or a bar—I realized that the lack of people at our opening hadn't been a result of no one caring. It had been a result of no one being *awake.* At 8:00 a.m., the city that *never* sleeps had, in fact, been asleep.

No sooner had I realized this than I called Steve.

It rang once.

Answer, I thought.

It rang again.

Come on, Steve, I thought. Pick *up.*

He picked up.

"What," he answered flatly.

"You have to come back," I said.

"Why?"

"Can you just come?" I said. "Please."

A long pause.

"No."

"Steve," I said. "Get your ass over here *now.*"

When he arrived an hour later, I met him at the door. He looked past me, then at me. The light in his eyes was back.

We walked past Fish's tubular window display—each tube displaying a different "switcher"—then into the store, and through the crowd. Our shoulders brushed with those of the coolest-looking people in New York City, many of whom stood over wood tables, their fingers tracing circles on newly solid-state iPod scroll wheels. Then we ascended the glass staircase and took a position overlooking the first floor. Neither of us said anything. Neither of us needed to. We simply stood in silence, soaking SoHo in. We heard the buzz, felt the store's heartbeat. The theater and Genius Bars, now *full* of people and life. The skylight through which light was streaming, reflecting off the glass staircase and illuminating the store. The windows through which Steve could stare at the water towers dotting SoHo's skyline, imagining what was possible in a world in which *everyone* saw his vision—and cared.

A different version of Steve emerged that day. The true version and the one I'd seen in our first interview. Passionate, lighthearted, at ease. I hired for these traits in store managers, and had I needed another one, I might've hired this version of Steve. The man in front of me wasn't the intensely private person I'd come to know. This wasn't the Steve whose ushering into the public eye at twenty-four and consequent ousting from the company he'd founded had him constantly ruminating about what he was doing, or why he was doing it, or who he was doing it with. This was a man at peace with everything exactly as it was. Steve had never been one to take it easy on others, because he'd never been one to make it easy on himself. But in an environment in which everything was exactly as we'd imagined, he did both. When he heard whispers from people around him wondering if that was, in fact, Steve Jobs, he turned, smiled, and told them that yes, it was. He was still hesitant to shake hands or be touched—quirks of his—but he spoke to customers with the warmth and kindness I knew was in him, even if I didn't often see it. For *seven hours*, he did this. The validation it gave me was unlike anything I'd ever known. Seeing our SoHo store open was one thing. Seeing it open Steve to the world was something else entirely.

The next day, Bob called me.

"Bob!" I exclaimed. "What can I do for you?"

"Nothing," he said. "I just wanted to tell you that I, well, I just met Steve at SoHo."

His tone was weird. Like, shaken, but in a good way.

"And?"

"And, well—he gave me a *hug.*"

"Who did."

"Steve."

"*Steve* gave you a hug."

"Yeah."

"Steve *Jobs* gave you a hug."

"Yes."

"What did he say?"

"That everything was changing," Bob said flatly. "And that he couldn't thank me enough."

"Why do you not sound thrilled about that?"

"Because," Bob said. "I just—I don't know. SoHo is good . . ."

He trailed off.

"But?"

"But it's not good *enough*."

"*That's* what you told Steve?"

"Yeah."

I paused.

"Were you even there yesterday, Bob?"

"I was."

"So, let me get this straight," I said. "Steve, who we've never seen do so much as shake someone's hand, let alone tell them what a great job they're doing, called you, brought you to SoHo, hugged you, told you that you were doing great, and you told him it wasn't good enough?"

"Yeah."

I shook my head.

"Everything is going to get so much better," Bob said.

Bob knew it, Steve knew it, and now I knew it, too.

□

SoHo didn't fix the financial picture for the stores, but it did something more important: it reinvigorated Steve. This bought us time. With that time, we would be able to grow and expand. We would also begin to move quickly toward the world I had once described for Steve: the one in which people couldn't think of Apple without thinking of the love they felt in our service, and the materials they saw in our stores. It was in the wake of SoHo, in other words, that we had the chance to figure out who we truly were.

SoHo was many things, but one of them was Steve's first glimpse of what could be accomplished with materials—like glass—in an Apple Store. We showed him what could be done with another material—steel—a few weeks later, when we opened our second two-story flagship store at the Grove in Los Angeles. We had worked with Rick Caruso, the leader of that mall and future candidate for mayor of Los Angeles, to develop it, and it was our first store (of many) that used a stainless-steel facade. But with sleeker stores and spectacular flagships, Steve recognized that everything else we'd done could get better, too. Amid stainless-steel facades and glass staircases, our light wood floors were beginning to look, in his words, "pedestrian."

For Steve, this was obvious. For Kramer, it was infuriating. New floors would cost money, and the floors Steve wanted would cost a *lot* of money. And given Apple's financial position, Peter's hold on the purse strings hadn't really loosened. But for these floors, it would have to. In 1985, Steve explained, he had visited Florence and been impressed by the gray-blue Pietra Serena sandstone of the city's sidewalks. We sent Bob to see if it was available, and for us—and, perhaps, Steve—it was. But it was also 25 euros per square foot, and using it would turn $15,000 floors—which did not, given Apple's still-precarious financial position, *really* need to be replaced—into six-figure expenses. The sandstone would be an absurd choice only months into rightsizing our capital costs, but Kramer—as he was so good at doing—tried to make it work for Steve. There was a functionally identical alternative to the Italian sandstone available in an Indiana quarry for one tenth of the cost, Kramer told Steve. But Steve shot it out of the sky, insisting it had to be authentic. Kramer threw his hands up. Working with visionaries was fun until it wasn't.

Steve's desire for authenticity followed Kramer like a bad habit. He wanted the best of everything, and would, according to Kramer, often find a way to convince himself that the most expensive item *was* the best. The tile in our first two stores' bathrooms had been from Italy. The sinks were from France. Each bathroom alone cost $300,000. And yes, that cost would be depreciated over ten years on an income statement. But the spirit of the amount spent—and what it was spent on—lingered. And Kramer didn't appreciate it.

Mike Fisher, our windows guy, shared Steve's taste, and served as an enabler. Kramer almost lost it when he found out that Mike had shown Steve a titanium ceiling sprinkler that was $125 when there were alternatives that would cost fifteen cents.

"They're from fucking NASA!" he said to me in 2002.

"Slow down, Kramer," I said. "*What* are from NASA?"

"The—the fucking *ceiling* sprinklers!"

Ah, I thought.

"I keep telling him," Kramer said to me. "I keep telling him that no one cares about this shit."

"But he does," I said.

"Yeah," Kramer said. "He keeps telling me that we will always finish the backs of drawers."

"Right."

"That there are no true craftsmen anymore."

"Mm-hmm."

"And then I've got Fish insisting on showing him the expensive shit."

"Yeah."

Sometimes, as a leader, I found it was my job to just shut up and listen.

Steve didn't win every battle, but he did win the one over the floors. The problem with the standard paving stone in Florence was that, as an organic material, it had veining and striations. When Bob visited Italy, he interviewed a few potential partners to see how he could solve this problem. One of them, Giovanni D'Angelo, offered a simple solution. All the stone was coming out of one quarry, Il Casone, in Firenzuola, about forty minutes outside of Florence. Giovanni took Bob to the quarry, where they discussed Apple's need. It turned out that Florence could only use so much of the stone, so Apple could have what was left over at cost, and Giovanni could hand-select the pieces without veining and striations to suit our need. What had been 25 euros per square foot was now 2.60 euros per square foot. We were thrilled, and so was Steve.

The first store in which we'd install sandstone was Pasadena, which was scheduled to open in January 2003. Bob explained to the installers that each tile had been cut such that if it was installed correctly, no additional cuts would have to be made. The tolerance for error in spacing between tiles required for this was less than a millimeter. (Or, as Bob put it, "effectively zero.") It was a level of craftsmanship that few had seen, and fewer still could execute. But even after a flawless installation, Bob noticed a problem. Veining had been easy to get rid of because it was visible in each piece. Slight differences in *color*, on the other hand, weren't something any of us had seen, because none of us had seen multiple tiles laid out in one place. But now, with all the tiles installed—and only days to go before Pasadena's scheduled opening—those color differences were all that Bob could see.

That night, Bob called me in a panic.

"It looks like a *checkerboard*," he said.

I'd lost Steve's trust once before and wasn't about to lose it again. So, Bob and I called him to head the problem off. Sometimes, we'd learned, if someone Steve trusted told him that something "sucked," he would often try to convince them that actually, it didn't.

"It's bad," Bob said to Steve. (And it *was* bad.)

"It can't be that bad."

"No, it is," Bob said. "We're going to take it out."

"Well, no—let's just go see it."

"Now?" Bob asked. It was seven on a Sunday night.

"Now," Steve said. The urgency in his voice was clear.

That night, we took Steve's plane down to Pasadena. Bob kept telling Steve, all the way down, that the floor was "fucked up," because Steve liked that phrase.

"Fucked up."

And then we walked into the store, and we looked down at the checkerboard-like floor, and then we looked up at Steve.

"This *is* fucked up," he said.

Within forty-eight hours, Bob was on a plane back to Italy. When he saw Giovanni, he explained that we were committed to using the stone in hundreds of stores going forward. This inspired Giovanni to help us. Working with Bob, he developed a process by which each store's stone could be preassembled in a warehouse in Italy to eliminate the checkerboard, and numbered so it could be reassembled identically on site. It was also more proof that we were becoming who we wanted to be and who Steve wanted us to be: a team that always finished the backs of drawers, yes, but also did right by our partners.

Still, while we had Steve's support, we continued to struggle with retail skeptics at headquarters. As of late 2002, one of the many barbs being thrown at Apple Retail internally—aside from how few Macs we were selling and how much money was being poured into our steel facades and our sandstone floors—was that we couldn't even attach AppleCare to the few Macs we sold.

But around the same time that we opened our first store with stone floors, our Emeryville store—led by manager Art Diaz—matched our resellers' AppleCare attach rate at 40 percent. Art shared his approach with other managers, and soon our *whole organization's* attach rate was 40 percent. Then it jumped to *60* percent. And then we shared our success with the channel—still suing us, but perhaps slightly less upset now—and they iterated on it, too.

Our increasing confidence followed us to Japan, where we were scheduled to open our first international store in November 2003 with Cano as manager. In the weeks leading up to the launch, we were told that our stores' culture wouldn't fly in the country. George had found us real estate in the ultra-luxury Ginza business district, where everyone walked around in suits; our T-shirts and jeans, we were told, would not be well-received. We were also told that Japanese customers, who were used to bowing as a sign of respect, would not line up and high-five like Americans. I heard the concerns, but I didn't share them. Those in Japan would want to experience Apple's culture. That was why I believed they'd come. There was one good reason, though, why customers might *not* come.

A typhoon.

The forecast for our store opening wasn't good, and in the days that followed, it only got worse. We did what we could, purchasing thousands of umbrellas. It seemed, only forty-eight hours out from launch, a bit absurd, but Steve and Laurene had surprised us and come to Japan to attend the launch, so there was an added pressure to make it work. Regardless, thousands of umbrellas seemed way too many.

It turned out not to be enough.

By our 10:00 a.m. opening on November 30, 2003, the line outside of our Ginza store—forming with wind blowing, black clouds swirling, and rain falling—spanned *eight train stops*, or approximately *four* miles. And once the store opened, I watched as Cano's raised hand was met by that of our store's first customer, then another, then another. Japanese customers wouldn't line up—except, they did. Japanese customers wouldn't high-five—except, they had. Standing there in our T-shirts, it was clear that my intuition had been right. It was an intuition that Steve shared, too.

"You have to be yourself for someone to love you and trust you," he said.

We were, and in Japan, they did.

Of course, we could've tried—like so many did, and do—to design our store based on what we thought a country's people would expect. (In Japan, this might've meant hand-written price cards, or lots of sounds, motion, and color.) But I didn't think that this was what Japanese customers wanted, nor did I think it would be what would help us demonstrate the value of our products. Japanese customers were visiting our stores for the same reason anyone did: to experience Apple. They wanted to have an authentic Apple experience designed in Cupertino; they wanted to see what *they* could do with our computers. None of this required that we model our stores on typical Japanese retail aesthetics, but it would require authenticity. Showing people who they could be would start with being who we were.

In the end, this was a philosophy that would apply for Apple around the world. Steve had built Apple's brand on what other people could do, who other people could be. Our culture reflected that; our excitement and desire to high-five people was borne of belief in what people were capable of doing. In the end, people didn't just line up to buy something. They lined up because they were bought into something. With belief in people as the fundamental driver of our culture, we didn't have to encourage lines. We simply had to let them find us.

They had, and soon, many more would.

□

Today, everyone associates Apple with lines outside of the stores. But those lines only really began to form in earnest once Apple fully got into the music business, and even today, people forget just how staggered its foray into that business was.

Apple released iTunes in January 2001, a full ten months *before* the iPod. But the original iTunes was music management software. The iTunes *Store* didn't debut until April 2003, and even after Steve announced that the iPod would be "compatible" with the PC through the MusicMatch Jukebox, iTunes—and consequently, the iTunes Store—was still Mac only.

This, too, represented Steve's aversion to opening Apple up to competitors. In this case, that aversion was more philosophical than economic; the iPod was slowly proving that it could, in fact, do what Steve had quoted *Businessweek* columnist Charles Haddad saying it might do: that is, Trojan horse us into Microsoft's share of the PC market. With this in mind, there was really no reason *not* to develop iTunes for Windows, too—except that Steve had once said that the day he developed software for Windows would be "a cold day in hell." Still, Steve couldn't help noticing how bad the MusicMatch Jukebox was and realize that now that he'd opened the iPod to Windows, there was no reason not to pursue the strategy to its logical conclusion. At a special event on October 16, 2003, he announced, on a giant screen, what many thought he never would.

"Hell froze over," the slide read.

iTunes would now work on Windows.

This set the stage for what we had been waiting for since May 19, 2001: a truly great, reasonably priced product, or, to use my words, the small purchase that would eventually lead to a big purchase. And alongside that product came the latest and greatest piece of another thing Steve had told me that I wouldn't have to handle: marketing. It was just after his announcement of iTunes for Windows that Steve debuted a campaign he'd been working on with Lee Clow and his team at Chiat\Day that would cement the iPod's evolution from a Mac accessory into a cultural object: black silhouettes dancing across colorful backdrops on billboards and television sets the world over, each wearing Apple's white, corded headphones. And then, in February 2004—four months into that campaign's launch—Steve confirmed what I had always believed about design: that it didn't have to be expensive. The iPod gave way to the iPod Mini; $249 bought you four gigabytes of storage, while $299 bought you six. And now, we didn't just have lines out the door for store launches, but products, too.

The combination of the more reasonably priced iPod Mini and its being compatible with Windows had an unexpected side effect. The prediction that the iPod would serve as a Trojan horse to win over diehard PC fans had not really proven true with the original iPod, but it proved more than true with the iPod Mini. The product itself had a lot to do with this, as did the marketing—the silhouettes, the corded headphones. But so did the stores. Steve had once referred to a store for Apple as "Project Nexus," and now it was clear what that meant. The stores were at the center of Apple's emerging cultural magnetism. And that magnetism was pulling everyone in—Windows users and non-PC users alike.

To that point, we had been seeing repeat customers in the stores. What we hadn't seen as much was repeat *buyers* in the stores. But as everything came together for Apple—marketing, products, stores, inventory—we started seeing all kinds of customers who bought the iPod (Mini or otherwise) showing up later for the Mac. This was the beginning of what analysts would term the "iPod Halo," and who knows, maybe it was this phenomenon that got Apple's internal teams to drop their bets on the death of Apple Retail. One analyst in particular, Piper Jaffray's Gene Munster, would later analyze the lines in front of Apple Stores to predict demand for our products. In November of 2004, he doubled his price target on the stock, indicating a spike in Mac interest among PC users who purchased the iPod. Haddad—and Steve—had been right. And now, the stores were flying as a result.

As Munster's prediction aged like fine wine—between February and October 2004, Apple's stock price had doubled, and by early 2005, it would double again—so did my belief in the Genius Bar. The same PC users who Munster had predicted would buy Macs now needed a place to come for support. I never *wanted* people to have the experiences that would bring them to the Genius Bar, but it was rewarding to see it working as I'd imagined. And, of course, this wasn't the only reason it was working. Customers could—and did—simply come in to chat with Geniuses about other computer or tech-related issues. They trusted us, too. One of the guidelines we'd established for specialists and Geniuses alike was to never badmouth our competitors, and to direct customers toward competing products if we thought they served their needs better. This earned us trust and goodwill that we were now benefiting massively from.

"Love," wrote Paul the Apostle, "rejoices with the truth." And John—or, perhaps, Jesus—wrote that the truth would set you free.

For us, now, love was doing both.

As customers packed the stores, employees learned from them—and acted on what they learned. At Duke's store in Minnesota's Rosedale Center, his employees had been practicing another thing I'd been encouraging: to take time with each customer to satisfy their need as well as they could. And through that, Duke's team realized that many customers wanted to have their computer set up by the time they got home and had been helping customers set up computers in the store. The next time I visited Duke's store, he shared the idea with me, and I watched as customers got set up on their Mac before they left.

I *loved* it.

It seemed like something we'd do—and later, it would evolve, then expand in a novel way throughout all of Apple Retail.

An interesting thing was playing out at the Genius Bar, too. Not long after Denise and I discussed needing to hire for soft skills *and* hard skills at the Genius Bar, she gambled that perhaps, a lack of hard skills wasn't a dealbreaker. She focused instead on hiring for soft skills like communication, empathy, and patience, then *training* for hard skills. In the early years, without many customers who needed the Genius Bar, it was hard to know if it was the right thing to do. Three years later, though, the Genius Bar was packed, and soft skills—far from being "nice to have"—were suddenly essential.

The Genius Bar was slammed by two types of people—iPod users and Mac users. This led me to another idea that could work in SoHo, which had two Genius Bars. One, I proposed, would be the Mac Genius Bar, and the other would be the *iPod* Genius Bar. With all our momentum, there was no reason not to try it; in retail, I knew, if something didn't work, you could always just change it back.

We would not have to change it back.

The idea worked better than I could've possibly imagined. Most iPod questions had simpler fixes than Mac questions, requiring answers in the form of software updates or hardware restarts. But how easy it was to solve a customer's problem didn't take away from how it felt to help them. If anything, the ease of the solves made the experiences more meaningful. Many people had been conditioned to expect that someone they went to for tech help would, instead of making their problem feel small, make *them* feel small. As we soon learned, there was immense gratitude to be earned if, instead of making customers feel stupid for experiencing a problem, we began solving it by taking care to recognize how they felt about it. Customer loyalty wouldn't end with this feeling, but it couldn't be earned—and in our stores, was never earned—without it.

By the end of 2004, everything happening in the stores had rooted me even more firmly in a belief I'd always had: that people *love* being of service. Every time I saw a specialist helping a customer to their car with a Mac, I was reminded of just how often needs revealed themselves—and how much goodwill could be created when they were identified and met. I was reminded, too, that cool products weren't the only reason people shopped. Every reseller had iPods and Macs. Every reseller had a place where customers could buy an Apple product. People bought in our stores because we created a place where they felt at home. The service we offered was exceptional. The places we built were beautiful. The people we employed were interesting, fearless, and kind. All this created Apple's "nexus": a meeting point between what Apple built and the people Apple built it for; the space where customers didn't *have* to build their relationships with Apple but a place where customers *wanted* to build their relationships with Apple. A specialist launched the relationship, a trainer deepened it, and a Genius restored it. And all that combined with everything else—the marketing, the products—led to more lives enriched than we could've possibly imagined, and finally, yes, profitability.

The fourth quarter of 2004 came with $561 million in revenue, or $5.6 million per store. This more than doubled what we'd done a year earlier with only a 33 percent increase in stores, and those new stores opened weeks before the holiday quarter started or during the holiday quarter itself. If the trend held—and there was every reason to think it would—we would finish the following year having *obliterated* our break-even goal of $15 million per store. When we closed the books in 2004, we also had become the fastest retailer ever to reach $1 billion in annual revenue.

The Apple Store, which David Goldstein had once given two years before lights out, was actually helping Apple keep the lights on.

□

It would be easy—but not true—to say that from this point, everything went smoothly. It didn't. In fact, our lead-in to 2004 was a difficult period for Apple because it was a difficult period for Steve. He was first diagnosed with pancreatic cancer in October 2003 and had initially opted to treat it with alternative therapies. Prior to the iPod Mini, Steve was thinking about how to increase our coverage faster, and it was only a few years earlier that BMW had launched the MINI Cooper.

"What if we launched mini stores?" Steve asked.

I didn't like to say no to anyone, but I almost said no to this. Coverage only really mattered because people could come to our stores for service, and there was no way that we could match our service experience in a smaller footprint. But sometimes, Steve's aesthetic considerations trumped the economics, and this was one such case. He loved the idea of thousands of mini stores around the country, and I agreed—perhaps that was interesting. So, working with Tim and Wilhelm from Eight Inc., we created mini stores: six-hundred- to one-thousand-square-foot spaces with stainless-steel walls and gleaming white floors. It took a year to design them and open them, and the first opening was on October 16, 2004, in Palo Alto. It was also Steve's first public appearance since undergoing treatment for his cancer.

Unfortunately, the mini stores were disappointing from the get-go. Their service experience was limited, as I'd intuited. No theater, no places for the digital hub, limited third-party products, and a seven-and-a-half-foot Genius Bar. The aesthetic didn't work, either. Tim and Wilhelm had designed storage space into the stainless-steel walls, but opening those walls left fingerprints that looked terrible and were impossible to clean off. This problem was even more pronounced with the floors. Within hours of opening, they looked like those of a recreational basketball court. Teams had to clean the floors, and after a few days, I got sick of it.

I called Tim and Wilhelm on a Sunday morning.

"Guys, come on down to the mini store tonight after it closes," I said. "Let's discuss and digest learnings from week one."

That night, Tim and Wilhelm showed up at Stanford Shopping Center. Both were clad in typical designer garb: black on black, Tim in Armani, Wilhelm in Prada. I handed them soft cloths. They were the same ones the team had been using to clean the floor that week. Bob and I were holding them, too.

"Before we talk, we're going to clean this floor," I said.

The image of the two men on their hands and knees in their designer clothes, wiping down the same floors they'd created next to Bob and me, always makes me smile.

Steve used to say that design wasn't about how something looked, but how it worked. I agreed—and still agree—with him. As designers of stores, we were responsible for how they worked. This meant that when our stores didn't work, it was our responsibility to fix them—and consequently learn from our mistakes.

All those lessons we'd learned—from the mini stores, yes, but also from every experience we had during our difficult early years—would shape what we would do next. Flying past breakeven gave me confidence that we could be what we hadn't yet been and go where we hadn't yet gone. Getting there would require a gigantic leap, but we'd been strengthened by years of struggle; I knew we could make it. Now that we'd *shown* ourselves who we were, it was time to *find* ourselves anew—this time, on the biggest and best shopping street in the world.

CHAPTER 9

Wouldn't It Be *Great*?

We had wanted to put a store on Fifth Avenue for years. But it wasn't somewhere we would go until we had a proven model or space that compelled us to bet big, and for the first few years, we had neither. Still, we had two things going for us: a world-renowned brand and great traffic. Someone was going to find us a spot on Fifth Avenue. The question was *where.*

In the years that followed, nothing revealed itself. Nowhere felt historically relevant like the Station A post office, and no space was conducive to constructing anything that would be a unique and unmistakable statement of our brand. Most spaces were in low-ceilinged, mixed-use high-rises with columns that made those in Northshore Mall—which Steve had almost fired me over—look like chopsticks. Rent, too, was $25 million per year, which meant that we'd need $100 million in revenue to even sniff profitability. As of 2002, our highest-grossing store—SoHo—was doing half of that.

None of this bode well for our prospects. We needed something different, something others had overlooked—a space in which we could create the type of magic that would make people say, "Wow," or "Of course, only Apple." What we couldn't know was that when we found it, we'd reveal something in which each of us would find our own definition of significance.

□

For something to be significant, it doesn't have to mean the same thing to everyone. In fact, truly significant things mean different things to everyone.

Teams might share a goal like putting a store on Fifth Avenue, but it's actually better if each person involved with the project has their own unique reason for pursuing it. The health and vitality of an idea—much like that of, say, a city—is signaled by how many ways there are to get there. When we talk about there being health in diversity, what we're really saying is that the more ways there are to get anywhere, the less dependent a destination is on any one of them, and the more robust it becomes.

Of course, I can't speak to everyone else's reasons for putting a store on Fifth Avenue, but I don't think it's a stretch to say that for George, the idea of securing real estate on the best shopping street in the world was innately meaningful, or that for Peter Bohlin, the idea of designing a store there would be similarly interesting. And in fact, the conversations we had about a Fifth Avenue store revealed exactly this.

As we emerged from our difficult early years, George presented me with two options that I thought were worth reviewing with the rest of the team. One was the safe choice: the space Abercrombie was inhabiting on Fifth Avenue between Fifty-Sixth and Fifty-Seventh. The other was unusual: a basement location in the General Motors Building's plaza between Fifty-Eighth and Fifty-Ninth, two blocks north of where anyone shopping on Fifth Avenue walked. Both were interesting, and because it was Fifth Avenue, I knew Steve would want to be involved. So, I invited George to our next Tuesday meeting at Bubb Road, where he could present to me, Steve, Peter, and Bob.

When George arrived the following Tuesday, he pulled out his laptop, placed it on one of the tables at Bubb Road, then presented as he often did—starting with a "decoy" location, then revealing the one he thought we should pick. The decoy was, in this case, the underground plaza location. The one George wanted us to take was Abercrombie's space, and he got animated explaining why: proximity to other great stores, yes, but also presence at the center of the most heavily-trafficked stretch of Fifth Avenue. Steve had a different reaction.

"That's *ugly.*"

George sighed.

"Show me the other one again," Steve said. George tapped a key on his computer. The Abercrombie building gave way to the General Motors Building's plaza.

"I don't think we'd ever do this," George said. "It hasn't been leased for seven years. And you're not even really on Fifth Avenue. You're *under* it."

Steve stood there, rubbing his chin.

"Go back to the other one."

George flipped back to the Abercrombie Building. Steve exhaled loudly.

"It's *so* bad."

"It's above ground," George replied. The four of us stood there for a moment. Finally, I spoke up.

"George presented these to me the other day," I said. "And everything north of the General Motors Building is zoned for museum and residential. If we can figure out how to get people to go underground, we can *always* be the first store on Fifth Avenue."

Steve fidgeted. "*That's* kind of interesting," he said.

"But you'd have to put a store *underground*," George said. "Underground stores don't work."

Now it was Peter's turn to find something in the idea.

"We could design something with glass over it," Peter said. "Like I. M. Pei did for the Louvre."

I looked at Bob, knowing he'd get to build what Peter imagined. He was smiling. I could hear the words he'd shared with Steve after SoHo.

"We're going to get so much better."

I sat there, thinking, too, about the Seagram Building at 375 Park Avenue and its iconic plaza. Steve reiterated that we should explore the idea, but everyone was already exploring it. We were all creating our own unique path to it from our experience, our imagination, our geography.

"Who's the developer?" Steve asked.

"Harry Macklowe," George replied.

"Let's get him out here next week," Steve said.

In the meantime, Peter went to work on renderings of a glass shape that could go over an underground plaza.

□

Harry's arrival in Cupertino was just one step on a journey that began over thirty years earlier in 1968, back when he was working as a broker in Manhattan.

At the time, several historical forces were competing on Fifth Avenue. Prior to World War II, Fifth Avenue was dominated by luxury retailers like Tiffany & Co., Bergdorf Goodman, and Saks. But after the war, this began to shift. Banks located on Fifth Avenue to capture the expanding upper and middle classes, and airlines began putting ticket offices there to capitalize on demand for international travel. In 1968, the CEO of one of those airlines reached out to Harry about a ticket office.

That airline, Braniff International Airways, had positioned itself to reinvent the industry with a 1965 campaign by adwoman Mary Wells announcing "The End of the Plain Plane." Braniff's CEO, Harding Lawrence, was clearly open to bold concepts. But New York City's planning commission had wised up to the retail space that banks and airlines were hogging on the world's greatest shopping street and voted in 1969 to limit them to twenty-five feet of frontage. The goal was to preserve the life and character of Fifth Avenue by restricting the prevalence of businesses that transacted with people instead of serving them. Harry wondered why Braniff couldn't do both.

Most Braniff routes flew through Latin America. This gave Harry an idea: instead of opening an office that sold tickets to Latin America, he proposed that Braniff open a restaurant in the plaza of the General Motors Building and serve Latin American *food.* Then they could attach a small ticket office to the *back* of that restaurant, skirting the frontage rule while also creating a space that served people. Lawrence loved the idea, and he and Harry shook hands on it over lunch with the owner of Restaurant Associates, Joe Baum, who Harry brought in to manage the restaurant. But just as quickly as the deal had been done, it was undone. March 6, 1969, marked the beginning of the longest newspaper strike in New York City's history. Restaurant Associates got cold feet amid the economic uncertainty, and Harry's first development deal—and brilliant, first-of-its-kind vision—was dead.

Still, even as Harry spent the next thirty years whipsawing through the ranks of the global real estate elite, he continued to believe that the General Motors Building's underground plaza was secretly the best retail location in New York City. This idea became part of his personal geography—one of those experiences that would forever give shape to the ideas that could emerge from his imagination. There is some poetry to the fact that not long after he first met us—back in 2000, when George had first been looking for real estate in New York—the building in which Harry had once tried and failed to locate a next-generation retail concept went up for sale.

The General Motors Building wasn't just any building. It would be the crown jewel of any real estate investor's portfolio. Everyone in the real estate world knew what it meant, and a lot of them wanted it.

But no one wanted it more than Harry.

He could realize his crazy idea by putting Apple in this plaza, he knew, if only he could win a bidding war for the General Motors Building. When that war began, two dozen investors and developers joined the fray. When the dust settled, Harry—whose winning bid of $1.4 billion was the most ever paid for a piece of real estate at the time—was the only one left standing.

It was, in retrospect, an astonishing gamble. When General Motors completed the building in 1968, it stood at 706 feet—one of the tallest buildings in New York City at the time. But to build that high, General Motors had taken advantage of a 1961 zoning ordinance that rewarded builders with zoning credits in exchange for their creating "privately owned public spaces." The General Motors Building's sunken plaza was pitched as a place for people. There was just one problem, and it was the same problem that made Harry's gamble so gutsy: no one ever showed up.

Almost immediately upon opening, General Motors ran into issues with its plaza. It was extremely difficult to keep clean: trash blew in off the street and became caught in the plaza's pale green astroturf covering. The space quickly became one many people avoided, and a place retail was supposed to thrive became somewhere it went to die. But this didn't matter to Harry, nor did it matter to Steve. And part of the reason it didn't matter to Steve was because the shape that Peter created to put over the plaza had been lingering in his imagination for decades: a cube.

When Steve had been at NeXT, he had spent $100,000 on a logo for the company and told the designer to make it in the image of a cube. He described its purity, its playfulness, its gravitas. He then tried to launch a cube-shaped computer, which flopped. Then he tried it again at Apple with the Power Mac G4, only to watch it flop again. Despite these failures, he held on to the idea of using the shape, and when Peter showed the cube-shaped design for Fifth Avenue to him, he saw a way he could. A cube hadn't worked as a product, and Steve knew that. But maybe—just maybe—it could work as a store.

There was just one question: How big should it be?

Steve wanted the cube to be forty feet, so it would "stand out." But that felt too big to me, and I articulated to Steve what four years of running the stores and a lifetime of experience had taught me about people: we had to fit in before we could stand out. A week later, the debate led us to New York. Harry, Bob, Karl, and I gathered in front of the General Motors Building at 767 Fifth Avenue at 2:00 a.m., all clandestine-like, to blow up cube-shaped balloons. We had three different sizes: twenty-four feet, thirty-two feet, and forty feet. Forty feet was too large, and twenty-four feet was too small. But thirty-two feet was exactly right.

To get permission to build, Harry got us in front of the New York City Planning Commission. They, too, would need a reason to buy into this idea. So, we gave them one. We explained to them that the entire plaza would become a home for New York City. Our design would use only 1,000 square feet and the remaining 19,000 square feet would be dedicated to the public. We showed New York's City Planning Commission our vision: renderings with fountains, ponds, and Victoria chairs, and explained that the store would make free Wi-Fi—which no one else offered at the time—available for everyone. Approval came quickly and emphatically. Our enthusiasm was contagious.

Once we'd been approved to build, Harry and his team needed to prepare the space for the glass cube. This would take time. For most developers, it would've also taken the signing of a lease.

Harry was not most developers.

Working without a lease, he began removing concrete from the top of the plaza and adding steel reinforcements to the basement. For him, a legal commitment was a formality; he could feel that everyone's individual connection to this idea was strong enough to keep it alive on its own. We did end up signing a lease, but by then, it was largely irrelevant. The legal obligation to build a store described what we had to do, but it said nothing of why we were doing it. We all had our own reasons for it, our own paths to it. And it was precisely in their diversity that the strength of the idea existed.

□

When the cube was completed in spring of 2006, its height of thirty-two feet, six inches corresponded perfectly with the General Motors Building's cornice line. The cube itself was an architectural marvel, too. After 9/11, great attention had been paid to the possibility of another terrorist attack in New York City. One of the risks of a glass cube, we knew, was someone driving a car into it. We did surround the cube with small barriers meant to prevent this, but Bob's team also engineered it to withstand the impact of a *truck* being driven into it.

You never would've guessed this from looking at it. To connect the eighteen panes of glass comprising the cube, Peter Bohlin, his team at Bohlin Cywinski Jackson, and James O'Callaghan—who has since become the global authority on structural glass—fused them using not metal, but more glass. No one had ever done this. Nor had anyone used glass to support such a structure, which eliminated the need for steel beams and, to Steve's delight, columns. The design that emerged from Peter, his team, and James allowed light to pass through the cube unencumbered, illuminating a downstairs space accessible via spiral staircase or elevator, both of which were *also* made of glass. The unique entryway filtered light like a prism and glittered like a jewel box. If an underground store had pushed the limits of the imagination, this cube pushed the limits of physical reality.

Still, we faced an uphill battle with an underground store in this location. Retailers, as I'd explained to Steve in our mall walk years earlier, always aimed to be at the fifty-yard line, whether of a great shopping street or a great mall. And we could not have been any further from that line. The best retail locations on Fifth Avenue were then between Rockefeller Plaza at Fiftieth and Bergdorf Goodman just north of Fifty-Seventh, and even people who made it to Fifty-Seventh then diverted *east* toward luxury retailers on Madison Avenue. Foot traffic on the greatest retail corridor in the world, in other words, traveled not toward our new location, but *away* from it—and now we were gambling that we could redirect it with an underground store.

This was not our only concern. To keep the cube secret until unveiling, we wrapped it in black vinyl. This proved controversial to many in New York City's Muslim community, who associated the cube with the Kaaba in the Masjid al-Haram Mosque in Mecca. Our store's "bar," they further claimed, was an insult to Islam. We monitored the issue to see if it grew, and it never did. But in the weeks leading up to our opening, I still found myself nervous. This was our one chance to open a store on the best shopping street in the world; we could not lay an egg on Fifth Avenue. There had to be something more we could do, something that hadn't yet been imagined, something to make this store even more meaningful to the people who would make it a success.

There had to be, as Steve had said so many times, "one more thing."

□

As I thought about what more we could do, my mind returned to standing outside of the General Motors Building plaza with Bob and Harry to blow up balloons. We'd done so at 2:00 a.m. to make some effort at secrecy, but it was futile. People walked by. Cabs rushed along.

The city that never sleeps, I thought.

Then an idea hit me.

What if our store didn't sleep, either?

The question took my breath away in the same way the Genius Bar once had. I didn't even have time to ask myself if it would be great before telling myself over and over again all the reasons it would be. This was the plan that would change the game, the store that would break the scoreboard, the inevitable right answer to the biggest question I'd been faced with yet. The problem was that it wasn't yet an answer to a question anyone else had.

Like many novel ideas, it was met, at first, with resistance. I tried to give my team the time to make it their own—to come up with the questions in their minds of which a twenty-four-hour store was the answer. But Jerry and Cano were not reacting as I'd hoped; their questions were not at first about how this could work, but about how crazy I was for thinking that it would.

"Are you *nuts*?" Jerry asked.

"No," Cano said. "He's *insane.*"

And, well, I kind of was. Three weeks before opening a retailer's dream store, and now I wanted to do what no retailer outside of a gas station or convenience store had ever done: keep it open twenty-four hours a day. Both Jerry and Cano bombarded me with reasons why it wouldn't work. There was the near impossibility of staffing across all hours, they said. There were also concerns about security, theft, and vagrancy. But I wasn't thinking about any of that. All I was thinking about was how great it would be.

I aired the thoughts as they occurred to me. I found myself thinking back on every trip I'd ever taken to New York City with Karen and the kids, about how there was so much to do—see the Statue of Liberty, attend a play on Broadway, go to Katz's Deli, visit Yankee Stadium, take a walk through Central Park—and how we never had enough time to do it. I thought about the people who would visit New York and be able to tell themselves that the Apple Store was the one tourist attraction they could visit whenever they wanted. Maybe some would come in the middle of the day, or in the evening after a show. Maybe tourists from Asia or Australia would come at 3:00 a.m. as they fought jet lag. The point was that we could serve an incredible diversity of needs—and make an unbelievably powerful brand statement as a result—by staying open twenty-four hours a day, seven days a week.

"Wouldn't that be great?" I asked Jerry and Cano.

They couldn't say no to that question, of course. Who in their right mind could conceivably tell me that this *wouldn't* be great? But then I'd stop talking and they'd start telling me, gently, and then less gently, that it would be great . . . if it weren't impossible.

"This can't be done," Jerry said.

"But wouldn't it be great if it was?"

"We open in three weeks," Cano said.

"And wouldn't it be great if we opened with it?"

Finally, Cano started coming around. Maybe, he said, we could do it *after* we opened. But that wouldn't work, I thought. We couldn't start with standard hours and then *later* announce that we were going to open twenty-four hours. No one would care!

Cano pressed me, asking if I really wanted to compromise the store's service model for a PR opportunity. Since we had hired three hundred people to staff the store from 8:00 a.m. to 10:00 p.m., the team estimated that we would need to hire a hundred additional employees to cover the remaining ten hours—and do it in three weeks. But for me, this wasn't just a PR opportunity. I also didn't think we would need to compromise our service model, because we wouldn't need to staff overnight like we staffed during the day. We could, I thought, find a subset of our existing team who would *want* to work overnight, who would *want* to help create the first twenty-four-hour store on Fifth Avenue. We could spread the rest of the team over the day shift until we could backfill them.

"But we'll be *slammed*," Cano said. "The teams will be too busy."

Except, would they? And even if they were, was that such a bad thing? This was, perhaps, the origin of another phrase that I would share many more times in the years that followed: "We're at our best at our busiest." I couldn't help thinking of my mom, bouncing from one commitment to another when I was a kid, or about the team I'd worked with at Mervyn's, at their happiest and best with a full slate of customers. I didn't say any of this to Cano—I simply used the words as fuel to keep pushing for the idea of a twenty-four-hour store. And slowly—and perhaps, painfully—he and Jerry began to come around.

When I look back, I can see that the language I used to frame ideas—a sentence like "Wouldn't it be great if we were at our best at our busiest?"—did several important things simultaneously. It acknowledged the reality of the person (or people) in front of me—I agreed that yes, we'll be busy. But I encouraged them to see it as an opportunity (*great*, *best*), and reminded them that I was right there with them (*we*). In continuing to ask this question about a twenty-four-hour store, I was giving other people the chance to build their own bridge to it, to "get over" their fear of the idea. And while I'm not sure if Jerry or Cano ever got there, one other person did.

My head of people, Denise Young.

For Denise, a Black woman of faith who was educated in the arts and raised by a mother from Brooklyn, a twenty-four-hour store wouldn't only be great because it gave tourists the opportunity to visit the Apple Store at odd hours. It would be great because it would create a place for the communities in New York who she knew weren't served by retail stores' typical hours. It would be great, Denise said, because it would be a place for the artists, the performers, the craftspeople, of whom she was one. It would be great, Denise said, because it would be a place for those she had grown up with: family members who were night nurses, business owners, and round-the-clock service workers. It was a reason no one else in that room could've imagined, and a reason without which a twenty-four-hour store would've never made it out of my office and onto Fifth Avenue. But as it stood, it was Denise's geography—her life journey—that truly made the case for this idea; it was the knowledge only she had that made a twenty-four-hour store a necessity.

□

On May 19, 2006, I stood at the top of the glass staircase outside of our Fifth Avenue store with Denise. We were there to take the first night shift at what would be our first—and, to date, Apple's only—twenty-four-hour store.

A line had begun forming several days in advance of our opening. It had snaked down Fifth before turning along the sidewalk toward Park, then turned onto Madison and wrapped back around the General Motors Plaza. By the time we opened our doors at 6:00 p.m., there had been more than a thousand people in line, and its end was far past where we could see it. It was not the first line in front of an Apple Store—far from. Nor was it one that we made any effort to create. It was simply a line that emerged in response to what we had created. We couldn't know why, exactly, people were in it. But there they were, and there we were. Meaning-seeking creatures seeking meaning.

Lines had now been forming for years outside of stores like Ginza, or SoHo, or even for software launches at any number of the now 143 stores we'd opened. But truthfully, with Fifth Avenue, we'd been so preoccupied with trying to figure out how to make a twenty-four-hour store feasible that we'd spent almost no time wondering if it would be profitable. In the end, Fifth Avenue proved to be both. The first night we were open, we did a million dollars in revenue. The following year, we would do $350 million on a goal of $100 million. Perhaps most notably: by the end of 2006, the store was not only profitable, but it was profitable with just the revenue it made from 10:00 p.m. to 8:00 a.m.—the hours it was originally scheduled to be closed.

I visited the store a few times during those wee hours. I saw the people I'd imagined would be there—the tourists, the businesspeople from around the globe. But I also saw the people Denise had told us would come: the artists, the craftspeople, the night nurses, and small-business owners. I felt the vibe that emerged in a store that wasn't just somewhere tourists could visit, but somewhere people felt they belonged. And while builders had long sought to do significant things in New York City by building ever higher, with Fifth Avenue, we did the opposite. Its meaning to everyone involved—and to New York—not only made it the global face of Apple's brand but also changed the skyline of Manhattan at just thirty-two feet.

□

Years on from Fifth Avenue, I would look back on it fondly. The numbers we did were one thing; the meaning we created was another. Researcher Eric Fischer later analyzed millions of geo-tagged photos and found that in 2011, the cube was the most photographed site in New York City. Peter Bohlin, its designer, would go on to win multiple architectural and design awards, including the Honor Award, American Architecture Award, Award of Excellence for Design, and Excellence in Architecture Award. And yet, the revenue, the awards . . . so much of it was an outcome of having created something as significant as this store was. Leadership was an art because it wasn't a science. It wasn't a leader's responsibility to understand why other people found their art meaningful. It was their responsibility to keep making it.

In my dad's letter to me about my decision to join Apple, he had added a section relating to this idea—a section in which he described a "secret wish."

"You have talent beyond that of anyone I know," he wrote. "God gave you this talent and you must use it in significant ways. My secret wish is that you would get this business success behind you at a fairly early age, as well as financial security. Then you could fully address the issue of assuring 'significance in your life.' There are so many ways in which you can do this and I am not advocating for any specific one of them. Five years in this prospective opportunity, for example, if successful, would achieve this objective."

Reading that letter, I knew that for my dad, "this objective" was getting business success out of the way so I could do something that would serve people. But seeing the impact Fifth Avenue had on New York City, I realized that business success and public service could be one and the same. My dad's prediction on timing, too, was downright prescient. Fifth Avenue opened on May 19, 2006—*exactly five years after we opened our first stores.* My dad had been right, but I had, too: significance could be found in business.

I couldn't know exactly what "significance" would come to mean in the years that followed. But what I did know was that for as much as Fifth Avenue had ushered Apple onto the global stage, the most significant product for Apple—and one that many would come to describe as "genius"—was still waiting in the wings.

I also knew that the stores would have to get even better to reveal it.

CHAPTER 10

"This Is the Moment We Built the Stores For."

People I've worked with have described my enthusiasm as irresistible. It's irresistible for the same reason Apple and its products became irresistible. People want to be a part of something, but they also want to make their own contribution. That's what Apple encouraged, and that's what I always tried to encourage. I wanted people to make their own mark; I wanted my store managers to find what they would become famous for; I wanted everyone to be a star on a winning team. Not long before we opened Fifth Avenue, I told the team that we would be renaming our store managers to store leaders. I didn't just want to create a leadership culture but also attract one. The opportunity to lead is what's truly irresistible.

The desire to lead is irresistible because the desire to have an impact is innate. In the late twentieth century, psychologists ran experiments in which they attached infants' feet to pieces of string, then tied those strings to mobiles above them. They observed that once infants realized *they* were moving the mobiles, it was all they wanted to do. Sixty years earlier, a German psychologist, Karl Groos, had observed a similar phenomenon. He termed it "the pleasure at being the cause." If we derive pleasure from being the cause, Groos seemed to say, then we find that pleasure in imagining that something will happen—like, say, that a mobile will move if we touch it—and seeing if we're right. That was all I ever wanted: to see if things like design at Target—or delivering support through a bar—would work. And while I did think a twenty-four-hour store on Fifth Avenue would succeed, its actual performance blew my socks off. It was like we tugged on a mobile with our foot and ripped a hole in the ceiling.

Years on from Groos's observations, philosopher Dallas Willard would give theological weight to his conclusion. The drive to "significance," Willard writes, first appears as a vital need in a tiny child, and is not egotism. Rather, it is the extension of our God-given creative impulse, and it is directed outwardly at the good to be done.

"We were built to count, as water is made to run downhill," Willard writes. "We are placed in a specific context to count in ways no one else does. That is our destiny."

Now, calling a twenty-four-hour store my "destiny" might be a stretch. But it was another expression of what had revealed itself to me in this specific context, at this specific moment in time. Sharing the idea of keeping the store open all day was an outward expression of the good to be done, and doing it was like kicking the mobile. Retaining a childlike wonder as I ascended through retail allowed my imagination to play within specific contexts and reveal ideas that I could then share with the team. Most of those ideas ended up on the cutting room floor, but some—like the Genius Bar—ended up in the store. And others, like a twenty-four-hour store beneath a glass cube, ended up on Fifth Avenue.

In a sense, innovation and success are always contextual, always some marriage of opportunity and necessity. And when I think about what Fifth Avenue really did, I believe it expanded the possible contexts in which an Apple Store could exist. Suddenly, we weren't relegated to malls or even shopping streets. We could take contexts and imagine something within them that would change the game for, say, a landlord, or people, or Apple, or even a country. There was no way to know what, exactly, this meant, but that was the point. We would discover what we could mean in *each specific context.* We would leap into an arena and find our sword in the sand. Most of all, we would count in ways no one else could. That, I believed, was our destiny.

With that in mind, the question after Fifth Avenue became what an Apple Store could mean and where it could mean it. The US was largely covered; after five years of steady growth, 80 percent of Americans lived within a fifteen-minute drive of one of our 143 stores.[1] Inspired by the strength I now knew we had, I found myself dreaming.

Ninety percent of our stores to this point have been in the US, I thought.

Wouldn't it be great if over the next five years, 90 percent of the stores we opened were *outside* the US?

This was often how ideas started in my imagination—as simple questions. And I knew what country would answer this one in a meaningful way for Apple, too. I'd been reading about its growth for years.

China.

I'd visited Asia a few times while at Target in the 1990s. As of 2006, China was virtually unrecognizable. Market reforms were opening the country to foreign investment, which raised incomes

---

1 Fifth Avenue was our 143rd store.

and led people to leave the countryside for cities like Shanghai, Beijing, Guangzhou, and Shenzhen. Those cities were growing quickly into vibrant economic hubs whose shopping malls were filled with global, aspirational brands.

Wouldn't it be great if Apple were one of them?

When I brought the idea of going to China to Steve, he loved it.

"Just ask Peter how much business we do there first," he said.

I did.

"Tens of millions," Peter told me. "Fifth Avenue is doing more than we're doing in China."

I remember thinking that couldn't possibly be right. But if it was, I thought, what an opportunity for Apple. There were a *billion* people in China!

There was something else—a new product—that gave me confidence in going to China, too. 2003 was the first year that there were more camera phones sold worldwide than digital cameras, and Steve—hyperaware as he was of potential threats to Apple's success—had begun wondering what would happen if a mobile phone maker added an MP3 player to their phone. This could, he thought, spell the end for the iPod, and this thinking—or, perhaps, paranoia—led to another big bet. In early 2004, years after deciding Apple would open its own stores, Steve decided Apple was going to create its own phone.

The project took the name "Purple." The first prototype—"P1," as it was known internally—took its inspiration from the device it was supposedly going to replace: the iPod. It had a trackwheel, which made scrolling through an address book easy. It would also be simple to engineer and manufacture. But there was a second version, too, which utilized an all-screen, "multitouch" design. Steve loved the idea of a multitouch phone, but the engineering challenge was daunting. By the middle of 2005—at which point we were still developing the cube on Fifth Avenue—we were spending an inordinate amount of time in ET discussing the merits of P1 versus P2.

One day, Steve came into my office and asked me what I thought we should do.

"It's like Fifth Avenue," I told him. "You only get one shot to launch a phone and change the world."

"So . . . ?" he asked.

"If it were up to me, I would do the multitouch interface."

Steve nodded. The following Monday, he revealed that this was what everyone else had told him, too.

"We all know this is the one we want to do," he said of the all-screen P2. "So, let's make it work."

Steve had a working prototype within a few months. On January 9, 2007, he announced it to the world as "a wide-screen iPod with touch controls, a revolutionary mobile phone, and a breakthrough internet communications device."

He named it the iPhone.

A few months later, Steve sent me a note—he had an iPhone for me. I dropped by his office to pick it up.

"There's just one rule," he said. "No one can touch it."

I nodded.

Two weeks later, I was going through security in the airport in Chongqing, China, after scouting out real estate for our first store there. I emptied my pockets into a gray bin, including my iPhone, then sent the bin through the scanner while I waited in line.

And waited.

And *waited.*

Come on, I thought. Something was holding up the line.

In the meantime, a crowd gathered around the other side of the security checkpoint, and I immediately realized I hadn't put my iPhone in my bag. It hadn't even occurred to me that people in China would recognize it, and part of me held out hope that the source of their curiosity was anything other than exactly what I knew it was.

It wasn't.

"iPhone!" I heard one of them exclaim. Except they pronounced the *i* like an *e*, so it sounded more like "ee-phone!" Over and over again they said it, chattering excitedly.

"Ee-phone, ee-phone, ee-phone!"

"Hey, *hey!*" I exclaimed from the other side of the metal detector. "I need my phone!"

I grimaced as one of the security guards grasped the "ee-phone," holding it up for what felt like the entire airport to see, and motioned to me as if to say, *Is this yours?*

I waved, nodded, and eventually got it back.

When I landed back stateside, I told Steve what had happened, making it very clear that while yes, several people had touched the "ee-phone," no one had unlocked it. The spin I tried to put on the story was that a market we didn't yet have a store in—and the biggest market in the world—already knew what the iPhone was.

Both of us agreed that the iPhone was going to be big.

Neither of us had any idea what that truly meant.

□

In many ways, we had been preparing for the iPhone for years.

"Five down, ninety-five to go" was always about capturing the 95 percent of people who weren't yet using a Mac—but even then, it was little more than a rallying cry. We were never going to capture the entire PC market with a $1,500 computer. In our ad announcing *why* we were launching stores, Steve said as much, pointing out that 5 percent of the PC market equated to roughly twenty-five million people around the world using Macs. If only 5 percent of the remaining 95 percent of people *not* using Macs switched, he wrote, we would earn an *additional* twenty-five million customers . . . and the opportunity to reach twenty-five million more.

Of course, Steve was a storyteller, and storytellers are prone to exaggeration. Apple did not, in fact, have 5 percent of the PC market in 2001. We had about 2.5 percent of the PC market. By 2006, Apple's 6 percent share of the PC market did not represent a 20 percent jump from where we'd started, but a more than *100 percent* jump; Apple's market share had doubled in five years, and we—the stores—took pride in the role we'd played. Still, there were a *lot* of contributing factors. We were trying to switch customers to Macs, but the ads being run—Apple's "Switchers" campaign in 2002 and 2003, and its iconic iPod silhouette ads—were driving the awareness that pushed people into the stores and made it easier for our employees to convert them. Then there was the work being done by the design, hardware, and software teams. And Tim's work to get the products manufactured and in the stores. We were one oar in a much larger boat, and while I did what I could to keep us paddling, it was Steve who set the direction. And, of course, in a dynamic environment, the right direction was often a *different* direction.

Even today, people talk about Steve's "changing his mind" like it was some mythical ability. For me, there wasn't much mystery to it. Steve changed his mind when he was exposed to new information. It was that simple. And because he was obsessed with what he did and thus "doing" it constantly, his appetite for knowledge was insatiable, and his ability to digest it was unmatched. He would ask everyone on ET what they thought about everything. Heck, he walked into our Palo Alto store in 2002 and asked Cano what he thought about the iPod not being compatible with Windows. So, yes, Steve often "changed his mind." But what made him such a great leader wasn't just the *ability* to change his mind—it was also the *courage* to act on having changed it.

I saw Steve's courage for years. I saw it when he decided that we needed to redesign the store in October 2000, when he decided to make the iPod compatible with Windows, and when he decided to develop iTunes *for* Windows. But most notably, I saw it when Steve decided that he was going all in on the iPhone. He knew that a music-enabled, multitouch phone would cannibalize sales of the iPod—which, as of 2005, was driving lines outside stores and sales of the Mac through the roof. But he *also* knew that if executed well, the iPhone had the potential to create an even bigger switcher opportunity than we'd revealed with the iPod. There were six-and-a-half billion people around the globe, and all of them were going to need a phone. This was our chance to go beyond what we had opened stores to do. The iPhone wasn't just a path to the 95 percent. It was our chance to reach *everyone*.

Throughout 2006, conversations within Apple Retail took the form of how we would launch in China while also getting the stores ready for what would be our biggest switcher opportunity yet. I worked closely with my head of retail marketing, Christy Schrader, to create a new, formalized training program for those who switched to the Mac because they loved their iPhone. The idea felt novel, but a version of it had already been happening: One of the programs we'd launched in 2002 to go after business customers, ProCare, included group training, but it wasn't particularly effective, nor did it offer great value. What could offer both, Christy and I determined, was one-on-one training. I asked Christy to brand the initiative, and she got to work on what would become "One to One." The pitch was simple and easy. A typical personal training session—say, in a gym—

might cost you $100. At Apple, you could spend $99 . . . and get a session a week for an entire *year.*

Now that, I thought, was great—and truly better.

Training wasn't all we did. As we'd been ideating on One to One, another idea had been coming to me. The seed had been planted almost two decades earlier, back when I'd been working at Mervyn's. To keep me busy, Mervyn's COO Jerry Gallagher asked me to do a report on the cash wrap. He wanted to understand what worked, what didn't work, and what could work better. I spent a few days observing and making notes, but notes are no substitute for experience. So, I decided to work one of Mervyn's cash wraps.

At our flagship store.

On Black Friday.

This was in 1984. I told my roommate at the time, Greg Delgado—a good-looking guy who got lots of attention from good-looking girls—what I would be doing. When he mentioned that he might drop by, I immediately regretted it. It would be hot in the store, and nowhere would it be hotter than behind the cash wrap staring at a line of a dozen customers. Within minutes of starting, I had sweat through my shirt. After a few hours, I would've given anything to change it. My saving grace was that no one in line knew who I was. Then, at the end of the line, I saw Greg. He *had* dropped by. Worse, he had dropped by with *a girl on each arm.*

I stole a couple of glances their way between scanning codes. I caught glimpses of the girls checking Greg out as I checked everyone else out. The conclusion I eventually presented to Mervyn's was measured. The one in my head was not.

Everyone loves shopping, I thought. *No one* likes checkout. Ever since that moment, I had wanted to get rid of the cash wrap.

The more I sat with this thought over the years, the more strongly

I felt about it. Throughout the 1990s, I saw how crazy checkout could get at Target—the lines, the waits—and at all the other stores I visited, too. I thought about customers trying to pick the shortest line, then kicking themselves after realizing that another one was moving faster. I thought about their having to pull products out of carts and onto the conveyor belt, then I thought about the employee behind the cash wrap needing to line up UPC codes to be scanned, and how those codes might be smudged, which would mean inputting them manually. I thought about the customer having to punch in their loyalty number or their coupons, then waiting for the transaction to be approved while the line waited on them, then fumbling with their receipt and their wallet and their card, or their cash, or their change. All of this took time. All of this felt messy. And all of it could go away—except that I lacked the ability, the need, and the technical solution required to make it go away.

Now, I had all three.

The technical solution came in mobile checkout devices, which a fearless member of Apple's IT team—Khawaja Shams—had been testing in the years following our first holiday season with the iPod Mini. The need had been clear then and was even clearer now. Demand for iPhones would add to existing demand for iPods, and I knew that giving the hundreds of employees in our busiest stores mobile checkout devices would eliminate any constraint on sales volume. I also thought about how much employees would love the satisfaction of checking customers out—and how seamless the process would feel for someone who wanted to buy. And if Hertz, who I rented cars from when I traveled, could do purely mobile checkout, there was no reason we couldn't, too. So, in 2006, I proposed another big, bold mission: becoming the first 100 percent mobile store.

The response was . . . mixed.

Since the dawn of shopping, people had been conditioned to understand the cash wrap as the natural end point of a shopping experience.[2] Department stores had physical checkout. Apparel retailers had physical checkout. Heck, *open-air bazaars in Mesopotamia* would've had physical checkout. Customers would know that if they wanted to buy something, return something, or ask for help with something, they could do it at the checkout counter. The cash wrap wasn't just a place for customers to buy; it was a psychological and logistical anchor that would keep everything—customers, business—from floating away. And we were going to get rid of it.

Cano was particularly outspoken about the issues we'd run into if we got rid of the cash wrap in favor of mobile checkout. Sure, he said, customers who came to stores to learn about a Mac or an iPod would be met by a specialist who could guide them through the purchase process, but he pressed me on where customers would land when they walked into the store simply to buy a product off the back wall and got missed by a specialist at the front. The answer was that this was a trade-off: There probably *would* be customers who would miss the ease of grabbing a product off the shelf and taking it to the cash wrap to check out. Still, it was a trade-off worth making given expected demand for the iPhone. If it was anything like we anticipated, we needed hundreds of moving cash wraps in each store more than we needed a dedicated place for customers to check out.

Another thing that gave me confidence in this idea was knowing how it would dovetail with another initiative we'd been working on to make our stores better for the iPhone launch: Personal Shopping.

---

2 Try to imagine what any store you've visited—other than the Apple Store—would be like without a cash register. It's hard!

We knew some customers would want the convenience and certainty of knowing that if they came to a busy Apple Store, they could get personalized help learning about a product. And it didn't make sense to me that a customer who had just spent an hour building a connection with one of our specialists should have to check out with someone else. The specialist deserved the credit for launching that customer's relationship with Apple!

Now, those reading closely might be wondering: Why not just leave a cash wrap for emergencies and give every employee mobile checkout? It's a fair question, and I'm sure Cano asked it. The fact that I didn't answer it affirmatively was, if anything, a symptom of the faith I had in him and his team. If we'd fumbled a twenty-four-hour store on Fifth Avenue—which would've just opened around the time we first started talking about eliminating the cash wrap—maybe I would've felt differently. But we hadn't. That store was crushing its numbers on its mission to be the first twenty-four-hour store in the world, and a 100 percent mobile store would be another such mission.

We planned to debut the first store without a cash wrap in the fall of 2007, just after the iPhone was scheduled to launch. In the meantime, Denise and I had been approached by a Bain consultant, Fred Reichheld, with another fun idea. Fred believed that the key to understanding customer loyalty and business growth—two things that we were hyperconscious of in the year leading up to the iPhone launch—could be found in one simple question:

"How likely are you to recommend our product or service to a friend or colleague?"

That question had helped Fred develop "Net Promoter Score," or NPS. Fred explained that were we to implement it, customers would receive an email after their experience at the store asking how likely they were to recommend us to a friend or colleague.

Respondents were sorted into three categories:

- Promoters (9–10): Loyal enthusiasts
- Passives (7–8): Satisfied but unenthusiastic
- Detractors (0–6): Unhappy customers

The Net Promoter Score was determined by identifying the difference in the percentage of respondents that were promoters or detractors. If, of the one hundred people who responded in one day, eighty were promoters, ten were passives, and ten were detractors, that meant 80 percent were promoters and 10 percent were detractors. We would then subtract the detractors from the promoters to reach an NPS score of 70 percent.

With the iPhone coming, visualizing our stores' day-to-day performance had obvious appeal, and it gave us the opportunity to measure, for the first time, the quality of our service. But truthfully, the reason I greenlit our investment in NPS had almost nothing to do with the score itself and everything to do with something Fred mentioned toward the end of one of our meetings with him. There was a box at the end of the survey customers received, he explained, where they could write feedback if they wanted.

Wait, I thought. *What?*

The second he showed that to me, my mind started racing. This would give me the chance to appreciate my employees! I felt like I was back at Mervyn's walking through the store with Brian Bee, watching him greet every team member and congratulate them on a job well done. I'd been able to do this at Apple when we only had a few stores. But Fifth Avenue had been our 143rd store . . . and we had since opened dozens more in our steady sprint toward three hundred. I was in touch with my store leaders, but I couldn't make close connections with all their teams. This was a chance to reestablish my connection with them—and do it by showing how much I *appreciated* them.

And it's funny—maybe the same part of me that missed greeting employees in the stores was compensating for it outside of work. Most mornings, I would wake up around three thirty and go for a run. Once I finished, I'd then hop in my car and drive down from my house in Atherton to our local 7-Eleven to get a Diet Coke. But truthfully, those drives were at least as much about the drink as the guy I bought it from—the store manager of that 7-Eleven, Gurdip. He was a good-humored older guy in his mid-seventies, and I loved starting my day with him and learning about him. I also observed that he was the only one in the store overnight.

I mention this only because as I got to know Gurdip better, I *also* discovered that often, he was left to stock shelves with merchandise in the wee hours of the morning while customers waited on him at the cash register. This was clearly a pain. Then, one day, I came in and saw more merchandise on the floor than I'd ever seen: full palettes of soda, candy, everything imaginable.

"Was this one truck?" I asked Gurdip.

"Two," he said. I stole a glance up at the front counter where a customer was approaching from the coffee machine.

"Gurdip," I said, nodding toward the front of the store. "Go take care of that customer. I'll take care of this."

The look of relief in his eyes was gratifying in a way that little else can be. And truthfully, at 4:00 a.m., where else did I need to be than right there? What better way was there to start my day than by making someone *else's* day better? And, *and* . . . How cool was it that I knew how to stock the doughnut cabinet at my local 7-Eleven—that maple long-johns were on the left because I had put them there?

It was the best!

From then on, I visited Gurdip at his 7-Eleven every morning, and whenever it was obvious that he needed help, I jumped in and stocked the shelves. It deepened our relationship and was meaningful for me—there was no better way to start my day than by doing something for someone else.

After helping Gurdip, I would return home to forward notes to my employees, make calls to store leaders who were hours ahead—in Europe or on the East Coast—and respond to every customer who had submitted a note. And *then* I would get ready to take the kids to breakfast and drop them at school. It's hard to overstate how happy all of this made me. I was at my best at my busiest, and my happiest at my best. There was no better way to start a day than with a small act of kindness, and there was no better way to motivate people than with a note.

In the days after we launched NPS, I stayed current on the new notes we received. When we got a rating between zero and six, I emailed the customer directly, telling them I was sorry we'd let them down, then copied the store manager. Then, oftentimes, I would receive a reply from the same customer.

"I wrote feedback, Ron, you responded in *five minutes,* and five minutes *later* your store manager called, apologized, and fixed my issue!"

It wasn't always five minutes, but the emphasis on urgency was a symptom of what mattered: the person *behind* the number. If we didn't secure customers' good, our numbers wouldn't look good. It was that simple. And I articulated this to teams repeatedly with the same phrase: "You don't deserve to launch a new relationship with a customer until you've restored the relationship with the customer in front of you." Not particularly profound words, I didn't think. But they reflected a fundamental truth for me: every person I encountered—customers, yes, or someone like Gurdip—was a privilege. Every interaction was an opportunity. Best of all, every failure was an opportunity to do better.

This mindset would inform everything we did in the wake of the iPhone.

□

On June 25, 2007—the Monday before the iPhone was first scheduled to go on sale—I sat in ET with Tim, Phil, Jony, Scott, and the rest of the team. Steve arrived late, per usual. After providing a brief update for us, he pulled his iPhone out of his pocket and looked around the room.

"These things are team sports," he said. There was a long pause.

"This . . ." He paused, staring at the iPhone. "It all started in 2005 with Jony. Then it was yours, Phil," he continued, gesturing at him. He ran his hands over the stubble on his chin and cast his eyes downwards as he paced.

"Then yours, Scott, with the software," Steve said. "Then yours, Tim, to manufacture."

I felt the moment unfolding as Steve turned to me.

"And now, Ron, it's yours," he said. "It's your turn to make this great for Apple."

I nodded, knowing that he couldn't know just how much we'd done to make it great.

A line had begun forming in front of Fifth Avenue—where we would launch the iPhone—even before that ET meeting. At 5:00 a.m. on June 23, 2007, six full days before the iPhone was scheduled to debut, Greg Packer—a portly fellow who intentionally arrived early at media events to get quoted by reporters—planted himself in front of our Fifth Avenue store. Then, when the sun reached over the peaks of Manhattan's skyline and the temperature outside breached ninety degrees, he took off his shirt. The press loved it. Steve, who had been anticipating this moment for thirty years, did not.

That night, he called me.

"You have to get that guy out of line," Steve said.

"Greg?" I asked.

"I don't know his name," Steve said. "Just pull him out."

"No."

"Why?"

"It's wrong."

"You've *got* to move him."

"It'll become the story if I do."

Steve was silent for a moment.

"Okay," he said. "Fine."

Then he hung up.

Over the next few days, the press in front of Fifth Avenue only intensified. The line stretched. Tents appeared. Helicopters circled. And there Greg sat, sometimes shirtless, sometimes not, beneath them.

Two nights before opening, Steve called again.

"You've *got* to move him."

"We talked about this."

A long pause.

"Well, he's not getting the first iPhone no matter what happens," Steve said. "I don't want his picture to be all over the world."

"Okay."

"*Okay?*" Steve asked. "What are you going to do?"

"I'll handle it," I said. "Trust me."

I visited our Fifth Avenue store the day before launch to do one final sweep. It was another warm day, just shy of ninety degrees. I chatted with employees and connected with customers, learning their stories, asking what they needed, bringing them water. It was the type of day that reminded me why I'd joined Apple.

After a long day of setting up the store, I'd taken a break, making my way north of the cube, closer to Fifty-Ninth. The last of the day's sunlight glinted off the glass, and a warm breeze from Central Park had brought some relief from the heat. As I stood there in the plaza, my phone rang, and I knew it was Steve. This was when he always called: after dinner with Laurene and the kids, while he was sitting at home reflecting. I'd told Steve I'd handle Greg; this call wouldn't be about that. It would be the type of call I often got from Steve before big moments: reflective, philosophical, human.

I found an open white Victoria chair in the plaza, sat down, and swiped right over the shimmering Answer on my iPhone. The device emitted a satisfying *click*, and I held it up to my ear.

"How are you feeling about tomorrow?" Steve asked.

"Good!" I said. "Ready."

"You know how much this means," he said. His voice cracked just slightly.

"I know."

I looked back at the line, the people, the pale yellow lights starting to emerge through the canvas of the tents. I imagined the scene that was less than twenty-four hours away, the wave that would start here at 6:00 p.m. tomorrow before sweeping across the country, the product unveiling that would start a movement.

Steve asked me to describe it, and I did. I told him that people were camping out, and that the line of several thousand was stretching south from the cube on Fifty-Eighth before disappearing behind the General Motors Building.

"This is the moment we built the stores for," Steve said.

I could feel the weight of his words. These things were team sports, and my team was ready to play its role. Every journey, I knew, began with a first step. After six long years, we would take our biggest step yet.

CHAPTER 11

The Most Important Person Is the One in Front of You

"Reason went out the window."

That was the quote from Ryan O'Donnell, an Apple fanatic who waited six hours outside of our Union Square store in San Francisco on iPhone launch day: June 29, 2007.

Except, *did* reason go out the window? That was the question we were left to mull as we watched lines of hundreds—and in many places, thousands—form around the country.

It had been Ginza where we'd first seen lines of this length: miles' worth of people lining up simply to get into a store. But with the iPhone, the calculus was different. Now, the people lining up weren't just bought into something. Now, they were also there to buy something. It was this pairing that drove the lines, the unprecedented demand. The lines, far from being unreasonable, actually made perfect sense.

We had now been dealing with lines for years. They had formed outside of stores in the mornings and the evenings, in good weather and bad. When they began forming overnight, we brought people sleeping bags. When they formed in the rain, we brought out umbrellas. It was our job, I explained to the team, to support those in the lines, to love them, to secure their good. We learned about them, too—about people like Gary Allen, who would travel with his son to store openings around the country and launched the blog *ifoAppleStore* to track what we were doing. The most important customers were the ones in front of us, and that included the people in front of the stores. So, at the hundreds of stores around the US now preparing to sell the iPhone, we brought them what they needed. In the summer heat, most needed water. Then, when they got inside, iPhones.

The lines were crazy almost everywhere. At the Grove in Los Angeles, one had begun forming well before dawn. One particularly enthusiastic fan tried multiple times throughout the night to get into the mall, but was dismissed each time by security. By 4:00 a.m., the guards finally relented and let him stay. Another guy hid behind four large planters in the Manhattan Village mall at 3:00 a.m. to avoid detection. By the time the mall opened, he had secured his spot in line.

A few hundred miles north, Apple's cofounder, Steve Wozniak, had arrived at the Westfield Valley Fair mall in Santa Clara at 4:00 a.m. with a few friends. Seventy-five people were already outside asleep. Wozniak convinced mall security to let everyone inside, and the group tooled around the mall for a few hours. Even though Wozniak had not been the first to arrive, the group agreed that he should get the first iPhone in Santa Clara. When he signed his name, the cheering crowd included hundreds of people in line and dozens of employees in the store.

Similar scenes played out around the country. Three hundred people lined up outside of our Union Square store in San Francisco. Thirty miles south in Palo Alto, four hundred. Steve was there, too.

"It's part concert, part tech convention," he said.

That about captured it.

The vibe was similar at Fifth Avenue in New York, where I was. By launch time at 6:00 p.m. Eastern Standard Time, the line extended over a half mile—and there at the front of it was Greg Packer.

I knew how I'd handle the situation with Greg from the moment Steve brought it up. During the 2004 holiday season, we'd addressed excess demand for the iPod by turning the Genius Bar into a cash wrap. Now, two and a half years later, I would do the same at Fifth Avenue for Greg.

At 6:00 p.m. on June 29, 2007, I greeted Greg and congratulated him on being the first in line. Once I had, I led him through the double doors of the cube, down the spiral staircase, and into the underground space. But instead of ushering him toward the cash wrap—and cameras—on the north side of the store, I led him toward the Genius Bar on the south side. Several of my team members were there waiting for him. We processed his purchase of the iPhone, took pictures with him, and eventually he was on his way.

Meanwhile, on the other side of the store, the press was preoccupied with a svelte Asian woman holding her new iPhone. To the millions who saw that photo, she got the first one. But she didn't. And technically, neither did Greg. Both got their iPhones simultaneously, just as I'd imagined it. You could please some of the people all the time, I learned. But given the reaction to the iPhone launch across the US, it was hard not to think that we could please everyone all the time—and we certainly wouldn't stop trying.

□

At $499 and $599 respectively, the four- and eight-gigabyte iPhones were already some of the most expensive phones on the market. They were made even more expensive because the deal Steve had negotiated with AT&T hadn't included a traditional subsidy, as was standard for most other phones.

Now, subsidy or not, the Apple faithful had been quick to adopt the iPhone. But as their wave receded heading into the holiday season, Steve found himself in a tricky position. He knew how far ahead of the competition the iPhone was, how critical the holiday season would be in terms of establishing its foothold in the market, and how the bigger that foothold got, the more leverage he would have to negotiate with carriers and resellers to make it even bigger. And yet, the numbers made it clear that the iPhone's price was too high to create that leverage. So, on September 5, 2007, Steve announced that Apple was discontinuing the four-gigabyte iPhone and dropping the price of the eight-gigabyte iPhone by $200.

The rationale was clear internally. Still, it made early adopters furious. After fielding hundreds of angry emails, Steve released an open letter to early iPhone customers, explaining the decision and offering a $100 store credit to those who had bought prior to August 21. Then, at the end, he did something he didn't often do.

He apologized.

"We want to do the right thing for our valued iPhone customers," he wrote. "We apologize for disappointing some of you, and we are doing our best to live up to your high expectations of Apple."

It was a masterclass in communication: honest, clear, and concise. But it also set the stage for potential chaos—and Steve noted that.

"[Even] though the technology road is bumpy," he wrote, "we need to do a better job taking care of our early iPhone customers as we aggressively go after new ones with a lower price."

"Aggressively" was an understatement.

In retrospect, Steve's quote would prove a harbinger of things to come, but it also described what we in Apple Retail existed to do.

Yes, Apple had an aggressive *goal,* but our job in the stores was to marry it with compassionate *delivery.* This would prove to be the biggest challenge of the next few years, but the stores would prove capable of meeting it. We would do it, too, with new products, competitors, and challenges looming on the horizon.

□

We thought we'd known what it was like to be busy. Four years earlier in 2004, as the iPod Halo grew and more customers came in to try a Mac, I'd had another idea: summer camp. People told me it was crazy, asking what would happen if someone who wanted to buy a Mac came in and saw every computer occupied—first, with people who were using us as a free Wi-Fi café, and now with dozens of kids.

"If a customer comes in and sees us busy with kids, they'll leave knowing we're a great brand," I said. "You won't lose that sale. The customer will come back."

We launched Apple Camp in 2005. My kids, Will and Lizzey, both attended. For those in the stores, seeing participants' smiling faces was magical. That same year, Apple launched the Mac Mini, the iPod Shuffle, the second-generation iPod Mini, and the iPod Nano.

Sales continued to grow.

The products had been improving, too. In June 2005, Steve had announced that he would be transitioning Apple's computers from PowerPC chips to Intel to improve performance. He completed the transition in August 2006, three months after launching another iconic ad campaign: "Get a Mac" with actors Justin Long and John Hodgman. The introduction to each TV spot was unforgettable.

"I'm a Mac," Long said.

"And I'm a PC," Hodgman replied.

It didn't take viewers long to recognize who they were supposed to believe was cool—and what computer they were supposed to buy as a result.

The problem for the stores was that the faster Macs were often occupied by those who couldn't necessarily *buy* them: kids. YouTube launched in 2005. Facebook opened to the world in 2006. Teens, who couldn't yet meaningfully access the internet via cell phones, filled our stores to check notifications, post on each other's walls, and watch videos like Judson Laipply's "Evolution of Dance" or Chris Parnell and Andy Samberg's "Lazy Sunday." It was fun, but for the stores, it was also somewhat of a problem; customers who wanted to get their hands on newly Intel-driven Macs—say the first-generation MacBook Pro, or the dual core Power Mac G5—were, in some cases, left waiting. But the stores being busy helped more than it hurt, and Apple's brand got stronger as a result.

Still, there is a limit to how busy a team can be, and leading up to 2007, we had been trying to find it. "Get a Mac" brought customers into the store in droves. It also proved that the Genius Bars, which had once seemed too big, weren't nearly big enough. We had six stools at most of them. It felt like we could've used sixty. The Intel Macs could now run Windows via Boot Camp, which reduced the risk of switching for Windows users and brought more of them in for help at the bar. The iPod Halo got bigger and brighter. Data transfers from PC to Mac surged, and with them, issues that Geniuses could address.

And then Steve introduced the iPhone.

It was chaos almost from the get-go. The iPhone had launched in four countries in 2007, but the plan had been to reach eighty countries by the end of 2008, and we had wanted to open stores in the highest-volume cities to help meet the demand. 2008 would see us launch more stores in the United Kingdom and Canada, but also our first stores in Germany, Australia, Switzerland, and China. Marketing had to be translated. Every point-of-sale system needed to be compliant with local regulations. People needed to be hired and trained. And this is to say nothing of what it actually took to *build* stores in new cities. Bob had imagined a glass façade for our store in Sydney with 65-foot-tall panes of glass, and to construct them, he worked with a partner who built an entirely new kiln. When one of the panes shattered in transit, Bob got another one manufactured and shipped—via 747—in time for the store opening. He was at his best at his busiest. We all were.

In the meantime, the stores were as full as ever. Apple wouldn't release the App Store (and the Facebook app) until July 2008, so teens continued to visit the stores to get on social media. Steve had given the world another reason to visit the stores in early 2008, too: the MacBook Air. Also, Apple Camp continued that summer, reaching capacity in every market. We had also launched One to One, which brought in thousands of people—often, those in their seventies and eighties—to see what they could do with a Mac, and they filled the back half of stores day after day, week after week. We couldn't hire trainers fast enough, and we were finding that many customers didn't want to be trained so much as guided through creative projects. To find more people who wanted to do this, we renamed "trainers" to "creatives." Denise's team then put together a job description seeking experts in music (GarageBand), graphic and web design (Adobe, Flash, SQL), video (Final Cut Pro, Adobe Premier), and 3D rendering (Apple's "Shake" application). In Palo Alto, we were training more people in the digital arts than nearby Stanford was training in the liberal arts. As much as we were a store, we were also a place for everyone to learn—and create.

And yet, that wasn't all we were. I had tried to make us the first store without physical checkout in Los Gatos, which had opened on September 6, 2007—coincidentally, the day after Steve announced the iPhone price drop, and *also* the day after Apple launched another new product: the iPod Touch. It was immediately clear that getting rid of the cash wrap had been a mistake. Cano was right—customers *were* confused. We introduced a concierge at the front of the store, but I wasn't sure it would be enough. It also wasn't our only issue. Managers were responding to customers whose NPS notes I'd been forwarding to them, many of which described long waits for Genius Bar appointments and a lack of clarity on where to go upon arrival. If Geniuses were late to appointments, it was often because they were assisting a customer with the move from PC to Mac, or talking a customer who had lost something in a transfer off the ledge by doing what I had emphasized to Duke so many years earlier and taking *time* with them. Still, there had to be a balance between ensuring each customer felt seen and ensuring every customer *was* seen, and that balance was proving increasingly hard to strike. I was asking each store to be everything to everyone. It was a big ask. And then another product came in the summer of 2008 and made it even bigger.

Steve's gamble on lowering the cost of the original iPhone turned out to be prescient. It fed holiday demand and created the leverage he'd been looking for. By the following summer, Steve had not only iterated on the original iPhone, but managed to get AT&T to subsidize it. The new iPhone, named after the high-speed "3G" network it could access, was scheduled to launch in July 2008 with two models—eight and sixteen gigabytes—and each model came with a subsidized price of $199 or $299. It was, in many ways, the perfect storm. Steve had doubled the carrying capacity of Apple's flagship device, halved its price, and sped it up markedly. He had also been working now for years on another major feature for Apple—the App Store—which would dramatically increase what people were capable of doing with their iPhone. Demand in the stores went supersonic. For some, that's when fatigue began to turn into exhaustion.

I could understand this, but I knew we couldn't accept it. Less than a year earlier in 2007, Google had announced a new mobile competitor—Android—and Tim was trying to get ahead of it. He had begun the process of expanding into more channels by starting with Best Buy, and it was clear that all 700 of their locations would eventually have their own Apple store within a store. As a retailer, I also knew the channel expansion wouldn't be limited to Best Buy. Verizon, Sprint, and T-Mobile would later get the iPhone, too, and Walmart and Target would eventually have most of Apple's products. If we—the Apple Stores—wanted to maintain our leadership in the years that followed, we couldn't slow down. We had to speed *up*. We had to find new ways to serve customers, new ways to be the preferred place for people to buy our products, new methods of deepening customers' relationships with Apple.

As it turned out, one such way had been hiding in plain sight for years.

□

It had been in 2004 that I'd taken that trip to visit Duke and seen him setting up computers for customers. But since then, the initiative remained isolated to Minneapolis. Customers in other stores didn't seem to need setup, so we never formalized it.

Now, we had to.

Beyond the intuitive understanding that we needed to maintain the stores' leadership as Tim pushed the iPhone into the channel, activation data supported expanding setup. Customers were taking a week to activate their iPhones. As a parent, I understood why. People got busy. They might not have had time to activate their iPhone in the way customers originally had to: via iTunes, which first-time

Apple customers would have to download. I imagined parents waiting until they had a free moment to activate their iPhone only to realize they didn't know how. And as a parent myself, I could understand why finding a free moment to do anything—let alone something you weren't sure how to do—could take the better part of a week.

These thoughts came together in my imagination as a new initiative that we could offer in the stores. We could not only set up customers' iPhones; we could *personalize* them. Steve had described the iPhone as a widescreen iPod with touch controls, a revolutionary mobile phone, and a breakthrough internet communicator. It was our job in the stores to learn which of these three things customers cared about, then ensure that they walked out of the store knowing how to use them. It was also just *fun* to set people up. Specialists would share stories of customers smiling as they experienced features like cover art for the first time, or the "pinching" motion that would zoom in on a web browser, or the simple "flick" and "tap" motions to which the screens would respond instantaneously. We encouraged customers to try everything they wanted to do with the phone in the store, including making calls. Many would dial a friend and tell them, with a huge smile on their face, exactly what was true.

"I'm calling you from an *iPhone!*"

There was something cool about that.

The more we set people up, the more every specialist in every store realized just how many things there were for customers to learn. It was a reminder that one of the best ways to learn is to teach, because trying to explain something reveals what you don't know about it. Specialists who recognized gaps in their understanding would lean on other specialists. Sometimes, a customer might know something a specialist didn't, and those revelations enriched our culture. Groups formed in the stores around new discoveries—say, that fonts could be enlarged for someone whose eyes were bad. As much as we were revealing the genius of Apple's products, we were also letting customers reveal it to us.

In the end, setup was a savvy business strategy, too. There was a risk that the iPhone would lose market share as Google pushed Android into less expensive phones with bigger touchscreens. We found that helping customers personalize their phones created lock-in and spurred the type of word-of-mouth advertising that kept the stores full. People who knew what they could do with our products became evangelists. And while we had once thought that we could only deepen customers' relationships with their products when they came back to the store, we realized that now, we could do it *immediately.* This was a new standard for us and for retail. Perhaps most importantly, it was one that Google wouldn't be able to offer and our resellers couldn't replicate.

In the meantime, I had been on the phone with Cano daily discussing our first store in China, which was scheduled to open alongside the 2008 Beijing Summer Olympics. I was getting to know who Cano had hired as China's store leader: a longtime Apple guy, John Ford. Cano was updating me on the biggest issue John was facing: getting a business license for the store. It seemed an insurmountable hurdle, but then one day, Cano told me it had been figured out.

"Get the story from John," he said. "You'll love it."

Curious, I called John.

"I heard you got a license!" I said.

"I did!"

"How?"

"I bought a sewing machine repair shop."

"You *what*?"

John explained. In China, you couldn't open a store without a license, but you also couldn't get a license without having a store. His experience in China led him to believe that this rule had been created by incumbents to stifle competition, so he'd just gone to the smallest shop he could find, asked if they were for sale, and smartly avoided sharing who was buying. They said they were, for $300,000. Peter immediately paid it, and John got a business license. Then he crossed out the name on it and wrote *Apple*. Somehow, all this was legal—and it became the basis on which we opened stores in China.

John's freedom spoke to our culture: fun, scrappy, making it work. Every store leader had their own unique style. Some led their teams in yoga sessions to kick off the days. Every store felt a little different, but we all loved retail; we all loved people. We were a team of leaders focused on enriching lives, and we were kind. We weren't perfect, but we got better every day.

A few months later, I sat in the audience at our annual store conference. Cano sat to my left. Steve was onstage speaking. He went on for a few minutes, then opened himself up for questions. Hands shot up. Steve pointed to one a few rows behind me.

"When did you know Apple Retail was going to have the right culture?" a voice asked.

Steve paused for a moment, thinking.

"I believe that everything starts by picking the right seed crystal," he said. "If you select the right one, the outcome is perfect. With Apple Retail, we were lucky because we selected the right seed crystal: Ron Johnson. The Apple Store developed as a reflection of him."

Cano nudged me.

"Nice," he whispered.

I smiled. But looking around at everyone—our store leaders, Cano—I wasn't sure I agreed with Steve. I wasn't the seed crystal. I was just the guy who had been in the right place, at the right time, with the right experience. If anything, *Steve* was the seed crystal.

He created the organization in which we'd innovated; it was his mission I'd been able to take and improve with my own contribution.

That, it turned out, was precisely Steve's point.

A seed crystal is a template placed into a solution by industrial chemists to grow larger crystals, often in the semiconductor industry. If I had understood that, maybe I would've thought a little harder about the solution into which Steve had introduced me; maybe I would've realized that a culture where my thinking and leadership style worked as well as they did was anything but guaranteed. Instead, I simply let the words wash over me, like one might a solution they'd been dropped into, then moved on.

We had work to do.

□

In the fall of 2008, I traveled to Europe with a few members of my team: Bob; Ben Fay, who led store design for him; and Chris Braithwaite, who led European real estate. We were scheduled to launch a new country, Switzerland, for Apple Retail in two days, and the teams had timed the launch of these stores—and five others—with the week of my fiftieth birthday. My favorite thing in the world was launching stores, and they knew it; celebrating with seven stores in seven days would be a gift. But as we sat in Barcelona the night before Geneva was scheduled to open (we'd been there to scout *another* store location on Passeig de Gràcia), I felt restless. We had nothing planned for the following day—nothing to do on my birthday! I never *wanted* to do anything on my birthday, always telling Karen not to plan anything. But Geneva was a ninety-minute flight from Barcelona, and the store opening wasn't until 5:00 p.m. Sitting around all day felt wrong. There had to be something more we could do, something to keep our momentum up, something to keep us at our busiest, our *best.*

"Guys," I said as we sat at dinner. "Wouldn't it be great if we woke up early, had breakfast in Barcelona, then flew to Milan to look at another store site before the opening in Geneva?"

"It just isn't enough for you, is it," Bob said, laughing.

"Come on, Bob!"

"We can't get from Milan to Geneva by five p.m.," he said. "There are no flights!"

"We don't need to fly!" I exclaimed. "We can drive from Milan to Chamonix, then onto Geneva."

"Drive," Bob said flatly.

"Yeah!" I exclaimed. "Through the Alps! It's beautiful. And, *and*—we could have lunch in Chamonix for my birthday!"

"I don't know," Bob said. "I think we should get to Geneva!"

Bob's hesitancy was unusual. This was a guy who challenged the limits of physics for a living!

"Lunch with Mont Blanc hanging over us!" I said. "Come on, Bob! Wouldn't that be great?"

Twelve hours later, we were walking Milan's Via Monte Napoleone—the most expensive street in Europe and third most expensive street in the world—scouting locations for our next store. Two hours after that, we were seated around an outdoor table at a café in Chamonix looking up at the Alps while dining on raclette. Lunch went on for an hour, then another. I could've sat there until 5:00 p.m.—and in fact, almost did.

Finally, Bob looked down at his watch.

"Ron," he said. "It's *3:00 p.m.*"

"Shit!"

We had to *go.*

We paid, hustled back to the car, and told our driver to step on it.

With gravity on our side, we flew down the mountain, checking our progress against the GPS on my phone and watching as our ETA went from 5:04, to 5:03, to 5:02.

Thirty minutes out, we called Jerry, who was in the store.

"Where are you?" he asked.

"Coming!"

"You're going to miss the opening—"

"Hold it!"

I looked back down at my phone to see that our ETA had updated to 4:59.

We're going to make it!

Then I looked up to red taillights.

We're not . . .

We sat in bumper-to-bumper traffic for several minutes as we approached Geneva's city center from the southeast, the clock ticking ever closer to 5:00 p.m. Finally, at 4:58 p.m., I peeked my head from the back seat up over the console.

"Can you pull over?" I asked our driver.

He gesticulated at cars to his left and right. Stuck between several lanes of traffic, there was nowhere to go. I looked at Bob. Six blocks left, and we were both thinking the same thing.

Run.

Bob flipped open the back door of the car and we popped out.

"Can you guys pay the driv—"

"Yeah," Ben said. "Get in there. *Go!*"

I barely had time to thank them before Bob and I were sprinting through traffic on Rue de Rive, stomachs full of raclette. One block, then another. We saw the line before we saw the store, sprinting past blond heads and black coats. When we finally sidled past the first person in line and in the door, we were red-faced and sweating.

Jerry and Denise were there at the front of the store, waiting for us.

"5:03," Jerry said. "In *Switzerland,* of all places!"

"Just open the doors," I said, smiling through deep breaths. All I could think was that I hoped we still had waters at the Genius Bar.

□

The scope of executing the Geneva opening was familiar, but how I'd felt knowing I'd be late to it was not. For years, I'd arrived at store openings early—Glendale, Ginza, Fifth Avenue—to ensure that everything was set up perfectly. And often, things needed to be tweaked: a screensaver changed, a table moved. But with Geneva, I was only worried about being late because it would mean not getting to see the excitement of the doors opening, and how well everyone performed. It felt like coaching Will and Lizzey in soccer. When they were young, I coached their teams. Then, when they got older and moved into different leagues, I got the privilege of showing up at gametime and watching from the stands.

I stood there in Geneva, a proud parent of a store—and a team—that was firmly in a league of its own. I watched them execute flawlessly, embodying the ethos of enriching lives. I spoke to customers, too—of course—and while that energized me, by the time we left to catch our 8:00 p.m. train out of the Geneva Cornavin station, I was fried. I knew we had another long day coming—Zurich would open in fourteen hours—and I looked forward to doing what I always did on trains and planes: planting myself in a seat and falling asleep. Then, when I stepped onto the train to Geneva, I realized why Bob had seemed hesitant to celebrate my birthday in Chamonix.

The train car I walked into was covered in decorations. A banner with "Happy Birthday, Ron" was hung from the luggage compartment. The cabin was filled with people who had supported the launch but also people who hadn't—team members I hadn't seen as much recently, given how busy we were. The feeling could not have been more foreign: as a retailer, I had dedicated my life to planning for others, and it was strange to think that anyone would've planned anything for me. But if anything, it was a reminder of how much this team did that I didn't know about—how my plans for Apple's customers were only possible because of the sophisticated plans put together by those around me. I had spent years keeping an eye on them only to realize that now, they were keeping an eye on me.

As a birthday gift to me—and a gift to those on the train—Denise performed a song she knew I loved: "For Good" from the musical *Wicked.* She picked the song precisely because of its meaning: the people we encounter show us who we can be, and our relationships with them make us who we are. And sitting on that train, I was overwhelmed by the scope and depth of the relationships we'd built. I thought about my team, about Steve, about Apple. I thought about Apple's relationships with its customers—nearing a hundred million, now—and imagined the relationships yet to come. The impact we'd had on the world was clear, but I was taken aback by this unexpected view of what I'd meant to the team. I was also realizing, for perhaps the first time, that they no longer needed me.

Raising the stores had always felt like parenting. The stores were Steve's and my children, but their people were mine. And like Will and Lizzey, I tried to raise them as best I could. I tried to give team members the space to make decisions—some good, some bad—so they could learn to make better decisions. I tried to give those in each store the space to make memories out of mistakes, and meaning out of memories. I also had the benefit of a leader in Steve who made my kindness look downright heroic, especially early on; I was the one who everyone knew was keeping them "safe" from his outbursts—an internal defender, a light in the dark. And as I sat there reminiscing about Steve—thinking about the debates over who would present to him first at Bubb Road, or the angst of the moments after Northshore Mall, or the fun, albeit desperate attempts to sell computers after his 2002 outburst, I realized just how far we'd come. The initial twenty-five stores felt like a lifetime ago and three hundred stores felt inevitable. Apple Retail could continue getting bigger because the team had grown up.

Still, I remained focused on what I had outlined so many years earlier: ensuring that getting big wouldn't have to mean *feeling* big. I maintained—and still maintain—that staying small is as much an organizational trait as it is a mindset: a team's tendency not to withhold information, but to share it, to communicate. As anyone who has ever been in a poor relationship knows, the size of a team has almost no bearing on how playing on that team feels. A small, two-person team can feel painfully slow, sluggish, and unfamiliar, but a big, communicative team can feel dynamic, powerful, and still *small.* Everything we were doing was proof. Apple Retail had tens of thousands of employees by 2008, but we were innovating at a clip that was unimaginable to other retailers. We could continue to grow while maintaining a "small" feel. It would just be, as success had once been, a matter of will.

And yet, there was something nagging at me, too. I knew that building higher would depend on a stable foundation; I also knew that the one beneath my feet was starting to shake. Steve was getting sicker, yes—visible weight loss was leading to questions about his health, and he would take six months of formal leave come January 2009 to address complications related to liver and kidney function. But the bigger part was that running the stores, which had been endlessly creative work, was becoming an operational challenge, which was less appealing. It had taken us 660 days to sell a million iPods, then 74 days to sell a million 2G iPhones, then *three days* to sell a million 3G iPhones. I had come to Apple to help Steve reach the 95 percent, but with the streets abuzz with people in white corded headphones and the iPhone a global phenomenon, it felt like the company was set up for success whether I was here or not. My journey at Apple wasn't over, to be clear. But it was evident to me that I was, perhaps, on its final leg.

In the meantime, I had to find a way to inspire a team that had done what felt like everything to do even more than that.

□

Steve used to get credit for rallying his team around missions—say, by pitting the Macintosh team against big, bad Microsoft; the Rebel Alliance to their Galactic Empire. I had no such enemy to pit us against—we wouldn't be competing with our resellers so much as growing with them. But I did understand that retail stores could get weighed down by protective, "this is how we've always done it" thinking, and pulled back to earth. Gravity exerted its force on all things. Crashing back to Earth was inevitable.

Except, was it? Maybe it was Denise's singing of a song from *Wicked* on that train that inspired me to think it wasn't. Maybe it was the reminder of Idina Menzel closing out the show's first act with a song that had, when I first heard it, made me want to leap out of my seat and cheer. Maybe it was the way she described herself and Kristin Chenoweth as the greatest team there'd ever been that made me think similarly about Apple Retail. And maybe it was all of that coalescing in my imagination that delivered me the "enemy" I was now going to pit us against: the invisible force we were going to defy.

Gravity.

It didn't matter that the world economy was, as of 2008, on the brink of collapse. It didn't matter that every other retailer was hunkering down and planning to weather the storm. All that mattered was what I knew: that we *were* the greatest team there had ever been, and we *were* going to defy gravity. For the next several years, at least. And in those years, we would help even more people around the world define the word my dad had once challenged me to define: *significance*. The team we'd built, the landlords we'd met, the cities and governments we'd found ourselves in front of . . . many of them *wanted* to do significant things. And sitting there on the train celebrating with my team, I realized that helping people do significant things . . . well, maybe that was what I'd always wanted; maybe that was what I'd always sought.

Maybe that was the true definition of significance.

CHAPTER 12

People Want to Do Significant Things

When our 2008 store conference kicked off in September, I didn't just have defying gravity as the theme. I also had it sung. By Kristin Chenoweth. She attended the conference and performed for our retail field and headquarters employees—now a team of nearly six hundred strong.

At that conference, I had processed some of my thinking from the train ride for my fiftieth birthday. I knew that success in the years that followed would require pushing leadership down to those below me. I also knew how busy the stores were, and understood that for them to be successful, their leaders needed to empower their teams like I'd empowered mine. Every hour has its leader, I explained to the audience of store leaders, and every leader has their time. When employees were speaking to customers, *they* were the leaders. Creating a leadership culture wasn't about taking on more responsibility. It was about giving it away.

It was Emerson who wrote that if you trusted men, they would be great to you, and that if you treated them greatly, they would show themselves great. By 2008, my entire team was proving him right. It felt like a new form of significance revealed itself every day. Bob had been navigating excruciating conversations with landlord Victor Comino over a store on George Street in Sydney by convincing him to buy the building across the street—which Victor later leased to Louis Vuitton. Cano had been figuring out China with John alongside operationalizing everything I wanted to put in practice. Jerry was navigating the minutiae of local payment processing regulation around the world and pulling all-nighters to ensure that international carriers were set up to handle the demand that would flood them once the iPhone launched in their country. Denise was ensuring that the pressure the demand was placing on the stores didn't tear holes in the fabric of our culture, and was beginning to explore something unprecedented in retail: expanding full-time benefits to part-time employees. Everyone's genius was being revealed. Everyone was at their best at their busiest.

In the meantime, there was still *plenty* for me to do. The Switzerland store openings had coincided with the September 2008 collapse of Lehman Brothers, and the world, already teetering on the brink of a financial crisis, was about to plunge directly into it. One of a leader's most important jobs is encouraging their team to meet the moment, and I had always found that the best way to do this was by telling the truth. Things, I explained to the team, were likely to get worse in the economy, worse for our customers, worse for our employees. But we would still act decisively. We would focus on what we had established. We would reduce openings in 2009 to twenty-five from the fifty we'd done in 2008, rolling out fewer—but more significant—stores around the world. Bob and I had been working with cities around the world to design those stores. Launching them was, quite literally, an act of defying gravity.

Perhaps the most notable store we opened in 2009 came in France. As far back as when Fifth Avenue opened, Steve had been keen on us having our own building built from the ground up in Paris. But as much as we had looked, nothing was available. There was, however, a retail area our team found in a subterranean arcade that connected the most significant museum in the world, the Louvre, with what was then a secret entrance known mostly to Parisians. The arcade was known as the "Carrousel du Louvre," and as we toured it and saw the space, I thought it could work. But as we walked out of the arcade and into the space beneath the Louvre's inverted glass pyramid, I saw a space that might work better.

"What about *that?*" I'd asked, two fingers pointing at an occupied space adjacent to the glass pyramid. The Louvre director looked at me skeptically.

"Ze food court?" he asked.

I nodded.

"Not possible," he said, the accent dripping from his words.

"But wouldn't it be great if it *was?*" I asked, my eyes boring into his.

Nothing was decided that day, but now that I had seen what I believed was possible, we were going to make it work.

In the weeks that followed, Bob and I worked with Karl Backus, who reported to Peter Bohlin and was the lead architect of all our "significant" stores, to develop a plan for what we imagined. We discussed what the Louvre team would be concerned about and how to address it. We even built a full-scale model of what we imagined, then set it up in the basement of the Louvre and covered it with red cloth in preparation for the big reveal.

When we presented to the Louvre team, I explained that it was our intent to bow to the Louvre's heritage—to honor it by *marrying* it with technology. Our store would bring a new layer of reverence to an already revered location, as well as new and talented technology people into the museum. I could see the nods, the lights emerging in their eyes. Finally, sensing the moment was right, I pulled the red cloth off our model. Oohs and aahs emerged from the Louvre team. The director lit up, too.

"Let us dream," he said.

And dream we did.

The store we dreamt of—and designed—was truly astonishing. Two floors in the basement of the most significant art museum in the world connected by a spiral glass staircase. The Louvre's inverted glass pyramid visible from the inside. Even in renderings, it was magical. There was no other word to describe it.

Bob's team would spend the next year building the store. During that time, we also rolled out updates to One to One. Denise's team had been hard at work finding more creative people (and renaming trainers to "Creatives" probably helped), and now, for $99/year, customers could get access to several different services. One was Personal Setup, which entitled members to the configuration of one new Mac over the duration of their membership (data transfer, software setup, etc.). Then there were Personal Training Sessions, Personal Projects, and One to One Workshops. People had been coming in for years to get help creating photo books for weddings, or personal movies, or music mixes. As much as we were encouraging people to be creative, we were also responding to the human impulse to create.

A few months after launching the revamped One to One, Denise's team had finished hiring for our Louvre store, and Bob's team had completed work on construction. Then, a few days before we were scheduled to open, I got a surprise from a team member I hadn't been hearing from quite as much lately—Khawaja. A little over a year earlier, two months after we'd launched the iPhone, we'd also launched the (Wi-Fi capable) iPod Touch, and I'd asked Khawaja why we weren't using it to do mobile checkout. He told me there wasn't a reason; we could—but it would take time. Now, over a year later, Khawaja's team had delivered. There were still kinks to be worked out, but mobile checkout via iPod Touch was ready for the Louvre launch. We called the idea "EasyPay," and it had started with Khawaja in 2004, reached me, and then reached Steve. Eight years into running the stores, it showed me the power of staying small.

The night before the Louvre was scheduled to open, I did one last walkthrough. Everything was perfect, save one thing: the entrance. The spiral staircase was in the center of the store, with a cash wrap immediately adjacent to it. I could see the checkout line limiting access to the second floor and creating a bottleneck for those entering. With EasyPay set to go, the fix would be easy—and it was one I'd wanted to implement for twenty-five years.

Get rid of the cash wrap.

I found Khawaja in the back of the store at 10:00 p.m. the night before and explained what needed to be done. Then I wrapped my arm around him.

"Are we ready?" I asked. "Do we have an iPod Touch for every employee?"

"Yes," he said.

"Let's go!" I exclaimed. "*Allez!*"

The following morning at 9:45 a.m., cheers erupted in the halls of the Carrousel du Louvre as our employees, clad in red t-shirts, ran through it and into our store. Just after 9:59 a.m., a countdown echoed through the atrium beneath the Louvre's inverted pyramid as people and press stood gathered outside. And when the doors opened and customers flooded the store, mobile checkout via iPod Touch worked flawlessly. Traffic flowed seamlessly up and down the stairs. Perfect store, perfect execution.

This was becoming the norm.

After the Louvre opened, I thanked Khawaja for his work. I also thanked Jerry. But what I was really trying to articulate wasn't so much gratitude as a sense of solidarity—this feeling that we weren't separate.

"What I love about you, Jerry, is I just say it and it's done," I told him. This would've been about ensuring our compliance with local payment processing regulation in France, which made mobile checkout via iPod Touch possible. But there were so many other things he'd done that he hadn't burdened me with, and while I thought I knew how hard he'd been working—how hard *everyone* had been working—I didn't. I couldn't. And this benefitted me. Leading takes belief, and doubt saps it. Jerry knew I didn't want reasons to doubt what we were capable of. I think everyone on the team knew. So, they didn't give them to me. Or maybe I just chose not to see them.

By the middle of 2009, I believed—correctly, I would argue—that I was planted firmly where I'd always wanted to be: a culture in which genius can emerge, in which there are no limits. The limit, I told the team, was our imagination. In the iPhone, we finally had the product that would help us reach the 95 percent. In the iPod Touch, we had another one. With the updates to One to One, Personal Shopping, and eliminating the cash wrap, we'd gotten better in the stores. Mountains of obstacles had once felt like speed bumps, but now I wasn't feeling them at all.

We were flying.

□

It had never felt inevitable that Apple would succeed—especially in those early years. But by early 2009, Apple was, by every measure, a success. Demand felt like a given. Our share price, too, was up 1,700 percent from its low in 2002.

I never thought particularly hard about my own role in Apple Retail's success. There was no reason to. Everyone doubted us at first, so all I could do was focus on willing a vision no one else saw to success. All I wanted to do was be there with my team, for my team. If it did occur to me that my work would be perceived externally, it was in moments like the weeks leading up to Fifth Avenue, when my nervousness pushed me to think about what more we could do for customers, which led to keeping the store open twenty-four hours a day. My instinct whenever I've felt that something isn't good enough is that it isn't good enough for others—and to find ways to do more for them. That's why I love retail. It's always about doing more for someone else. It keeps me—it has always kept me—outside of myself, rooted in something bigger than myself. But in the fall of 2009, something happened that, strange though it may seem, put a mirror up in front of me.

My mom passed away.

Her passing came out of nowhere. She had just visited our family on the West Coast for her oldest granddaughter's graduation. She was at her absolute best on that trip—talking to everyone, taking us to dinner at Benihana, spending time with each grandchild. The only thing that had limited her was mobility: a bad knee. So, after returning to Minnesota, she decided that she wanted to get her knee replaced, which meant going off blood thinners she'd been on for years. Not long after the procedure, she had a stroke. A few days later, she was gone.

When a parent passes, there's always a moment when, in your wonderings about their legacy, you begin thinking of your own. The same thing happens in nature, too: when a fruit-bearing tree experiences the type of stress that it associates with its own mortality, it will produce more fruit than it did in previous years. It's as if a living organism's knowledge of its mortality spurns a desire to see itself continue on, to leave a legacy. My mom would be remembered for her kindness, her service to her family, and her undying loyalty to us, her kids.

How, I wondered, would people remember me?

At a store conference in the fall of 2009, I had processed some of this thinking. I had thought about the stores' culture of kindness and explained to the team that it was my mom who inspired it. It was hard to talk about it without getting choked up, and I saw the same mist in the eyes of my store leaders that I felt as I spoke about my mom. She was gone, but her impact would remain.

As I spoke to my team, I framed the year's success in terms of one of the things that had always mattered to my mom: serving others. That year, we'd served 170 million customers. We'd also seen 2.5 million people for the updated version of One to One, up from one million the year prior. Coupled with the eight million people who had received product support, I told the team, that meant 10.5 million people—or, the entire city of Paris—had visited our family rooms for training or gotten help at a Genius Bar. And even though we didn't grow on a per-store basis that year, we still grew—albeit slower—just like I'd said we would, and unlike virtually every other retailer in the world, whose 2009 sales were marked by double-digit declines.

Meanwhile, the success of stores like Fifth Avenue and George Street had been attracting attention from city governments who wanted to do what we had done in their cities. In 2010, we opened a three-story store in London's Covent Garden, having pitched ourselves as the tenant that could reinvigorate the space by blending old and new. Bob, Peter, and Karl had worked tirelessly on the store design, knowing we were battling to unseat Abercrombie as the space's tenant. When we'd unveiled a physical model of our plans, a hush had fallen over the room. The decision was obvious. We were inevitable.

Later in 2010, we also launched our store in Pudong, China—a glass cylinder that we positioned as a figurative "splash" emerging from our store being dropped, like a pebble into water, at the center of a new development in the city. Angela King had led the presentation of the design, and the leader of the development, Raymond Kwok—who we had initially struggled to get in front of—was so enamored with it that he decided right then and there that he wanted a store like this in every one of his centers. Then he looked directly at his team of leasing agents, who had been skeptical of what betting on us would mean for their relationships with luxury retailers like Cartier, Louis Vuitton, and Prada, and told them, in no uncertain terms, exactly what to do.

"Figure out whatever you need to do to achieve this and make it so!" he exclaimed. Then he thanked us for our perseverance.

That gratitude reinforced everything I had come to believe: As a leader, it was my job to lead people through the anxieties, to be the means by which the greatness of others revealed itself. As creators, it was in our DNA to improve things.

"Never let people be skeptical," I had said to the team in 2008. "They will get in the way of your creativity."

Of course, by 2010, the external skeptics were all but gone. Everyone seemed to want to work with us—even the authorities we had to present to in Shanghai to get final approval for our store in Pudong. When they saw the pebble-in-water idea, they didn't just sign off on it. They changed their entire pedestrian circulation plan to create a corresponding circular walkway around Pudong's primary intersection. Seeing this happen, I couldn't help but think about people who walked around believing there were limits to what they could accomplish as a business, or a person, or a country. There weren't—or at least, there didn't seem to be. There were no limits to our success, either.

Around that same time, Raymond had brought us another opportunity: Hong Kong's IFC Mall. Already one of the biggest and most valuable pieces of real estate in China, the opportunity was nothing if not significant. I sent Bob to do a site visit, and as he left it, he noticed that he was staring out at Victoria Harbour, which separated Hong Kong island from the Kowloon Peninsula. Wondering why he hadn't seen that same view from inside the mall, he turned back to look at it. The mall's entire harbor-facing facade, he realized, was covered up.

That night, Bob called me and said something that sounded like what I would say.

"Wouldn't it be great if that whole facade was open to Victoria Harbour?"

Of course, my answer was yes. By 2010, the answer was always yes. We pitched the idea—a glass facade that would give people in the Apple Store an incredible view of Hong Kong, and people arriving in Hong Kong an incredible view of Apple—to Raymond. He loved it. Executing it required moving mountains—literally, a half dozen tenants—but Raymond shared our vision and helped us realize it. In 2008, it had felt like we were caught in a hurricane.

Now, we had become the storm.

□

2010 was chaotic. It was also the year that proved to me why Apple had launched stores in the first place.

My push for eliminating physical checkout with the iPod Touch had been met with skepticism when I'd started making it in 2008, but in April 2010, Apple launched a new product that made it look genius: the iPad. Giving a significantly faster mobile checkout experience to every employee enabled them to manage the demand. Hundreds of employees filled our busiest stores, each with their own iPod Touch to check customers out. The iPad couldn't have done the numbers it did without every employee's ability to check customers out in the store. But of course, the stores wouldn't have had employees to give iPods to without Denise's work to keep people happy—and attract talent.

This had proven to be one of the biggest challenges of the last few years, and it was part of why Denise had been exploring extending full-time benefits to part-time employees. We needed more smart, capable people in every corner of every store; more specialists would help us address demand for products, more creatives would help more Apple customers create, and more Geniuses would help us address more customers' questions. It had gotten to a point where we couldn't build Genius Bars big enough; one of the ideas we'd pitched to Raymond at IFC Hong Kong was that the store could have the biggest Genius Bar in the world: *ninety* seats. But what might've seemed gratuitous was, in fact, necessary. Our busiest store, Fifth Avenue, had taken five years to do $500 million in annual revenue. IFC Hong Kong would do it in twelve months.

The chaos of 2010, it turned out, had been somewhat of a long time coming. When the original iPhone launched in 2007, it had issues. Sometimes it failed to activate via iTunes. Other times, its buttons didn't work, or its speaker was defective, or its cellular radio failed upon activation. And it wasn't just customers who had purchased at the Apple Store who were frustrated, but those who had purchased at an AT&T store, too. The Apple Store was the only place where customers could get support, and the Genius Bars were already full of customers with Mac questions. The priority, as of 2007, was to relieve pressure at the Genius Bar while keeping first-time

Apple customers happy. This led to an internal retail initiative that we called "Get to Yes."

The idea behind the initiative was as simple as it sounds: get customers to say "yes" when asked if they'd recommend us to friends and family. And at first, it was a relatively simple endeavor. If a customer came in with a defective handset, we replaced it for free. There had also been a small percentage of customers who had been dealing with an equally frustrating issue: cracked screens. But getting to yes with them, while costly on a per person basis, wasn't terribly expensive for Apple; the original iPhone's glass screen was surrounded at the edges by a metal bezel, so while screens did crack, they didn't do it often. The same was true of the iPhone 3G (launched in July 2008) and the iPhone 3GS (launched in July 2009), both of which had rounded plastic backs. Unfortunately, it really wasn't true with the iPhone 4, which launched in June 2010.

The iPhone 4 was a monument to beauty and performance. It had flat, squared-off edges, a glass front and back, and a stainless-steel frame. It also had a gorgeous high-resolution Retina display and Apple's first front-facing camera, which enabled a new feature: FaceTime. And specialists were excited to show customers how to FaceTime friends in the store. The problem was that when people tried to FaceTime their friends, they found that the iPhone 4 would randomly drop the call.

As it turned out, the issue wasn't random. It was the design. The iPhone 4's cellular antenna had been built into the stainless-steel band that wrapped around the phone, and when customers held it in a certain—and very normal—way, they lost service.

The issue was dubbed "Antennagate," and it was the stuff of nightmares. Recalling the phone would've been tantamount to admitting defeat in our battle with Android for market share, so we needed a solution—and fast. Eventually, we found one. Some customers reported that putting a case on the phone fixed the call dropping issue. Apple developed a "bumper" case that wrapped around the edge of the phone without obscuring the beauty of its all-glass design, and I advocated that we give it away. A few weeks later, Steve announced that any customer with an iPhone 4 could come into the store and get one for free. He had given another masterful demonstration of how to handle a PR crisis, too.

"You know, we're not perfect," he said. "Phones aren't perfect, either. But we want to make all of our users happy."

But of course, the iPhone 4's antenna wasn't its only issue. I'm not sure who figured out that a case would keep the phone from dropping calls, but I can't help wondering if the solution didn't reveal itself to someone who was trying to address another issue with the iPhone 4's design: fragility. It might not have been such a problem if not for two other things—first, that the device itself looked so good "naked," and second, that its glass was branded as "30 times harder than plastic," so customers were given every reason to believe they didn't need to cover it up. But as everyone was learning, they did. The iPhone 4 had an all-glass back and didn't have metal bezels at the edge of its screen. When people dropped it, one—or both—tended to shatter.

In July 2010, the stores became the front line between customers and Apple's second PR crisis in a month. AppleCare didn't yet offer accidental damage protection, so the typical repair cost for a cracked screen was $199. This felt crazy to me. We were locked in a battle for the future of the phone, had just released one that couldn't reliably make calls without being held a certain way, and now, when customers realized it *also* couldn't survive a drop from four feet, we were going to tell people that they had to pay $199 to fix it?

I had a different idea: repair their phones for free.

Now, internally, I was certain that this decision wouldn't be popular. But the calculus in my head was simple. At a time when Samsung, HTC, and Motorola were growing as they shipped an increasing number of Android devices, the word of mouth about the iPhone 4—our *only* device—could not be that it dropped calls, shattered, *and* was expensive to repair. The idea that we were going to charge customers to fix a device that was breaking because of how we had designed it was simply not acceptable. But of course, to some at Apple, neither was the idea of fixing devices for free.

Not long after the iPhone 4 launched, I walked into an ET meeting. Phil followed me in.

"What the hell are the stores doing giving away repairs?" he asked.

"Good morning to you, too," I said.

"I'm serious," he said. "We can't do this."

"We have to."

"We don't," he said. "*Customers* are breaking the phones. That's on *them*."

"Phil," I said. "If we design a phone that breaks when it's dropped from four feet, that's not on the customer. That's on *us*."

"Tell them to buy a case!"

I was about to say something when Steve walked in. He looked at Phil, then at me. We both fell silent.

Steve dropped by my office after the meeting.

"What was that earlier?" he asked.

"I decided not to charge customers to repair broken iPhones," I said. "Phil didn't like it."

"What's your thinking?" Steve asked.

It was as if my entire personal geography unfolded in front of me in that moment. I could see my mom's emphasis on service, my dad's on doing the right thing for people. I knew that Phil believed he was protecting Apple's brand, but when I thought about the great brands

I knew, I didn't think of those that looked to absolve themselves of responsibility. I thought of those that looked for ways to take on more of it. And one brand in particular—a department store—stuck out to me.

Nordstrom.

Back when I had been at Mervyn's, my boss had told me that a Nordstrom clerk offered to have her brand-new Mercedes repainted after learning that it had been keyed in their parking lot. That story had always stuck with me, and I found myself thinking that if we repaired phones for free, people would tell everyone in their lives a similar story about Apple.

And yet, there was another question: would we repair phones only for those who had purchased them from us, or for those who might've bought from AT&T, too? Here, I recalled another story—this time about a customer who had walked into Nordstrom with a Goodyear tire, insisted they'd purchased it there, and told the clerk they'd wanted to return it. The kicker, of course, was that Nordstrom had never sold tires, but *they took it back* anyway—and that story had proliferated forever. If they were willing to take back a product they had never sold, we had to help *every* customer with a shattered iPhone. And if Nordstrom had once paid to repaint a *car,* we could pay to repair phones.

Still, just because we *could* do this didn't mean we should. Steve echoed Phil's concern about the expense. I told him to trust me—I'd figure it out. In the meantime, I got Steve to agree with me that eventually, Jony would figure out how to design a phone that was less prone to shattering, and Tim's team would get us the parts to repair the phones for free until he could. If this was my intuition speaking, its voice was some marriage of values and context. Winning the battle with Android would require the same tactic that I'd once believed would help us win the battle over the future of the PC: service. NPS data would prove how powerful addressing a customer's negative experience was, too. Those who had a bad experience with Apple resolved in a store were *seven times more likely* to recommend us than those who simply had a good experience. Delivering a great experience mattered, but repairing a bad one arguably mattered more.

As a leader, you often have to balance doing things that are popular externally—and giving away free iPhones was—with their being unpopular internally. But what I believe happened, at least in this instance, was that culture influenced policy; by the end of the following year, Apple would update AppleCare such that it covered accidental damage. In the meantime, yes, the stores were *supposed* to enforce Apple's policy of charging customers $199 for a broken screen. But, as I explained to store leaders, it wasn't our job to be the policy police for Apple. Some readers may have experienced this first-hand with a Genius looking for any opportunity to repair (or exchange) an iPhone for free—say, by running its serial number, finding that it was associated with a battery recall, and asking the customer, with a wink and a nod, if they'd been noticing their iPhone dying faster than usual. The simple truth was that I liked leading stores that tried to do right by customers. And I was proud of having created a culture in which Geniuses were led not by policy, but by their own inner voice.

Of course, this isn't to say that a customer-first culture wasn't hard on the store teams. It was, and I knew it. I knew that Geniuses appreciated variety in their work and that spending a significant part of their day replacing screens wasn't their favorite; I knew that store leaders had been relying heavily on part-time help without the ability to offer the same benefits we were giving to our full-time people. But I *also* knew what Denise had been working on, and at a store conference in the fall of 2010, she got up on stage and announced what many in retail thought they'd never hear: that we *would* now be extending full-time benefits to part-time employees. In light of the chaos of the last few years (and particularly the last few months)—the packed Genius Bars, the overflowing stores, the emphasis on getting to yes and enriching lives and being compassionate and kind with customers who sometimes weren't—the reaction was as overwhelming as it was expected. Hundreds of store leaders leapt from their chairs to give us a standing ovation. Many were in tears. There were a lot of magical moments during those years, but that one felt different.

In the years that followed, this extension of benefits would unlock even more magic in each Apple Store. Yes, the stores were able to hire more Geniuses to address customer issues and more specialists to keep up with demand. But they also attracted more creative people by offering what most part-time jobs didn't: health insurance. Suddenly, our Creatives weren't just people who understood GarageBand or Final Cut Pro. They were true creative professionals who helped us further realize Steve's dream of stores filled with interesting people. The Grove employed Hollywood writers who might've once drafted scripts on our computers. Fifth Avenue employed Broadway performers who might've once found a home—at 3:00 a.m.—in our twenty-four-hour store. These people embodied Apple's ethos and our mission: that the truest way to enrich a life was to create something with someone else. We revealed Apple's genius through the relationships we built with customers. Enriching lives wasn't just something we said, but something we lived.

In the end, I'm not sure what would've happened with Apple during the iPhone 4 if the stores hadn't existed. Maybe the company would've been fine. Maybe the brand was strong enough to withstand Antennagate and a shattering device without retail behind it. But I was proud to be part of an organization that did what I thought was right for customers and for the brand. I pushed hard, but I was on a mission. We all were. And I was overjoyed to be able to say that on September 25, 2010—my birthday—we not only opened seven stores in seven different countries, but also reached the milestone that so many had once thought we wouldn't: three hundred stores. It had been an ambitious goal, but its pursuit revealed who we were. The crazy ones. The round pegs in the square holes. The people on a mission to enrich lives.

□

Every part of me wishes the story ended here. But it doesn't. And understanding why requires understanding everything else that was going on at that time.

First, I knew that everything I'd done happened in decades. I'd spent my thirties at Target helping the brand better compete with Walmart, and my forties at Apple helping the company reach the 95 percent. My fifties were a chance to do something new, something different, something significant. And what that could mean was shaped by everything that was being done around me at Apple.

By 2011, we had run out of superlatives to describe our success. In 2010, Best Buy—who sold everything we did and a million things we didn't—was doing approximately $1,000 per square foot. That year, Apple Retail touched *$5,000* per square foot. We also welcomed over a million visitors—*every single day.* Then, in 2011, we launched a formal version of the program that had emerged from Duke's stores years earlier: Personal Setup. Some within Apple questioned why, as busy as we were, we would try to get busier. To me, the answer was obvious. Mervyn's had once been busy, and now it was gone. The same was true for CompUSA, and Blockbuster, and Circuit City. The right to exist as a retailer wasn't guaranteed. We had to keep innovating, keep finding new ways to serve customers, keep finding ways to enrich lives. Good things happened when people came to the store, and it was our job to give them more reasons to come.

Personal Setup proved itself immediately. Customers could come in and get any product they purchased set up—Mac, iPod, iPad, iPhone, or Apple TV—but amid our battle with Android for market share, it was the ability to deepen customers' relationships with their iPhones immediately that made the program indispensable. And people *loved* it. After a week, 90 percent of customers who bought a product in an Apple Store were leaving with it set up. And for those who just wanted to buy something, we would soon debut another solution: checkout via UPC code. People would be able to come in, open their Apple Store app on their iPhone, scan a product's UPC code on their own (and pay for it), and walk out of the store with it. Some argued that people would "rob us blind," but I didn't agree, and we could get security to address it if they did. The point was that our people would be freed up to do what only people *could* do: launch, deepen, and restore customer relationships. If someone only needed to transact, they could do it using our technology.

In the meantime, dozens of other significant stores were in development. We were expanding and remodeling spaces we had opened nearly a decade earlier on Santa Monica's Third Street Promenade and in Seattle's Bellevue Square. We were also putting the finishing touches on a store in Grand Central Terminal—our fifth store in New York City. Every day, it seemed, came with a new renovation, a new expansion, a new idea for something we could do. But as gratifying as it was to look out from the mountaintop, I missed being at the bottom. I missed the challenge of having taken over Target's home department as the brand struggled to compete with Walmart and figuring out a way to compete better. I missed the days when, far from operating an Apple Store, I'd been *imagining* the Apple Store. I missed the earliest days with my Edina West Cougars, dreaming about how it would feel to be at the state tournament and imagining what it would take to get there. I wasn't yet searching for anything new, to be clear. But the team at Apple had turned my work into a hobby, and I was open to a new beginning.

There had been a moment in that soccer season with my Edina West Cougars when, after imagining us getting to the state tournament, we'd gotten there, and in our semifinal game, I'd had a penalty kick to put us up early. But perhaps because all I'd imagined was *getting* to the state tournament, and not actually *winning* the state tournament, I found myself unprepared for the moment. I rushed my routine. I sailed the ball over the crossbar. Eventually, we lost—by one goal. I returned to that moment as the Apple Stores sat atop the retail world.

Never, I thought, would I allow anyone to be limited by their imagination.

As of early 2011, there was no limit to what I could imagine. I was open to what was next, what there was to do with all of our—of my—momentum. I was open to what was possible in a world in which everyone felt like a collaborator, a world in which everyone wanted to *be* a collaborator. I knew that excitement didn't have to be limited to Apple. It could extend to partners, to customers, to the world. Everything could get better. More resources could be freed up for innovation. The world seemed as if it had an inherent tendency to aggregate itself around people with passion—those "crazy ones" who Steve once said could change the world. Maybe, now, I had become one of them. Maybe *I* could do something that would change the world.

Maybe.

Had I spent more time lingering on this thinking, what came next might've played out differently—or not at all. I might've realized that I couldn't bottle the magic of what I'd created at Apple—that the culture here was not one I'd be able to take with me. But I didn't. I was ready for a new challenge—a "problem child" only I could adopt and only I could fix. After doing what felt like everything, I was ready for *another* thing, for the *biggest* thing, for one *more* thing.

Of course, you can't always control what opportunities find you. And another opportunity would find me. When it did, *significance*—the word my dad had once encouraged me to define, and the one I used to describe the meaning we created for our people, our customers, the world, and ourselves—would come to mean something very, *very* different.

CHAPTER 13

"How Much Success Do You Need?"

When I returned from Harvard for my second year of business school and narrowed my choice of destination down to Goldman and Mervyn's, I didn't immediately pick the latter. I took time. Six months.

During that time, I signed up for a retail field study.

The project's subject was a storied American institution: the department store. The historical background was the rise of specialty stores and big-box retailers amid post–World War II suburban flight. In a climate that seemed sure to kill the department store, our task was to reinvent it. It was my favorite project in business school, and as I worked on it, I met retail CEOs who had started in stores and made their way up, earning their way into a position in which they could serve others. I loved all of them, save one: a fellow named Boake Sells, who was then the CEO of the Dayton Hudson Corporation.

"There's only one question you should be asking," he told me.

"What's that?" I asked.

"'Can I become CEO of a retailer?'" he said.

The question stuck with me only because of how arrogant it felt to let myself ask it. I had no idea if I had what it took to be a CEO. I believed you had to earn your way into that position. I told Boake as much.

"I don't know if I have what it takes to be a CEO," I said. "It depends how I perform. Why?"

"What do you mean, 'Why?'" he asked. "You're a Harvard Business School guy! You *want* to be a CEO! We all do!"

If I'm capable, sure, I thought. But am I?

My mindset wasn't that I'd eventually be CEO. I didn't let myself think that way. At the time, I didn't even know if I'd be a good *merchant*! I thought I could probably lead a store, but all I really wanted to do was put my head down, do one job at a time, and let things play out as they would. But now, after twenty-five years, I realized that maybe I'd earned the opportunity to be a CEO; maybe I did have what it took.

Then, in 2011, I received a note from a recruiter.

□

At first, the scope of the opportunity, while interesting, felt limited. In October 2010, Pershing Square's Bill Ackman and Vornado's Steve Roth had disclosed a 27 percent stake in the same store that had laid its claim to the northeast corner of Southdale Center in 1972, the same store that I'd walked through for years as I'd sought ways to improve the men's shirts and ties department at Mervyn's and the kids' department at Target.

JCPenney.

As part of their investment, Bill and Steve had gotten JCPenney to expand its board from ten members to thirteen. They had each taken one of the three new seats, but the third—pending board approval—was left to fill. Bill asked if I'd be interested in it, and I was. Then he asked me if I thought the department store could be saved, and fresh off the Louvre, Covent Garden, Pudong, and countless other significant stores around the world, I told him what I believed.

"The department store can be *more* than saved," I said. "If someone has the courage to completely reinvent it, it can become significant again."

My answer might have surprised Bill and Steve, but it didn't surprise me. I'd always believed that department stores were significant. They had once been what the Apple Stores were now: places to belong. I associated significant moments—birthdays, graduations, engagements—with the department store. This may seem quaint now, but it's true.

A few weeks after meeting with Bill and Steve, they attended JCPenney's February board meeting, where they discussed my joining the board. Then, six days after that meeting, the CEO of JCPenney, Mike Ullman, severed his spine in a car accident. He survived, but the tenor of the discussions around my joining JCPenney shifted. The board was spooked into considering a succession plan. Now, Bill told me, the board was wondering if I'd be interested in joining as CEO.

My reaction was immediate and unequivocal.

Yes.

Leading JCPenney felt like a new beginning and a *huge* challenge—*exactly* what I was looking for. And when I spoke to people about it—my pastor, John Ortberg, and close friend Peter Stamos—they wondered if it wouldn't also give me the chance to embody my faith. I had been blessed, and now I could be a blessing;

I had been given much, and now I could give back. My roots, too—Southdale, Mervyn's, Target . . . I was, at my core, a retailer. I loved the idea of finishing where I started.

Once Ullman recovered from his car accident, I flew out to Plano, Texas, to meet him. We spoke for several hours. I was struck by how different his leadership style was from what I knew. At Apple, we did everything via email. Mike used pencils and notepads. At Apple, anyone could attend a meeting or air an idea. In Mike's ET meetings, only certain people were allowed to speak. He even had different-colored notepads for different teams. Yellow for his executives. Blue for their direct reports.

"I pay more attention to the yellow ones," he said.

If I hadn't been so caught up in believing that I was being called to reinvent—and save—the department store, maybe I would've paid more attention to this clear cultural difference between Apple and JCPenney. Instead, I found myself seeking reasons to confirm what I already believed. Then, toward the end of our meeting, Mike gave me one.

"Fifty percent of Americans shop at JCPenney once a year," he said.

Wait, I thought. *What?* If the average American shopped at JCPenney once a year, that meant half of Americans were within reach of their stores. Now, if we could just get them to shop *twice* a year . . .

I thought of everything we'd done at Apple, all the initiatives that drew people in the store not once but over and over again. And JCPenney wasn't a store that sold technology people bought once a year. This was a store that sold things people needed *all the time.* Getting people to shop more than once a year seemed . . . *easy.*

A few weeks later, I traveled out to Plano, where I met each member of JCPenney's board. Many of them expressed how excited they were about the opportunity to change. Or maybe it was just a few. It didn't really matter. *I* was excited about the opportunity for JCPenney to change, and so it was that excitement that I chose to see. When I received a formal offer to become CEO of JCPenney, I was ready to go.

Not long after, I called Steve.

"There's something I need to talk to you about," I said.

"What's up?"

"Well . . . It's going to be a tough conversation."

Steve knew what it would be. There was only one thing it could be.

"Come on over," he said. "Let's discuss it in person."

□

By May 2011, Steve's cancer had further metastasized. Tim had taken over day-to-day leadership duties at Apple. Steve was still CEO by title, but he was spending more and more time at home.

For Steve, home was a single-story brick house on a quiet suburban street in Palo Alto. Unlike the house of a typical, high-profile CEO, Steve's had no security. I'd visited countless times over the years—several times with Mike Fisher to discuss windows, other times with Bob to review store designs. Most recently, I'd been there with architect Rafael Viñoly to discuss designs for the new Stanford hospital that I'd been championing as a board member of Stanford Medicine. Some of the most meaningful conversations I ever had with Steve took place in that house. This would be our most meaningful conversation yet.

I got there and parked on a side street, then walked along the driveway behind the house. The back door was unlocked, as it always was. I pressed the handle and walked in. Laurene was often there when I arrived, but that day she was out—working or walking, I'm not sure. I also wasn't sure where I'd find Steve. With his health hanging in the balance, every day was different. Some days he was up and moving around. Others, he could hardly summon the strength to get out of bed.

"Steve?" I half said, half shouted. Words didn't carry in the old craftsman home.

"In here!" he replied. His voice was coming from the living room.

I followed it, walking into the cozy, dimly lit space. Its small windows and old light fixtures cast uneven light over beaten-in furniture. The living room gave me the same feeling every time I walked into it. This was a place people lived.

I sat down on a chair, Steve on the couch.

"So, what's up?" Steve asked.

"I've got an offer that's making me think it's time to leave Apple," I said. "JCPenney—they want me to be CEO."

"JC*Penney*," he said.

I could hear the faint note of surprise in his voice.

"Yeah."

"And you want to go."

"I do," I said. "I think it's time—with Apple Retail, I've done everything I came to do. *We've* done everything we wanted to do. This organization . . . It doesn't really need me anymore. But JCPenney—it does. And it's retail. It's everything I love. It's one last chance to reinvent the department store, to do what no one else has done."

There was an eternity in the pause that followed, and my imagination ran with all the ways Steve could fill it. But when he finally spoke, he wasn't upset. He was understanding, kind.

"I get it," he said quietly.

The words lifted a cinderblock off my chest.

"You do?"

"Yeah," he said. "I do. I know you love retail. I can understand wanting to leave after being here for twelve years."

"I'm so grateful for my time at Apple," I said. "I think this is the time to move on."

A few days later, a version of Steve many struggled to recognize delivered a Worldwide Developers Conference (WWDC) keynote at the Moscone Center. He spoke about the PC as the digital hub, explaining that the strategy built around that idea had run its course. I knew this from experience; both my iPhone and iPad could do music, photos, and video, and keeping my content synchronized across my devices could be a headache. The solution was a new service, iCloud, which would store people's content and push it to *all* their devices. Steve positioned it as a new beginning for Apple, and something that "just worked." I wasn't in the audience for that keynote, but if I had been, I would've smiled. Steve's quest for perfection was admirable. Still, if the iCloud experience was anything less, I knew a few thousand people ready to help.

By the end of the week, I had collected my thoughts on my future. I called Steve and told him I'd made up my mind: I was going to accept the offer to become JCPenney's next CEO. He asked when I would be announced, and I told him the following Tuesday, June 14. I had anticipated that this would be it, that this was the end, and almost found it natural when Steve invited me over again. Maybe we'd sit, relax, and talk about the good old days. But when I got there, it was clear he had something else on his mind.

"Guess it's my turn to have a tough conversation," he said. I felt a pit forming in my stomach. I knew what he was going to say, but every part of me hoped he wouldn't say it.

Then he said it.

"I'm not going to make it."

The words landed like a comet in my lap.

"I know Tuesday's the big announcement," he said. "But the doctors are saying I have six months."

There was a long pause before he looked up at me.

"Will you stay on until I pass?"

I never struggled for words, but at that moment, I did.

"Ron?"

"Of—course," I finally said, choking the words out. Then I said it again, steadier. "Of course."

I got up, said goodbye, walked out through the kitchen, the door, the garden. I felt empty. All the excitement was gone. I called Mike to explain that I'd be staying at Apple until Steve passed, which meant we'd need to announce that I wouldn't be starting as CEO of JCPenney in June but likely November. But when Mike announced this, his messaging wasn't clear; he said I was going to start by overseeing merchandising and marketing, which created confusion about whether I was actually going to be CEO. Ackman, who had been championing this transition for months, went ballistic due to the miscommunication. Still, the market seemed to get the message. When the day ended, JCPenney's stock was up 27 percent.

In the days that followed, the press descended on the story. I'd been glancing at Yahoo News in the months leading up to being announced as CEO, and there had been one story a month about JCPenney. Now, *every* story was about JCPenney. Every story was about *my leaving* for JCPenney. Many were supportive. Many more were surprised.

The *Apple* guy is going to JCPenney? The *tech* guy?

The thing was . . . I wasn't a tech guy. I had never been a tech guy. That was part of why the Apple Store worked! Retail was my first love. And JCPenney—well, now it could become the object of that love, the *ultimate* act of securing the good. For me, the opportunity wasn't just something worth leaving Apple for. It was the *only* thing worth leaving Apple for.

And yet, I couldn't help but think of the words Steve had shared with me only days earlier.

"The doctors are saying I have six months."

The eventual arrival of November 2011 took on a new—and unwelcome—significance.

Six months, I thought, until I'd start as CEO of JCPenney.

Six months until a world without Steve.

□

Steve, it turned out, was not the only one in my life battling illness. My dad was, too. For years, he'd been navigating a variety of cancers, and while they were under control for the time being, the long-term prognosis was grim. Still, he cared more about what I was experiencing than anything he was navigating, and I had been speaking to him every day, updating him on everything. I told him that my plan for the next six months was to spend a week each month getting to know the JCPenney teams. Then, when I formally joined as CEO in November, we could hit the ground running.

In June, a week after I was announced as CEO, I flew to Hong Kong with the JCPenney sourcing team. Mike had told me that they were the best in the world, and I believed him. But it wasn't true. They weren't *bad*, but they weren't the best. Zara's parent company, Inditex, was running circles around JCPenney. So were Gap and Target. But no one *within* JCPenney's sourcing team seemed willing to admit this. I mentioned things like this to my dad over calls and periodic visits to Minnesota, and his excitement—like mine—began gradually turning to apprehension. Still, his sense of humor and general ebullience never wavered. Our calls continued. I relished every one, trying to avoid thinking about how many I had left.

In July, I traveled to Plano and spent a week at JCPenney's headquarters. I had hoped to find out that my experience with the sourcing team was an outlier and that I'd be able to share some good news with my dad. It wasn't, and I wasn't. I met countless people as I shadowed Mike's daily routine. I listened as he told his teams that they were the best in the business, and that it was their customer—not JCPenney itself—that was struggling. And while I didn't blame Mike for trying to encourage and motivate his teams, I couldn't help but wonder: If they believed what Mike was telling them—that they *were* the best in the business—then why would they *want* to change? And who was I to suggest that they *should*?

Those thoughts turned to conviction after I traveled to New York City with JCPenney's merchandising team in August. We were there to visit suppliers—Ralph Lauren, Tommy Hilfiger—during Market Week, and the conversations echoed those I'd been listening to for months. My dad asked how they'd gone, and I was honest. I was honest with Mike, too.

"I don't think the teams want to change," I said.

"You're reading them wrong," he replied.

But I was certain I wasn't. I'd encountered skeptics at every company I'd worked for. Apple, Target, Mervyn's. More than knowing how skepticism looked, I knew how it *felt*. And every interaction I had with the JCPenney team felt like that. Every blank stare was a reminder that they didn't want this, that they didn't want me. I had seen myself as the hero. They saw me as the savior they didn't need.

Eventually, the doubt became overwhelming. I aired my concerns to Karen on a trip we took in August—less than ninety days from my scheduled start date as CEO of JCPenney.

"You've had such a great career at Apple," she said. "The kids are going into *great* years. These can be the best years of our life! I don't think you have to pursue another big career challenge down in Texas. *Especially* if you don't think they're up for the challenge!"

I nodded. But I'd already accepted the job, and I didn't want to go back on it.

When we got back to California, I spoke to my brother-in-law, Mark.

"Ron," he said. "I respect you. And I'll support whatever you want to do. But I don't understand Penney's."

I'm not sure I understood it, either. But Mark's words didn't dissuade me. Perhaps recognizing this, he recommended I talk to Apple board member Bill Campbell, who he was coaching Will's football team with. So, I did. Bill came over and we sat down in my backyard. He listened, as he was so good at doing, as I explained the doubts that had crept in since accepting the offer.

"Ron," he finally said. "You shouldn't do this."

"Why?" I asked.

"Well, you're beloved at Apple," he said. "But most importantly, you're a dad. Your kids need you."

"But the business opportuni—"

"I don't *care* if it's a great business opportunity," Bill said. "Your family doesn't need you to be a CEO. Will and Lizzey need their *dad*. Karen needs her *husband*."

I sat with his words for a while. I thought about how I could be the dad and husband I wanted to be and still be CEO of JCPenney. Then I called my dad. I knew that he would never tell me what to do, that he would simply ask questions.

I hadn't anticipated precisely how pointed his questioning would get.

"How much success do you need?" he asked. His tone was, as it had always been, genuinely curious. If anything, that made the question hit even harder.

"It's not about success," I said.

"What is it about?" he asked.

"Significance?" I ventured. The word felt hollow.

"What's more significant to you right now?" my dad asked. "Your family or JCPenney?"

I sat with that question through the afternoon, the evening, and well into the night. The following day, I'd made up my mind. Or so I thought.

I called Ackman.

"Bill," I said. "I'm not going to be able to do this."

"Ron," he said. "Ron, Ron, *Ron*. Where is *this* coming from?"

Where *wasn't* it coming from?

"The team isn't ready to change."

A long pause.

"Let me call you back," Bill said.

A minute passed. Two minutes. Then my iPhone rang.

"Bill?" I answered.

"We're having dinner tonight."

"What?"

"I'm flying out."

"No, you—"

"Pick a restaurant," he said. "Bring Karen if you want."

And then he hung up.

I stood there for a moment. Then I told Karen about the dinner, about Bill.

"I don't want to meet him," she said. And honestly, I didn't either. I knew what was going to happen, and I think she did, too. I was going to capitulate. That was the double-edged sword of wanting to make people happy. Great when interests overlapped. Not as great when they didn't.

Bill and I met at 7:30 p.m. at a French brasserie, Bistro Vida, in Menlo Park. It was a warm August evening, so we sat on the patio outside. The sun had just dipped below the single-story buildings on Santa Cruz Avenue.

"You're going to do *so well*," Bill said.

I shook my head and aired some of my doubts—about the people, about the lack of willingness to change. Bill listened intently, then stopped me.

"Ron," he said. "We've got three board members. And if you have to fire people, well, you fire people!"

I didn't want to tell him how much I hated firing people, so I just nodded.

"I'll be here to help you," Bill said. "I've got your back."

I remained silent.

"Listen," Bill said. "The board is meeting again in September. Come out for that, present, and you'll see how much support you have."

"Okay," I said.

The problem was that however much support I had, I didn't have my own.

I searched for it in everyone else. I asked my son, Will, what he thought, to which he reminded me that he was fourteen and not exactly in the position to guide me on this decision. Then I asked Lizzey. Maybe I went to her last because I thought she'd say what I already believed.

Then she said it.

"Dad," she said. "You can't back out now."

But, of course, I could. I just wasn't going to.

In that moment, I recall looking at Lizzey, sixteen, her entire life ahead of her. I thought back to pushing her through Walmart as a toddler, and to everything she'd done since: starring in musicals, singing the National Anthem at Stanford's basketball games. I could see every bit of myself in my daughter—the courage, the conviction, the enthusiasm. The tendency to believe she could make things work, to see possibility where others might've seen peril, to dream greatly, unreasonably, fearlessly.

What am I telling her if I *don't* go? I wondered. And if I *do* go . . . Am I not showing her—and Will—that their dad can take on a hard challenge? I sat with the thoughts, failing to recognize that the hardest challenge—at least for me, personally—wouldn't be to say yes but to say no.

"*I* think you should do it," Lizzey added.

I smiled, realizing how well I knew my daughter.

That's my Lizzey, I thought.

That night, visions flashed through my head. I saw my two-win Edina West Cougars at the *state tournament*, design at a *mass-market retailer*, a technology store that would win on *service and love*. These had been big, bold, *crazy* ideas. The only thing crazier would be trying to reinvent JCPenney.

In that moment, I decided I would do it. I'm not sure what pushed me over the line. Maybe it was not wanting to disappoint people. Maybe it was not wanting to disappoint *myself*. Or maybe it was something simpler: the need to answer a question no one else dared ask.

What could the department store become?

The following morning, I set myself to the task of figuring it out.

CHAPTER 14

When Vision Becomes Blinding

For the next two months, I imagined JCPenney's future. Outside of daily calls with my dad to share ideas, I did this largely alone.

I thought back to meetings with JCPenney's marketing team. At one point, they had run sixteen ads in *one week*. That wasn't true to James Cash Penney's vision of "one price for every customer." It was also hurting the company! Every sale required new signage, new marketing, new tags—and that meant endless work for the store teams.

The solution was to offer "everyday low prices."

I believed that everyday low prices had a chance to work for a few reasons. The first was that countless retailers were growing by offering it. Marshalls was one. Ross was another.

The second was my experience at Target. Bob Ulrich, the CEO while I was there, had tested entire stores of everyday low pricing in Texas, and it hadn't worked, so he'd shelved it. But when I'd done design, we had effectively reintroduced it—we just hadn't called it "everyday low prices." We had simply offered exceptional merchandise at the same price all the time—and the performance was *extraordinary.* Each of my six buyers in home had a sales number, gross margin number, inventory turnover number, and gross margin return on investment (ROI) number. The numbers represented competing priorities, so making two of the four was standard. For any buyer to make all four was rare. For *every* buyer to make all four was unheard of. But after launching design, all my buyers not only hit all their numbers—they *smashed* them. There was no reason, I thought, that the same couldn't be true for *JCPenney's* buyers.

JCPenney's customers were already getting every product at 60 percent off its sticker price. Sixteen ads a week, and the average customer—as I'd learned from Mike—shopped at JCPenney *once a year.* This made two things very clear. The first was that everyone was ignoring the ads. The second was that everyone was still getting the products at 60 percent off. So . . . why *wouldn't* we just offer the same prices JCPenney was spending millions to promote all the time? And if we did that, couldn't we get customers to shop way more than once a year? Wasn't that just . . . obvious?

To me, it was. And as I followed the logic, I found more ideas. The elimination of money spent on discounts—and additional cash flow generated by the increase in customer visits—would free up cash that we could invest into better merchandise, including brands that I had already begun working with.

Joe Fresh, Martha Stewart, Bodum.

Disney, Marchesa, Jonathan Adler.

Michael Graves.

We would reorganize a traditional department store into a series of a hundred unique specialty stores, which customers would navigate through wide, welcoming aisles. We could, I thought, even do a version of one of the great department stores—Selfridges—which I'd walked through numerous times when I worked at Target, and had now been walking through for years on trips to Europe with

Apple. This would bring a unique history to JCPenney—a pairing of old and new like what we had done at Apple with our Covent Garden store. Merchandise would be curated to create an experience. Every brand would be merchandised in its own shop, including the private labels that JCPenney had developed over the years. Sales of these products—along with faster inventory turns—would create more cash flow that we could invest in institutional advertising to introduce the new JCPenney. Except it would no longer be JCPenney. We would rebrand as JCP: America's Favorite Store.

Our streamlined presentation of brands would also enable us to create an open, airy space in the middle of the store for events. It reminded me of the plazas I'd visited in Europe. There was a plaza in front of Apple Covent Garden where people gathered, and we could create something similar at JCPenney. Our plaza—our "town square," as I took to calling it—would be like the Genius Bar: the soul of a store beloved not just for what it sold, but what it meant. We'd become an economic hub like Selfridges or Dayton's, but also a meaningful institution and cultural engine. And sure, we'd offer free haircuts for back to school; we'd be the place for formative childhood moments; we'd have a candy store for kids, and would offer, among other things, five round, colored chocolates wrapped in cellophane. But we would *also* use the trust and goodwill we generated to attract the best brands in the world and direct-to-consumer upstarts that would need physical retail to reach new customers. I could see it. All of it. And as I did, I saw something I had never previously seen nor sought: a world in which I had not only done something significant but also become someone of significance. Jim Cramer had once called me "America's Greatest Retailer." Now, I had the chance to prove him right.

As I imagined all of this, I grew increasingly confident.

This can *work*, I thought. I saw JCPenney's future like I'd once seen

Target's, or Apple's. And I was excited! I began seeing the types of connections that made America's Favorite Store feel inevitable. Truth and fairness were fundamental aspects of my faith, and as I thought more about the constant price changes at JCPenney, I decided that the company's coupon strategy was unfair, and truth began on the price tag. I didn't want people to have to get a PhD in our pricing strategy to get value in the store. I didn't want customers to wake up the day after having visited, see a flash sale, and realize they should've waited to shop. I wanted them to feel good about shopping at JCPenney all the time. If we told customers the truth and treated them fairly—if we modeled our store on the Golden Rule, on which James Cash Penney had *founded JCPenney*—every day could be a great day to shop!

Of course, I also wanted to make every day a great day to come to work—and they weren't. JCPenney's sales and coupons were a nightmare for employees. Signs on racks, shelves, and walls needed to be swapped out weekly, or even daily. Sometimes this needed to happen mid-shift—say, for a flash sale. More often, it took place late at night. Associates then had to double-check that the prices in POS systems matched the prices on the floor. If they didn't, associates then had to manually override prices to adhere to advertised signage. This led to frustrated customers. So did expired coupons. And the storewide 40 percent off sale not also qualifying for the special JCPenney cardholder discount. And the $10 off $50 coupon not applying to a $55 purchase because some of the items were brands versus private labels. And, and, and . . .

Everyday low prices would solve all of this. Customers could get the *products* they wanted at the *prices* they wanted *whenever* they wanted. Employees would be liberated from the monotony of managing sales and empowered to serve customers. JCPenney itself would be freed up to become what its founder had always imagined it to be: a store with one price for every customer. All of this would make

America's Favorite Store a reality. Calls with my dad took on a new significance. I was excited and so was he.

□

In September 2011, I went to the JCPenney board with a full presentation of my vision. I had been working on it now for a month. My first slide was full of once-familiar department store logos. Dayton's. Marshall Field's. Rich's.

"There used to be *sixty* department stores," I said. Then I tapped a key. Fifty-six logos disappeared.

"Now there are *four*."

I let the words hang in the air for a moment.

"JCPenney is one of those four," I continued. "But its stock is lower now than it was in 1963. And sure, there have been some ups and downs. But this is a company that has lost its way as others have come in. Specialty stores, off-price, online retail. *All* department stores are going away."

Having set the stage, I switched gears.

"But *going* away doesn't mean it has to *go* away," I said. "The department store can still win. But *for* us to win, we've got to learn to compete. And not just with the remaining department stores. We've got to compete with *everyone* in the retail landscape. Target. Walmart. *Amazon*. We have to have the courage to change. JCPenney has been around for a hundred years, and it can be around for a hundred more. But only if we're committed to making it America's Favorite Store."

I looked around the room.

"I need to know that you guys are up for this," I said. "I'm not coming to operate JCPenney. I'm not even coming to improve JCPenney. I'm coming to *transform* JCPenney."

"That's exactly what we want," one board member said.

Others nodded. I looked around at their faces, and though I was hearing what I wanted to hear, I wasn't seeing what I wanted to see. The light in their eyes was dim; the conviction in their nods, seemingly, forced. It felt like they were afraid, like my team had once been at Mervyn's.

Except, I thought, did it *really* matter?

No, I decided. I'll make it work.

For the next six weeks, I worked on a presentation of my vision for JCPenney to share with the company's rank and file upon my arrival in November. I filled open positions with those I trusted: Mike Kramer as chief operating officer, Mike Fisher as chief creative officer, Ben Fay as head of real estate and development, Dan Walker as chief people officer, and others. I also took the step of securing a space like the one we had on Bubb Road at Apple. JCPenney's store in Dallas's Valley View Center had three stories, so we consolidated them into the bottom two and turned the third floor into an experimental space. We would prototype the new JCP there—the new shops, the new presentations, the new signage—just as we once had the Apple Store. I thought of everything we could do, everything JCPenney could become.

What would America's favorite *kids'* department look like? I imagined asking my merchants. What kind of service would you deliver in a town square of America's Favorite Store?

What I wasn't thinking about, clearly, was that we were launching a strategy targeting hip, urban customers in tired, suburban real estate. What I was also not wondering about was whether my whole idea of relationships at Apple wouldn't also apply, in reverse, at JCPenney; if, perhaps, some customers—and in fact, most customers—wouldn't see coupons as I saw them, as obstacles to the shopping experience, but as part of an experience that they actually liked. I was lost in my thoughts, lost in my imagination, lost in the dream of America's Favorite Store.

Then, on a cool fall day just a few weeks before I was scheduled to take over as CEO of JCPenney, the ringing of my iPhone brought me back to reality.

□

On September 29, 2011, I got my final call from Steve.

"Will you come visit?" he asked.

I made the drive I'd made so many times before—north on 85 from 1 Infinite Loop, then onto 101, then off at the Oregon expressway before turning left onto Waverley. I parked in the same spot up against the rolled curb, walked the same steps I'd come to know so well: along the path, up through the garden, into the kitchen. Laurene was standing at the sink when I walked in.

"How are you?" I asked. No sooner had the words left my mouth than I wished I'd asked a different question.

"We're . . ." She trailed off. "Not great," she said. She ran her hands through her hair and kept her eyes averted, staring through the kitchen window into the garden.

"I'm sorry, Laurene," I said. "This . . . it's hard."

"It *is* hard," she said.

We stood there for a moment.

"Is he in the living room?" I asked.

"Bedroom," she said.

I knew what that meant.

"And, Ron . . ."

I turned back.

"If there's anything you need to say, I . . ." She trailed off again.

"I will," I said.

I walked from the kitchen through the hallway, my hands brushing the familiar stucco walls. The last time I'd seen Steve, he'd been in the living room, but when I walked into his bedroom, it was clear that he wasn't making it there anymore. He lay on his bed, his gaunt figure propped up by a few pillows.

"Ron," he said weakly.

"S.J.," I said.

He smiled over the edge of his MacBook, which lay open in front of him.

"You're never going to give it up, are you," I said.

"Like you and retail," Steve said, shuffling the laptop to his left on the bed and propping himself up. "I guess we just love this stuff."

I sat down on a chair facing him. Sheets of paper were strewn across the bedsheets—designs for new iPhones, iPads.

"Look at this," he said, holding up a drawing. I squinted at it. It was a boat he was designing with Philippe Starck.

"I'll never get to ride in this thing, but it's been energizing designing it for my family."

I nodded.

The conversation shifted to everyday things. Where our daughters were applying to college. How funny it was that, because their names were next to each other alphabetically, Erin Powell Jobs and Lizzey Johnson had lockers next to each other at school. How Reed, Steve and Laurene's oldest son, was liking college. It felt like a normal conversation, apart from the toll it clearly took on Steve. After an hour, he could hardly form words, and I could barely articulate them. It was time to go, but I didn't want to leave.

The two of us sat there for a while longer. Neither of us said anything. Neither of us needed to. The weight of the moment—of *all* the moments—hung in the air.

Finally, Steve broke the silence.

"You and Campbell," he said. "You both like to hug people."

"We do," I said. I felt a lump forming in my throat.

"But you've never given *me* a hug."

"You were never the hugging type of guy!" I said, the words tumbling out through laughter and tears.

"I'm really not," Steve said. "But I could use one today."

"Can I ask for something in return?" I asked.

"What?"

I paused.

"To say a prayer."

Steve looked at me for a while.

"Okay," he finally said. "Sure."

I closed my eyes and bowed my head in the chair.

"Dear God," I said. "Please meet my friend Steve. Take care of him. Amen."

I got up from the armchair, walked around the foot of the bed, laid myself down next to Steve, and shuffled my body up against him. I laid there, feeling his body shake gently against my own. I could feel my heartbeat against his back, what remained of his hair tickling my cheek as my head rested awkwardly on top of his. I have no idea how long I lay there, how long I held him. However long it was, it wasn't long enough.

Finally, I pulled back and lifted myself from the bed. Steve rolled over gently to look at me and smiled.

"That wasn't so bad," he said.

"Not so bad," I repeated. I stood there for a moment.

"Good luck," Steve said.

"Thanks," I said. "For everything."

"Thank *you*."

Steve passed away on October 5, 2011. The world mourned the loss of a titan. I mourned the loss of my friend.

□

Outside of Apple, Steve was a regular guy. He was a father, a son, a friend. He was a human being, and human beings are imperfect. But at Apple, Steve was something different, something more. For many at Apple—and for many of the company's faithful—Steve was seen as a god.

How do you pay tribute to a god? How do you honor someone whose light you fought to reveal for a decade? Those were the questions running through our minds in the wake of Steve's passing. They were also the questions running through the minds of millions of people around the world who visited our stores the day after Steve passed. Tributes poured in. Bouquets of flowers rested against each store's glass facade. Notes filled matte black coverings that we'd placed over those facades to indicate that—at least for today—the stores were closed. We had been the places where customers went to get close to Steve, and now, we were the place they went to commemorate his life. But it wasn't just people who commemorated Steve.

It was the stores themselves.

Perhaps to honor Steve's wishes as we'd built the stores, we'd designed the glowing Apple logo above each one without an off switch. If a store leader wanted to turn their store's logo off, they had to get a ladder, climb it, then remove the plating behind the logo with a screwdriver and manually shut it off. This was not easy to do, period. But on October 6, 2011, all 357 stores did it simultaneously.

This had not been planned. There was no talk of doing it before Steve passed. All the necessary coordination happened in less than twenty-four hours—and it all happened *without my knowledge.* Apple IFC dimmed their logo starting at 12:00 a.m. local time; Apple Ginza, 1:00 a.m.; Apple Sydney, 3:00 a.m. Those times corresponded with 9:00 a.m. in California, ensuring that the lights would be dimmed by 10:00 a.m., when customers would arrive at the Palo Alto store—Steve's store—to pay their respects. That 10:00 a.m. opening was symbolic, too: Steve had always opened Mac keynotes at 10:00 a.m. before closing them with "one more thing." Except on October 6, 2011, there was no "one more thing." There was only one less thing. One less person, one less light. On October 6, 2011, dimmed lights represented that the world had lost one of its brightest: a man who empowered me to be myself, to let everything I believed seep into the culture of an organization, and to reveal his—and Apple's—genius by meeting my own.

There was, at the time, no real way to understand the degree to which everything at Apple enabled what our team had accomplished. But soon, I would learn the hard way that not every organization is like Apple, and not everywhere has someone like Steve.

Three weeks after his passing, I began my tenure as CEO of JCPenney.

□

November 2011.

Two weeks had passed since I started as CEO of soon-to-be JCP. I had been developing a presentation and was planning on delivering it on the lawn in front of our headquarters. I would be announcing a new day for JCPenney, and I felt like being outside would be a breath of fresh air.

On November 14, the team had completed arrangements for my presentation. It was a perfect fall day in Plano: seventy degrees, a cloudless sky. The lawn was framed by a lake, and its surface was a mirror: glassy and undisturbed. My brother Dwight had told me he was coming, too, and I'd looked forward to seeing a familiar face amidst the sea of new ones. He called me when he arrived, told me he was out front. I walked out of my office, took the elevator down through the rotunda, and stepped outside. Dwight was there. But so was someone else.

My dad.

Something broke in me in that moment. I don't know what it was. But I do know that it pressed me forward, into my dad's arms, as tears ran hot down my cheeks for the second time in the last month. I hugged him hard, too hard, noticing just how thin he'd gotten since I'd last seen him. I realized that cancer had taken its toll on him, too, and I tried not to think about when he'd cease being able to pay its cost. I was a kid again in that moment—a third baseman or forward eyeing the stands for his dad before kickoff or the first pitch, and finding him, always finding him.

"Good luck, Ron," he finally said.

I don't know what I said back. I simply took everything that had been rattling around in my head, the lifetime I'd lived in the last six months, and buried it in is shoulder.

When I took the stage to give the presentation to this team—to *my* team—I felt a calm like I'd once felt at Mount Olivet Lutheran as a child, as confirmation president. The words flowed out like water. I saw my dad in the audience, Dwight at his side. More importantly, I saw that he had seen me, here, as CEO. It was a perfect moment, a perfect day.

It would be the only one I'd have for the next eighteen months.

□

I treated JCPenney's culture like Apple's, where the trust I'd developed as creator and leader of the Apple Store gave me unilateral ability to run it as I saw fit. Before I even joined JCPenney as CEO, I was inking partnerships. Once I did join, I went to meet Chip Bergh, the CEO of Levi's, at his office in San Francisco. He told me about a new concept that they'd just launched at a store in Costa Mesa: the Denim Bar.

"Like the Genius Bar!" he said.

"Let's go see it!" I replied.

"What—you mean now?!"

"Sure!"

I had the JCPenney jet. We hopped in an Uber to SFO. Two hours later, we were in Levi's Costa Mesa store. An hour after that, we were shaking hands on an agreement to put Levi's in six hundred JCPenney stores. We already carried Levi's, but the denim bar would give us the strongest presentation of their brand outside of their own stores. Typically, a negotiation like that would've taken months. We did it on a plane ride.

I remember Chip being excited by that partnership, and he was. But I think there was also an element of surprise: a sense that this autonomy I was operating with was less a result of being connected to my team, as it had been at Apple, than operating as my own division. I was CEO, sure. But I didn't know the team yet. I assumed people would get on board, but as it turned out, more than a few didn't.

One of the early dissenters had insisted that eliminating discounts would alienate our existing customer. He had no way of knowing that I'd heard the same thing from colleagues at Target about design before launching it to great success—that his pushback, far from dissuading me, was actually signaling that we were on the right track. His position was redundant, too. So I let him go.

Three weeks later, I met with JCPenney's board for the first time as CEO. I updated the board on the progress of our transformation, which was moving fast. I then initiated a conversation about when we should launch. I explained that retailers typically launched overhauls at the beginning of the year, so we could either launch in February 2012—a month away—or wait until February 2013.

"What do we have to lose?" Ullman asked. "Let's go now."

The board agreed with Ullman, and I went along with the board. I'm sure it occurred to me that I'd had far more time at Apple, but with all the momentum of having created the vision and presented it, I was pleasantly surprised at the board's desire to move quickly. Looking back, I would have welcomed—and should have encouraged—a more cautious voice.

Throughout January, I led the team in preparing for the transformation. I also held a major meeting at Chelsea Piers on the west side of New York City for suppliers, analysts, and the press to introduce the new JCP. The difference between my first few months at JCPenney and my first few months at Apple couldn't have been starker. At Apple, very few had supported us—not internal employees, not the board, and certainly not the media. But Steve did. At JCPenney, I didn't have Steve. I was supposed to *be* Steve. I was supposed to inspire the media, the employees, and the board with my vision. At Chelsea Piers, I did, and a lot of them got caught up in it.

A lot, but not all.

As part of my presentation, I unveiled that Martha Stewart would be joining us. For the first time, she would have six hundred of her own stores that would anchor the new JCP home department. At the time, she had an exclusive agreement with Macy's. Our legal counsel had reviewed the Macy's contract and advised that bringing her into our store would not violate the terms of their agreement. What was less clear was whether it would violate the unwritten rules of their relationship. I had gambled that it wouldn't, and I was wrong. The day we announced the Martha Stewart partnership, Macy's filed a lawsuit arguing that we had broken their exclusivity. In other words, they claimed that she was cheating on them—with us.

This was an early sticking point, but I'd seen lawsuits before; we pressed forward with the transformation inside the JCP stores anyway. I offered my expertise in places where it felt like the team could use it. Marketing. Signing. Emails. I proposed ideas for our circulars. I offered thoughts on trend reviews. The team embraced the change. We updated every price in the store, remerchandised as much as we could, and went live on February 1. It was a sprint like I'd never experienced, and the team's effort to execute was heroic. Still, I couldn't help thinking that this speed—while I had adopted it and knew it was what the board wanted to appease the shareholders—was a bit reckless. If this team was a garden, it needed time to grow. But efforts to speed up that growth would be better for shareholders, who wanted to reap what hadn't yet been sewn. Balancing the two speeds—or, perhaps, failing to—gave me a renewed appreciation for Steve.

But of course, it wasn't just that stakeholders wanted to move at different speeds. It was also that many seemed to want to drive us in a different direction. Along with overseeing the overhaul, I had been working on a beautiful, gentle advertisement illustrating the new JCP as America's Favorite Store and a place for everyone. Meanwhile, our marketing team had been developing an advertisement announcing the end of coupons. It portrayed three different women reacting to discounts . . . poorly. One was under a sale sign, another was holding a coupon, and a third was opening a mailbox overflowing with discount mailers. Each of their reactions was the same: a long, guttural scream of the word *no.*

"Enough. Is. Enough," the ad's final frame read.

I didn't like the ad, and I said as much. But I was told that loud and brash was necessary, and with a million other fires to put out, I went along. I was reminded of something I'd once said at Apple—that leaders say yes—and began to think that maybe, I'd oversimplified it. Maybe, leaders didn't *just* "say yes." Maybe, leaders also got the privilege of things they wanted to say yes to by leading as I'd once encouraged people at Apple to lead: *through conversation*. And no sooner had the ad been launched than everyone panned it. Sure, it got our point across—no more coupons! But it got another point across, too: that we no longer cared about our customer. Days into running it, I got a call from JCPenney board member Colleen Barrett.

"You have to stop running that ad," she said. "I can't *stand* it."

That, at the very least, was something I could say yes to.

Of course, if the ad had led to financial results, maybe it wouldn't have been so controversial internally. But it wasn't having the intended effect. Investors were calling board members and asking them, quite pointedly, if they had set foot in a JCP store since we'd launched. They couldn't yet know the numbers, but they could see the traffic. It wasn't great.

Steve Roth called me only a few weeks into the change and invited me out to meet him in New York City.

"Can't we just run one discount?" he asked.

The answer was, again, no—but I didn't use that word.

"I told you this would take one hard year," I said. "We have to have the courage to stick it out."

And we did. Everyday low prices were the linchpin of the strategy. They unlocked the savings that we could reinvest into the brand. If we went back to discounts, the whole strategy would fall apart. That was why we needed to have courage. That was why we needed to stick it out!

I pulled Michael's coupon ad not long after the call from Colleen. It didn't save us from the financial reality. We had planned to be down 15 percent. When the quarter ended, we were down *19* percent. This wasn't a disaster, but for investors, it seemed to be. The same ones who had been calling board members already called again, incensed, asking how they could let me walk away from nearly 20 percent of the customer base that JCPenney had spent years building. I continued to insist on patience, that it would take time for customers to adjust. As the months went on, this belief became harder and harder to sustain.

□

Sometimes, when business gets hard, the pressure can become as much personal as financial. This is why self-esteem matters for leaders. You have to believe in yourself when almost everyone else doubts you. I say "almost" because in my own experience, I always had someone who believed in me. My dad. Every day after work, I called him. Every day after work, he'd ask the same question.

"How was your day?"

And every day, I'd reply with the same word—*Good!*—before launching into all the reasons it wasn't.

And there were a lot of them.

My dad was never quick to offer an opinion.

"Seek ye first to understand," went his favorite quote. "Then be understood."

The best way to understand, he knew, was to listen. And I had a lot to say.

After one particularly difficult day—the *New York Post* had come out with an article claiming I was having an affair with Martha Stewart, the latest in a string of hit pieces that it was hard to think weren't somehow tied up with the hedge funds that had been shorting our stock—my dad finally decided it was time to make himself understood.

"Ron," he said quietly. "I want you to know something. And I say this as your dad. You've led a charmed life. You've always worked with people who have loved and supported you. So much of what you've done—in fact, maybe *everything* you've done—has worked.

No parent wants to see their child go through tough times. But what they want even less is to see their child fail to ever encounter one."

I was silent.

"Everyone faces adversity," my dad continued. "You're facing it now."

My mind worked furiously, trying to come up with some magic phrase, something to dissolve the truth of my dad's words. I started to say something, but my dad cut me off.

"Think about what *other* people go through," he said. "You're not the only one who's heading into a challenge."

I sat there on the starched white sheets in my hotel room thinking about my dad's battle with cancer and couldn't help but think that he was handling dying better than I was handling leading.

"You're right," I finally said to him. "You're right. But *this* challenge—*my* challenge—it's so *public*!"

"You wanted this job," he said. "That was *your* choice."

Except, *had* I wanted this job? Hadn't I tried to back out?

More than that: What *had* I told my dad?

The truth was becoming harder to discern. The more one plays with it, I was learning, the more flexible it gets.

Regardless, there were no excuses, my dad seemed to say. I had the power to change my circumstances because I, unlike my dad, had been the one who chose them. I shuffled on the bed, realizing—for perhaps the first time—just how hard it was to sit still in a marketing posture.

Then I sighed.

The next day, I went back to work.

As 2012 went by, I did my best to keep us moving. It was all I could do, and often, it's all you can do. I visited the Valley View warehouse most days, working to refine the store-within-a-store prototypes. It was energizing to visit Valley View after walking the hallways of

JCPenney's cavernous headquarters, where I always felt like an unwanted outsider. In June, I walked through our first ten store-within-a-store concepts that we were scheduled to launch. They were stunning. They also worked! The Levi's shop drove sales up 40 percent year over year. Joe Fresh was an exciting addition, too. We launched an entirely new JCP label, which merchandised modern, everyday items. And we relaunched some of our most popular heritage brands. Still, the second quarter was no better than the first. Sales stayed down 20 percent with no improvement in sight. The NPS of the 80 percent who shopped at JCP was way up from the prior year, but the stock was down, as were the spirits of the company and the board.

Steve once said that if he had too many days when he woke up and wasn't excited to do what he was doing that day, he knew he needed to change something. By October 2012, I'd had nearly 365 of those days. They were made no easier by what I was missing. Will and Lizzey had been playing sports, getting their drivers' licenses, going to prom. At night, I sat alone in the Ritz-Carlton in Plano and scrolled through photos of the moments I was missing. The isolation was breathtaking. My pursuit of a vision that many in the company weren't supporting was draining me. All of those I'd hired—Kramer and Dan, in particular—encouraged me, as I did them, but we were busy, and when we had time to speak, we tried to avoid getting dragged into the depths. The only person with whom I could share honestly was my dad. Then, in the fall of 2012, it became clear that I was about to lose him, too.

Of course, the loss wouldn't just be mine. It would be my sister's, my brother's. It would be that of the entire family who looked to my dad as a patriarch. Throughout the year, Dwight, Diane, and I had visited my dad periodically. Then, in late October, his health took a turn for the worse, and Dwight and I flew back for what would be the final time. Every night, along with saying goodnight, we would say goodbye.

"If we don't see you, we love you," we'd say. "We'll see you on the other side."

Then, each morning, we'd go into his room, where he'd greet us with the same good-natured humor we'd come to know.

"Am I still here?" he'd ask, eyes half open.

"Yeah, Dad," one of us would say. "You're still here."

This went on for a few days. The joke was funny, and Dwight and I always laughed at it. Then, on November 2, 2012, we didn't. That morning, our dad wasn't there to say it.

Losing a parent is never easy. Neither is losing a best friend. When my dad passed, I lost both.

His passing marked one year since I'd joined Penney's.

□

A celebration of life took place for my dad on Saturday, November 10, at Wooddale Church in Edina. Dwight, Diane, and I organized it. We didn't expect many outside of our family to attend—at 87, my dad had long since outlasted most of his friends. But that day, more than 700 people showed up to pay their respects. Most of them were those my dad had mentored in his spare time—even towards the end. I hadn't been the only one headed into a challenge, my dad had said. Now, I realized I also wasn't the only one he had been helping navigate one.

That realization stuck with me in the weeks that followed—and they were a blur. I've heard it said that grief is the brain's effort to keep making a connection it no longer can, and every day as I drove back to the hotel in Plano from Penney's, I realized how true that was. Every thought tried to take me somewhere I could no longer go. The memories were good, but the muscle memory was painful. Everything led me to reach for my phone, to dial my dad. At least once, I did it just to hear his voicemail. The relief was temporary. I had never felt so alone.

My faith got stronger during those weeks. I figured there was something I was supposed to learn from this—how to walk a path alone, how small I was in the grand scheme of things, the perils of situational arrogance. But I did still have a company to run, and things had been progressing. Kramer had reduced inventory by nearly $600 million, freeing up much needed cash. Mike and Ben had built out nearly 40 percent of the store in the Valley View warehouse. Dan had been working with store leaders to articulate the new strategy and ensure that the stores were on board. Our Net Promoter Score continued to be well above the score JCPenney received before I arrived. But none of this was revealing itself in our numbers. The sales report, which had ripped me out of bed at Apple and inspired me to drive downtown on Sundays to snag it off the printer at Target, offered no comfort. Eventually, I couldn't even get myself to open it. But I held out hope that perhaps Christmas, for which JCPenney had *historically* promoted heavily, would bring in customers who recognized that we were the place that *always* had good prices; that we were the place they could get *all* their shopping done.

It didn't.

As December turned to January, I tried hard not to dwell on what had been. Sometimes, I succeeded. More often, I failed. Less than a year earlier, it felt like I had everything. Now, it felt as if I'd lost everything. Steve, my dad, my reputation. My confidence. I couldn't understand why, after almost a year, customers *still* hadn't embraced our better merchandise at everyday low prices. Was it, maybe, that we hadn't given customers some anchor to understand how good these prices actually were? Were the everyday low pricing strategies at Ross and Marshalls really only working because of the signs they put outside—"60 percent off department store prices"? Had design at Target, which we hadn't promoted, worked because *other* departments—say, health and beauty—had brought customers in with promotions?

Maybe.

The uncertainty was unfamiliar. The only thing that was certain was the board's desire to return to the previous strategy, but that wasn't what I thought we should do, and it wasn't what the best CEO I'd ever known—Steve—would've done. As I saw it—and as I believed he would've seen it—we had already lost JCPenney's savvy, coupon-clipping customer; if we returned to the old strategy now, we would lose whoever we had been starting to gain, too. But with pressure mounting from the board, news stories filled with headlines about our lack of financial performance, and little evidence of a light at the end of the tunnel, I was losing the will to keep going.

Finally, in January—with "one hard year" since the launch of the overhaul ending—I went to the board and offered to resign. Giving them an out felt like the right thing to do, and I knew that if they wanted to go back, the sooner they did it, the better. But I also explained what I believed to be true: that a U-turn at this point would be far more damaging to JCPenney than continuing with the transformation. This got the board's attention, and they encouraged me to stay. I explained that I would, but only if they wanted to stick with the existing strategy, and that to keep pursuing it, I would have to make cuts. Some would be headquarters people who were related to board members. Things had the potential to get ugly, but, of course, they already were. The board decided—at least, for the time being—to continue on.

In the weeks that followed, I tried to address the slow uptake of everyday low prices by communicating the strategy better. I thought back to Steve's words outside of SoHo in 2002, back when Apple, five years after his return, seemed doomed.

"No one gets what we're trying to do," he'd said. That felt true at Penney's, too. We had to communicate our strategy better—to help people "get" it, to get *us*. So, at first, I proposed doing what Ross and Marshalls had done: adjusting our labels to better indicate value to customers. Nothing was "on sale," but a $10 price tag on an item would look more appealing, I thought, if it *also* said what was true—that we had previously sold the same item for $40. I got pushback; apparently FTC regulations required that to say this, it had to be the exact same item, and we had to have sold it for $40 "recently." And in most cases, the items *had* undergone small changes—perhaps its manufacturer was using a different button, or type of fabric—and even if they hadn't, "recently" was a stretch, as it had now been a year.

I struggled with this, and I didn't try to hide it. Ross and Marshalls were selling goods for $15, then slapping them with "compare at $60" labels, referencing different (though similar) department store items. But while, yes, the word *compare* implied only that the item was "comparable" to something sold at a department store, this was apparently a legal gray area—and not one anyone else was keen on entering. (Maybe this had something to do with our already being embroiled in a lawsuit with Macy's.) I asked how I was supposed to convey the pricing strategy. The answer was that to use the "compare at" language, we'd have to buy samples of *every piece of merchandise we wanted to compare* for review. I shook my head. There were barriers everywhere I looked. Years after these conversations, I can see their logic. In the moment, I was seeing red.

Perhaps unsurprisingly, I later learned that internal Penney's people had been saying I needed to go for a while. Some gave me six months. I only lasted three. I made one more failed effort to resign in February 2013 before my final effort in April. Finally, the board agreed it was time. They were scheduled to meet that week in New York. I stayed home. The same morning that they discussed a succession plan, I woke up and went for a run. After a few miles, I stopped, sweat pouring off me, and looked up at the sky.

"I'm *free*," I whispered.

It was the first great day I'd had in eighteen months.

□

I wanted out of JCP *badly*. But now, fifteen years later, I wonder what would've happened if I'd stayed. I have perspective now that I didn't have then. But of course, I've also lost the perspective that made me want to leave in the first place.

One of the hardest parts about being a CEO is realizing that it's all on you. It's your responsibility to outline the mission, to tell the story, to create the context. I had been doing this my entire life, but I had been doing it in contexts created by others. At Apple, the context was Steve's vision for how people could relate to technology, and I built on that by showing him that he could use a store to reach everyone. At Target, the context was a strategy of differentiation, and I built on that by also making us better with design. At Mervyn's, the context was creating a slightly upscale—but still value-focused—department store, and I built on that by layering a brand into our men's shirts and ties department. I was exceptional at taking what was expected and doing even more than that, at finding missions within visions. I thought that's what I was going to do with JCPenney. But once my mission was the vision—and it was clear that no one else seemed to want it—I couldn't keep pushing for it. Belief is a two-way street. I've always needed people to believe in me for me to believe in myself. Once they didn't, I couldn't. It was that simple.

The biggest question I'm left with in the wake of JCPenney—and the one whose answer is, I believe, the most instructive for future business leaders—is what would've made staying bearable? In the moment, I thought the answer was positivity. I've always been positive. But maybe part of why I've always been so positive is because I haven't encountered much hardship. When I have, I've dealt with it alone. Maybe that was the nail in the coffin. I wonder now if I couldn't have been more open about what I was experiencing. Maybe I could've told Dan and Ben and Fish and Kramer that I was struggling, that I didn't feel like I belonged, that my dad had just died, and given them the chance to support me. That's what Steve did. Maybe if I'd been more honest with my team, I would've learned that they felt like I did. In the moment, I was afraid that admitting how bad I felt would send us hurtling towards rock bottom, but I wonder now if that wouldn't have been the foundation from which we could build, and if honesty wouldn't have been the shovel we'd use to get there. Steve did once say it was the highest form of kindness. Maybe he was right.

I have a lot of regrets about JCPenney. I wish I'd been more open with those closest to me, of course. But I also wish I'd had the courage to go slower. I wish I'd spent more time building trust with the team, with the board, with customers. A lot of success in business gets retroactively attributed to the quality of a vision, and sure, visions matter—they garner resources and support. But the world is dynamic. It can take visions that should've worked in one context and make them look silly, just as it can take visions that had no business working and make them look genius. The point is that when you go too fast, you miss the opportunities that reveal themselves along the journey. You don't feel your impact in a way that allows you to react to it, and you don't create the tight-knit team that can react faster than one person ever could. Everything great in business *is* accomplished by teams, and teams require focus and trust. It's a simple lesson. But if there's anything I learned from Steve, it's that there's power in simplicity.

Of course, in the heat of the moment at JCPenney, with the pressure mounting, I remained focused. I fought every effort to return to promotions. I believed I was right, and I recall bolstering the position in my own mind by reminding myself that Steve wouldn't have compromised, so neither would I. But I know now, having written this book, that Steve wasn't as uncompromising as I thought. Maybe I manufactured an image of him in my head to justify myself. Maybe I forgot that even though he *hated* the idea of opening the iPod to Windows, he did it. Maybe I forgot that this quite literally saved Apple *and* the stores, and maybe I failed to act on what I do think some part of me knew to be true: that contexts shift, and while confidence in your convictions is valuable, so is the humility that enables you to release them. I have no idea if promoting at JCP would've solved anything. I can't know. But I do know that a lack of willingness to compromise was not a solution. I also know that rushing towards the end was the surest way not to reach it.

My dad used to say that I often made up my mind very quickly "without counting to ten." I think he was right. My tendency my entire life has been to want to move quickly. I believe in the power of momentum—starting it, building it, preserving it. I've always believed that people will get behind me if I pursue a direction boldly, fearlessly. But in the wake of JCP, I can't help recognizing that so many of the things I did were only possible because of what was happening around me, and that for as fast as I thought I moved, I often benefitted from being circumstantially slowed down. Steve's willingness to postpone launching the Apple Store so we could redesign it gave our store and headquarters teams an additional seven months to train, to get to know each other, to establish a culture. I joined the home department at Target just after the team had picked that year's assortment, so as much as I might've wanted to push design immediately, I was forced to take a year and get to know the team. Even my election as confirmation president, which I always attributed to "kindness," came after a decade of having attended Mount Olivet with parents who understood, as any retailer understands, that the most important part of selling anything is making it *visible.* I like to think I created contexts throughout my career. I am more grateful now for the ones I found myself in.

One of the hardest things about leaving Apple was leaving people behind: Jerry, Cano, Bob, Christy, Denise. Everyone in headquarters; everyone in the stores. They understood, I think. But others within Apple didn't. I know there were people who wondered how I could consider leaving with Steve so close to passing. I wonder, too, if the people I worked with at JCP felt similarly when I left—if Kramer, Fish, Ben, and Dan wondered what the heck they were supposed to do now that the guy for whom they joined the company was gone. But if I'm being truly honest, I wasn't thinking about them. I've heard it said that an animal will gnaw off its own leg to escape a trap, and that's how it felt at JCPenney at the end. I wasn't as afraid as I was frustrated. But the point of being a CEO is that you're supposed to tolerate what others can't—to block out what you need with what the company needs. I believed that a U-turn would be more damaging to JCPenney than continuing with the transformation, and I was right. But by the end, I couldn't bear to keep acting on that belief. My hat is off to anyone who could.

In the end, the world is a complicated place. Plates are shifting; waves are forming, curling, crashing. Tim Cook once said that you can't control the opportunities you get, only your preparation for them. I like that idea because it speaks to a fundamental truth about the future: It is unknowable. The only place where you can even catch a glimpse of it is in the present. That's where—and when—our inner voice speaks to us: not in the past or the future, but right now. Still, for as much as I've lauded my own inner voice throughout this book, the truth is that it is always shaped by the outer voices. In many cases, it might simply be their echo. I'm sure there were countless times when I shared what I thought was a novel idea only to have someone—Jerry, Cano, my dad—wonder if they hadn't said it to me in conversation the day before. God only knows how many times that happened. Maybe someday he'll tell me.

A lot of people have joked with me—or written op-eds arguing—that like Icarus, I flew too close to the sun at JCPenney. That's probably true. But I've heard different points made about that story, too—that perhaps it wasn't so much that Icarus flew too close to the sun as it was that he didn't spend enough time building his wings. I don't know what the lesson of his story is; it's probably some combination of both. But I like to believe in the power of what we can build. I think Steve did, too. People with passion *can* change the world for the better, and the things we create—wings, or anything else—can help us do it. I've always believed that people soar with their strengths, but I realize now that strength develops slowly. It's hard to build things up, but it's more worthwhile—and a lot more fun—than tearing them down.

In the end, I'm grateful for my time at JCPenney. I think it made me a better person. I do regret things about my time there, but the only thing I'd regret more was never having tried. If we'd gone slower, who knows, maybe we still wouldn't have created America's Favorite Store. But I do think we would've had the chance to do what we did at Apple: create *our* favorite store. And if we had . . . Well, I guess we can never know. But maybe things would've gone better. At the very least, I know they would've been different.

CHAPTER 15

What's Next, Now?

Today, the most common question I get asked is what's next for the retail industry. Of course, if there is anything my time at JCPenney taught me, it's the danger of utter certainty. But if there is a hint at where the retail world is going, I believe we can understand it by looking back.

In 2000, the same year I joined Apple to develop and launch stores, venture capitalist Marc Andreessen predicted that physical retail would die. His logic was simple. Before the internet, customers had to go to a local store to buy a product. After the internet, people could buy products from anyone, anywhere, and have them delivered to their home. Why would you ever go to a store when shopping could be that easy? The answer, according to Marc, was simple: you wouldn't. But this was a bold prediction, not the least of which because, two miles east of Marc's office on Sand Hill Road, sat one of the world's most respected and productive shopping malls: Stanford Shopping Center. If Marc's prediction was right, Stanford's parking lot seemed destined for condominium conversion. Twenty-seven years later, it's the hardest place to find a parking spot in Silicon Valley.

Walking through Stanford today, it's easy to see why. The all-outdoor center boasts thirty-six different food vendors—Blue Bottle for coffee, restaurants like the Melt (or True Food Kitchen, or Shake Shack, or . . .) for lunch, and places like Pinkberry for dessert. Stanford's west wing is then a de facto who's who of global luxury brands—Hermes, Louis Vuitton, Zegna, among others—and the mall's northeast end is dominated by expanded versions of the same retailers that once gave me the confidence to bet on design at Target: Pottery Barn, Williams Sonoma, Restoration Hardware. A decade after my gamble that JCPenney could become a direct-to-customer (DTC) launchpad, Stanford has realized that vision and more; along with hosting DTC brands, they have also created a place where international brands can open stores and discover new customers. Even the owner of Stanford Shopping Center, Simon Properties—the same landlord who once referred to the Apple Store as a "six-thousand-square-foot Radio Shack"—has since added a flagship, *twelve*-thousand-square-foot Apple Store to Stanford's west end, right next to the same department store, Neiman's, that I pointed out to Steve on our walk through Stanford in 2000.

This story is not limited to Stanford Shopping Center. In fact, it has been playing out—and continues to play out—across the country and around the world, in the best shopping malls and on the best shopping streets, over and over again. Of course, tired stores have always eventually gone away. But they have always been replaced by fresh, new entrants.

Put simply: the internet has not killed physical retail.

So, what has it done? The best answer to that question comes in understanding the history of the DTC brands I once imagined in JCPenney.

□

The DTC movement birthed by the rise of the internet suggested that there was no need for stores. Brands could reach customers anywhere. Without that barrier to entry, Casper—one of the first DTC mattress companies, and pioneer of the mattress in a box—was able to put up an online storefront, tell an *extremely* compelling story about their model to investors (zero fixed costs, no overhead), and convince them—and people—that they were the future. People love stories like this, especially when they speak to their experiences—and this story did. Casper told everyone that shopping for mattresses didn't have to "suck," and it struck a chord. In 2011, Marc Andreessen doubled down on his 2000 prediction, saying that software would eat retail. And a lot of people asked: Well, who needs stores?

Well, apparently . . . Casper.

Several years after Marc doubled down on his prediction about the death of physical retail, Casper *opened* their first retail store.

Why?

The answer is simple: There is virtually zero barrier to entry online. Not long after Casper launched, countless other DTC mattress brands—Avocado, Birch, Leesa—emerged to compete with them. As the battle over eyeballs online launched Casper's customer acquisition costs into the stratosphere, they were also forced to ask themselves what made them different. And while the answer had been their distribution model, that quickly proved mimicable. With Casper's online customer acquisition costs skyrocketing, they realized that they had to go offline.

Enter: stores.

The verdict has since come down on how effective that strategy proved to be. Casper's plan had been to open two hundred stores—many of them in the same malls George got us into at Apple—but their store count peaked at seventy-three, and as of this writing, it sits at forty. Casper was never profitable and has since been taken private. And yet, even as late as 2022, Casper's CEO was pointing out that their stores—while not profitable—were *still the best way to show Casper's products*. The numbers bear this out: Even after hundreds of millions of dollars in funding and a dozen or so companies that tried to sell mattresses purely online, 80 percent of mattresses are bought in stores where you can test them.

The point I'm making is this: Stores are not guaranteed to work, but they are always guaranteed to be necessary. They are responses to our need to consume and our impulse to create; they are downstream of the human impulse to seek meaning. Unless we stop creating and consuming physical things—and unless businesses stop mimicking other successful businesses—there is simply no world in which physical retail ceases to exist. Stores are not just *for* us. They—to use the words of a certain defunct toy store—*are* us. And yet, there are *still* people who believe they're going away.

□

If you ask just about anyone—other than a retailer—about the state of retail today, or the future of retail tomorrow, you'll hear one very familiar refrain.

"Stores are dying."

Except . . . Are they? What percentage of products are purchased in stores versus online? Would it surprise you to know that it's 70 percent in-store . . . and in some places, higher? And that the average transaction size in stores is higher than online? And that sales in physical stores are growing *faster* than online sales?

The list goes on. Yes, the retail industry went through a painful period when the internet emerged and supposedly "killed" stores. But did it really? Throughout the 1990s, cheap capital fueled mall overdevelopment ("B" and "C" malls) as Wall Street rewarded retailers for growth in store count. Leases in those malls were cheap, which meant that stores didn't have to do the same volume as locations in "A" malls to be profitable. Some retailers overextended themselves, betting that people would eventually find their way to these stores, but when the internet revealed itself as an easy way to buy things, there was less of a reason for people to visit mediocre malls. In the years that followed, people attributed those malls—and the stores in them—feeling dead to the internet having killed them, and though there was truth to that, it wasn't the full story. The internet didn't kill stores. It revealed the brands that had too many of them.

What happened because of the internet was what always happens: Retail evolved. It adapted. And in this case, it consolidated. The internet wasn't the end of physical stores. It wasn't the first horseman of the retail apocalypse. It was, actually, a necessary correction, with tired, redundant stores going away as retail pushed into an omnichannel equilibrium. Today, 70 percent of products are purchased in stores and 30 percent are purchased online. And even of those 30 percent, about half are delivered by the online stores of physical retailers who embraced online shopping. The other half are from primarily online retailers, like Amazon, who has been trying for a decade—with bookstores, grocery stores, and convenience stores—to break into physical retail.

All of this is to say: The internet, far from killing physical retail, has actually given it new life.

Today, we can see this life in malls around the world. Gen Z and Gen Alpha, in their search for authenticity, personalization, and education, are pulling digitally native brands *back into malls.* Successful brands in *all* categories—Apple, Zara, Restoration Hardware, Dior—are launching bigger and better flagship stores in the biggest and best cities around the world. Global fast-fashion giant Shein—who, to this point, had been running their business entirely online—recently drew more than sixty thousand people to their store launch in Paris. Stores are clearly more than just places where people go to buy products. They are places where people go to make connections with brands that they cannot make online. They have the potential to be the most important marketing a brand ever does. This is because they are places where we—humans—go to do the things we do: express ourselves, see what other people think, find meaning. The internet cannot kill those desires. It never could.

With this said, I think the more interesting question than whether retail will *survive* the next technological revolution is what it will do with it. We know that retail is collectively doing better than ever because of the internet. We know that the present state of retail is omnichannel, that 70 percent of sales happen in stores, and that a significant portion of the 30 percent of sales that happen online *originate* in stores. What we *don't* yet know is what retail will look like when we pair human intelligence with artificial intelligence. But we would be foolish to say that anything bad will happen. In fact, there is profound opportunity in the pairing of artificial intelligence and human intelligence in a retail store. If the present state of retail is omnichannel, the future of retail—and, perhaps, people—will be omni-intelligence.

Some people are afraid of AI, and I respect their opinions. But I am an AI optimist. AI is an immediate path into the information that has been made available to it: a repository of what is known. But if there's anything my career has taught me, it's that revealing what isn't yet known is a human activity. Combining our personal knowledge with AI's general knowledge might spark new ideas, but passionate teams working together will reveal genius. AI doesn't have to be a threat to the world. It can be a path to a better one. It can be, as Steve believed computers could be, a tool that we use to imagine a better world, to create the things that end up in stores, to plan the things that make us excited about the future. AI can be—as Steve envisioned technology would be—something that will enrich lives.

Now, I want to clarify: I do not believe that we are currently in this world. But my hope is that we can eventually get, if not to it, at least somewhere close. It is always our relationship with technology that shapes what emerges from it; it is always our choice to either be consumed by it or create with it. And while some might choose the former, I can say with virtual certainty that there is a significant group of people who are going to choose the latter.

Retailers.

Many retailers are wondering how to use AI to improve their customer interactions, to offer insights about customers that could be used to better shape in-store experiences. And yes, they're trying to sell products. But the truly successful ones will be those that, like the Apple Store, see sales as outcomes of having served their customer well. Every retailer can secure their customers' good in a different way. That's all it really means to enrich a life, and retail has always been an inherently creative, life-giving industry. I've always felt this way. I feel even more strongly about it now.

If you walk any of the greatest shopping streets in the world today, you can probably feel it, too. The best malls, shopping streets, and stores have never been better, and the premium on in-person experiences has never been higher. Prada recently spent nearly $1 billion to buy their store on Fifth Avenue—a location they had been leasing since 1997. LVMH just did the same with their real estate in London, Tokyo, and Paris. The smart money is betting that in a world in which we can do everything alone, the premium is back on being able to do things together. And I agree! The internet is where we go to check out; the real world is where we go to check in. With people, with ourselves. We are realizing that life is made richer not by transacting, but by interacting. And I can't help but think that Marc's prediction about the end of physical retail, predicated as it was on the assumption that online would beat it out because of "convenience," was based on a fundamental misunderstanding of what convenience actually means. In a world isolated from itself, maybe the real convenience is the ability to *convene*. And maybe stores that invest in omni-intelligence will create places where we do it.

I believe this about people, too—that our human intelligence can be augmented by artificial intelligence. If there is anything AI has revealed, it's just how much knowledge is now a commodity. The only thing we have now—and arguably, the only thing we've ever had—is our own unique knowledge. Businesses can talk until they're blue in the face about how to differentiate, but the reality AI has made clear is the same one Steve and I both understood when we met in 1999, even if we were approaching it from different places: The only true differentiator is people. Apple's brand was powerful because it was about what people could do. The people in the Apple Stores embodied the best of humanity—kindness, courage, love—to show people what they could do: what they could create with the knowledge only they had. This, in the age of AI, is the fundamental question. What is the knowledge only *you* have? What lights *you* on fire? Who—or what—is right in front of you, asking for *your* attention?

Retailers in the future will succeed by answering these questions. And the path to meaning for the rest of us starts with asking them.

CHAPTER 16

Choose Kindness

In the summer of 2005, not long after the vision of enriching lives had begun to pay off financially in the Apple Stores, I got a call from Steve. We hadn't been speaking as much. There was no reason to. The stores were doing well, and he was busy building what would become the iPhone, along with guiding a million other projects. But he told me he needed my help. He had been asked to give the commencement address at my alma mater, Stanford. He'd been putting together some notes but wasn't sure about them. As someone who hadn't graduated from college, he wasn't sure what graduates would want—or need—to hear.

I don't remember exactly what I said. I think I probably asked him what *he* wanted out of the speech. He likely wanted what he always wanted. Something honest. Something that would endure. Something that would resonate not just that day but every day. I told him I was sure he'd figure it out. I probably mentioned something about keeping it simple. Not that Steve needed any reminder of the power of simplicity.

A few weeks later, I went to Stanford Stadium to listen to the speech. Steve shared three short, simple stories from his life and encouraged students to pursue what they loved.

"Your time is limited, so don't waste it living someone else's life," he said. "Don't be trapped by dogma—which is living with the results of other people's thinking. Don't let the noise of others' opinions drown out your own inner voice. And most important, have the courage to follow your heart and intuition. They somehow already know what you truly want to become. Everything else is secondary."

When the ceremony ended, I got up and began making my way toward the exit. Before I even got out of the stadium, my phone buzzed in my pocket.

It was Steve.

"What'd you think?" he asked.

"People really seemed to like it!"

"I didn't ask what people thought," Steve said. "I asked what *you* thought."

I paused. I'd loved his content—of course I had. But I'd been struck by the tepidness of its delivery. I could have kept that thought to myself, and with anyone else I probably would have. But as I walked, I was reminded of what Steve had once said to me—that honesty was the highest form of kindness.

"It was . . . *different*," I managed.

"Different how?"

"Well, take Macworld," I said. "Those aren't presentations. They're performances. They make me feel like the only person in the room. This didn't."

"Why not?"

"Your delivery," I said. "That's your strength. Your content is always good, but your delivery is exceptional. You spend days rehearsing so that when you're onstage, you can truly connect with the audience. With this speech, you did the opposite. You just read from a piece of paper."

"Well, these things get transcribed," Steve said. "So, you have to script them perfectly."

"Fair enough," I said. "I guess that just made it harder to connect with you."

"Makes sense," he said. "Thanks for the feedback." And he hung up.

Not two minutes later, my phone buzzed again.

"Give me a grade," Steve said.

"What?"

"A *grade,*" he repeated. "For the speech."

"I'd give you a B plus."

There was a long silence.

"Okay," he finally said. "Thanks." And then he hung up again.

In the weeks that followed, I watched as critics lauded Steve's commencement speech as one of the best ever given. Day after day the reviews came in, each more glowing than the last. Finally, I shot Steve an email.

"I think I was a little harsh with my initial assessment of your Stanford speech," I wrote. "I'd like to change my grade. I'm going to give you an A minus."

Two minutes later, I got a reply.

"Thanks," Steve wrote. Then he added a smiley face.

I really don't like criticizing people. And while I respected Steve's belief that honesty was the highest form of kindness, I didn't believe it was helpful—or necessary—to speak the truth in a way that diminished other people. As I saw it, the truth was best communicated with a desire to love another person.

My whole life, I've tried to communicate this way. Even today, I try not to be critical of people—and after my experience at JCPenney, I try even harder. People will ask me if I still believe in people like I did at Apple. I tell them I do. It took me time to recover from my failure at JCPenney, but helping others—and seeing them grow—has helped me do it. Today, I still try to model the behavior that worked so well at the Apple Store—greet people with warm welcomes, learn about their needs and address them, then issue fond farewells. I do this with the people I share boardrooms with, people I share advice with, people I share moments with—in bars, or restaurants, or stores. I'm friendly. Life eventually ends, but in the interim, I try to stay open to beginnings.

Of course, sometimes, when I claim that the people with whom I share these beginnings—these simple, shallow moments—are "friends," I'll get flack for it.

"They're not your '*friends*'!" people will say of me and the bellhop, or me and the bartender, or me and the board. "You don't really know them."

Fair enough. Maybe I don't. Maybe I don't know their deepest insecurities, what keeps them up at night, what they bury in the depths, and maybe I can't claim someone as a true friend if we never go there. But I do wonder: Isn't it only possible to get there—to reach the depths—by wading through the shallows? Isn't that where every conversation starts?

Yes. It is. And the most important conversation is the one we have with ourselves. So, perhaps there's a final word to be said about the man who stuck with me in the shallows. Each day I tried to convince myself to take a path that wasn't mine, his kindness reminded me that the conversation in my head could sound different.

□

Ten years after I first met Dayton's greeter Jim Fuhrmann in 1984, a photojournalist by the name of David Dennison took an interest in his story. Maybe it was because so many other people had insisted on telling it. So, David—who was then working for Minneapolis news network KARE 11—sought Jim out. And when he found him, exactly where you'd expect, doing exactly what you'd expect—he learned, completely by coincidence, that Jim was planning on retiring.

Now sixty-three, Jim had been at Dayton's since he was *nineteen.*

David proposed that he come and tape footage of Jim's final day outside of Dayton's entrance. This was long before social media, and even so, news of Jim's retirement spread far and wide. Of course it did. Before people talked online, they just . . . talked. To each other. In front of—and inside of—stores. Jim asked people what was new with them, and they asked Jim what was new with him. Most days, the answer was the same. But in the days leading up to Jim's retirement, the answer was different. Now, along with telling everybody hello, Jim had to tell everyone that he was going to have to say goodbye.

And then everyone told everyone else.

On the day the segment was filmed—the day of Jim's retirement—thousands flocked to Dayton's entrance. A life-size picture of Jim on a white piece of paper filled up with notes and signatures so fast that Dayton's had to print a second, then a third. In the video segment, Jim is spinning like a top. All his trademark idiosyncrasies—like giving you a name if he didn't know yours—were on full display. One little girl was "Sunshine." An older woman was "Nice Person." Another was "Helper." You can almost hear the smile in the voice of the reporter narrating the video as he describes Jim as a "smiling, heel-spinning, hand-pumping jolt of caffeine."